Frameworks for

MALLARMÉ

Frameworks for

MALLARMÉ

THE PHOTO AND THE GRAPHIC OF AN INTERDISCIPLINARY AESTHETIC

GAYLE ZACHMANN

STATE UNIVERSITY OF NEW YORK PRESS

Portions of this book have appeared in other publications. Chapter 4 includes material originally published as "Developing Movements: Mallarmé, Manet, the 'Photo' and the 'Graphic,'" *French Forum* 22.2 (May 1997): 181–202, reprinted with permission from the University of Nebraska Press. Chapter 5 includes material originally published as "Frameworks for Mallarmé's Photo-Graphics," *L'Esprit Créateur* 40.3 (2000): 39–49, reprinted with permission from the University of Minnesota Press, and "Offensive Moves in Mallarmé: Dancing with *des astres,*" in *Confrontations: Politics and Aesthetics in Nineteenth-Century France,* edited by Kathryn M. Grossman, Michael E. Lane, Bénédicte Mouret, and Willa Z. Silverman (Amsterdam and Atlanta: Rodopi, 2001): 187–200, reprinted with permission from Rodopi. Sincere thanks to these publishers for granting permission to include this material in the book.

Published by
STATE UNIVERSITY OF NEW YORK PRESS, ALBANY

© 2008 State University of New York

For information, contact State University of New York Press
www.sunypress.edu

production and book design, Laurie D. Searl
marketing, Susan M. Petrie

Library of Congress Cataloging in Publication Data

Zachmann, Gayle, 1964–
    Frameworks for Mallarmé : the photo and the graphic of an inter-
disciplinary aesthetic / Gayle Zachmann.
        p. cm.
    Includes bibliographical references and index.
    ISBN 978-0-7914-7593-5 (hardcover : alk. paper)
    ISBN 978-0-7914-7594-2 (paperback : alk. paper) 1. Mallarmé,
Stéphane, 1842-1898—Criticism and interpretation. 2. Mallarmé,
Stéphane, 1842-1898—Aesthetics. I. Title.

PQ2344.Z5Z334 2008
841'.8—dc22

                                              2007052318

10 9 8 7 6 5 4 3 2 1

Drawing on the future

For Alexa

In Memory of Gordon

CONTENTS

Ilustrations

ACKNOWLEDGMENTS

THE IDEAS IN THIS BOOK were conceived as a thesis presented at the University of Pennsylvania in 1994 under the direction of Lucienne Frappier-Mazur, Frank Bowman, and Gerald Prince. Their insights, intellectual rigor, and profound humanity touched me in ways I could never have foreseen, and words cannot entirely convey my gratitude to them and to my other professors, my colleagues, and my friends from the University of Pennsylvania for their abiding support. With deepest respect, I thank you who have been there for me all of these years.

I thank the Department of French at Bryn Mawr College, the Department of Romance Languages and Literatures at the University of Pennsylvania, the Florence Gould Foundation, and the Mellon Foundation for the support that brought forward the thesis on which this book is based. I express my warm appreciation to Columbia University, Paris, and particularly to Mihaela Bacou, Danielle Haase-Dubosc, and Brunhilde Biebuyck for providing a home to my thoughts years ago at the Columbia University Graduate Research Institute. I am grateful for their daily inspiration and for the place to which I would return to complete the project.

I would like to thank the University of Florida, especially the Department of Romance Languages and Literatures and the College of Liberal Arts and Sciences, for supporting my research and international initiatives. I am grateful to have met there the mind that would rivet my own mind's eye, and to have the opportunity to work and think with extraordinary people, both on campus and at the U.F. Paris Research Center.

As it evolved, this project benefited from productive comments on my research presentations and helpful readings of early versions of parts of the manuscript. I am grateful to Lucienne Frappier-Mazur, Gerald Prince, Frank Bowman, Jean Alter, Nora Alter, Mihaela Bacou, Charles Bernheimer, Gordon

Bleach, Katharine Conley, Florencia Cortes-Conde, Ziad Elmarsafy, Jeannie Harpold, Nira Kaplan, Rosemary Lloyd, Diane Marting, Marshall Olds, David Powell, Jaymes Ann Rohrer, and Gwen Wells.

I thank the Bibliothèque Littéraire Jacques Doucet for permission to use "Photograph of Mallarmé, Renoir and Degas, 1895" for my cover, and Jean-Luc Berthollet for his quiet support over the past nine years. Thanks to the Bibliothèque littéraire Jacques Doucet and the Agence Photographie de la Réunion des musées nationaux (RMN) for providing illustrations. Warmest thanks to Jean Luc Berthollet, Fatima El Hourd, Yves Gaonac'h, Raphaëlle Cartire, Suzanne Nagy, and Helène Hubert for assistance with image production, selection, and permissions; Rachel Gora for administrative assistance; and the Musée Départmental Stéphane Mellarmé. Thanks to *L'Esprit Créateur, French Forum,* and *Editions Rodopi* for their generous permission to reprint material from my previously published articles.

Many thanks to my editor James Peltz at SUNY Press for his understanding, patience, good humor, and humanity during the harrowing metaphorical and nonmetaphorical life-and-death situations that coincided with the preparation of this book. Special thanks for their support and guidance go to all of the State University of New York Press staff and especially, Senior Production Editor, Laurie Searl, for her kindness and enthusiasm; Marketing Manager, Fran Keneston; and Copy Editor, Rosemary Wellner. I want to thank my family and my daughter Alexa, for the home for my soul that they have always been; Eveline Felsten, my first true teacher; and all of my colleagues for their readings, listenings, friendship, and support. Also, and unforgettably, to my dear friends, Mihaela Bacou, Katharine Conley, Jaymes Ann Rohrer, and Gwen Wells. Warmest thanks to Elizabeth Emery for pointing me to the recent sale of Dornac's photographs, auctioned at the Hotel Drouot in May 2008. Dornac's collection included a previously unpublished autograph-poem by Mallarmé. Special thanks to Gwen who read and edited the manuscript and kept me going.

I am fortunate to be indebted to so many.

ABBREVIATIONS

BOC Baudelaire, Charles. *Oeuvres complètes.* Edited by Claude Pichois. 2 vols. Paris: Gallimard, 1975 (Vol. 1), 1976 (Vol. 2).

Corr Mallarmé, Stéphane. *Correspondance.* 3 vols. Vol. 1 (1862–1871), edited by H. Mondor. Paris: Gallimard, 1959. Vol. 2 (1871–1885), edited by Henri Mondor and Lloyd James Austin. Paris: Gallimard, 1965. Vol. 3 (1886–1889), edited by Henri Mondor and Lloyd James Austin. Paris: Gallimard, 1969. In cases when letters also appear in Bertrand Marchal's recent edition of Mallarmé, *Oeuvres complètes* (*MOC*), page references are given only for the latter.

DSM Barbier, Carl Paul, ed. *Documents Stéphane Mallarmé.* 7 vols. Paris: Nizet, 1968–1980.

MOC Mallarmé, Stéphane. *Oeuvres complètes.* Edited by Bertrand Marchal. 2 vols. Paris: Gallimard, 1998 (Vol. 2), 2003 (Vol. 2).

MOC 1945 Mallarmé, Stéphane. *Oeuvres complètes.* Edited by H. Mondor and G. Jean-Aubry. Paris: Gallimard, 1945. Dual page references are given only when there are substantial differences between this edition and Bertrand Marchal's more recent edition of Mallarmé, *Oeuvres complètes.*

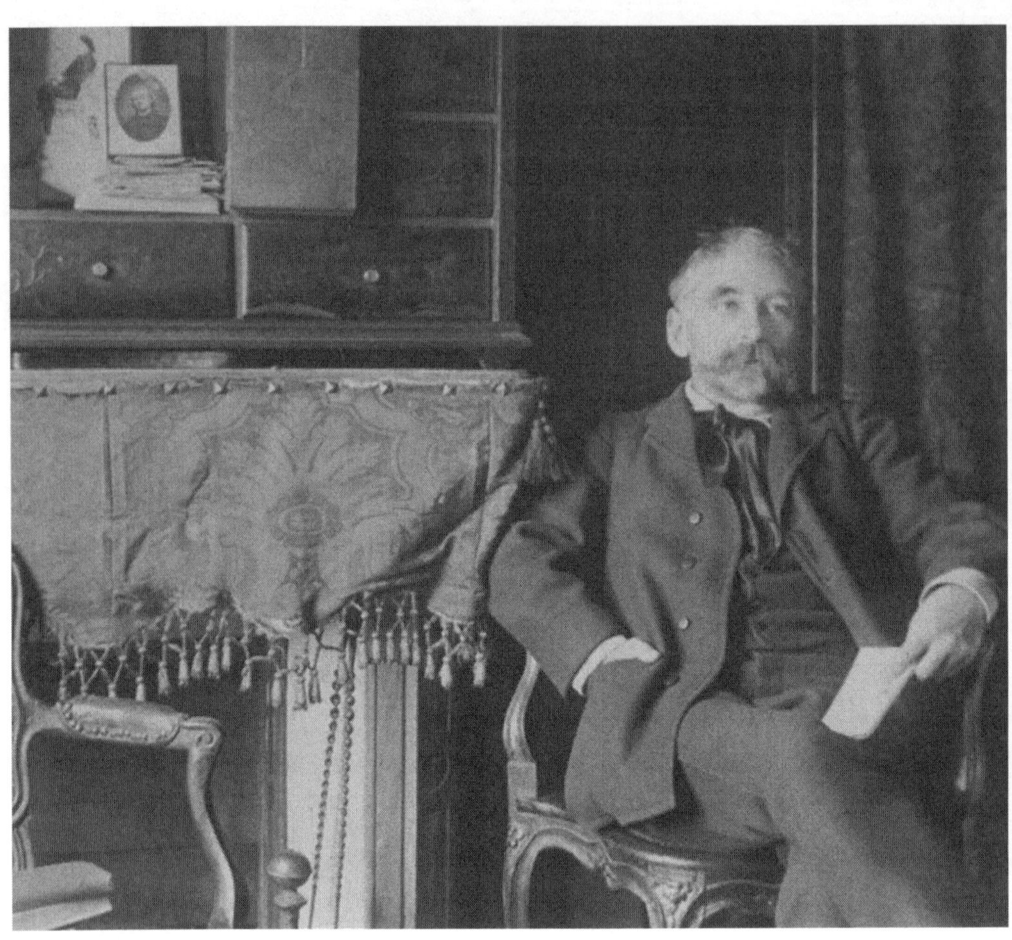

DETAIL OF PLATE 7
Dornac, Stéphane Mallarmé, poet. Series "Nos Contemporains chez eux."
Bibliothèque littéraire Jacques Doucet, Paris.

This photographic portrait shows Mallarmé posing for the series *Nos Contemporains chez eux*. Illuminated by the window and centered, is a framed photograph of Baudelaire. Recently auctioned at the May 2008 Hotel Drouot sale of the private collection of Dornac, the photographer's copy dons a mounting inscribed with a previously unpublished autograph-poem by the poet, who assimilates the privileged instant, the "lieu" of the autograph-poem, to the photographic process and to the signature of the moment:

> *Voici, lieu des instants élus,*
> *Que tu connais le photographe,*
> *Il reproduit jusqu'à ton plus*
> *Flottant songe et, moi, je paraphe.*
>   SM

INTRODUCTION

Picture this . . .

IN MY VIEW, a mere glance—*un coup d'oeil*—at this chapter's subtitle illustrates the principle lines of argumentation I draw in it, foregrounding the framing of our own discourses—and Stéphane Mallarmé's—as both encoded and simultaneously encoding acts. The metaphors that pass so transparently in the cliché "picture this," which asks that you imagine, and again in the rhetorical "in my view," which frames and exposes how I will illuminate the place and time of the visual in this study, inextricably link our verbal symbolic system to the act of looking, to the gaze, and to a visual epistemology, that codifies cognitive events and psychic phenomena with metaphors that appear like so many déjà vus, already seen, already there, in the realm of the visual.

Embarking on this verbal adventure, I remain highly conscious that the metaphors with which I write cannot be severed from the visual aspect of the universe that informs them, and that this act that any verbal adventure presupposes—the reading act—is, in the nineteenth century and perhaps even today, intimately linked to a visually metaphorized model of perception that is presently occurring, as the lines and curves and blanks on this page trigger a flurry of physiological responses between the visual faculties and the brain. The visual model of psychic functioning to which I allude might appear to support Susan Sontag's affirmation that "humankind lingers unregenerately in Plato's cave, still reveling in its age-old habit, in mere images of the truth" (*On Photography*, 3). And yet the visually encoded critical paradigms I exhibit here surpass the questions of image and copy that such a declaration assumes, aspiring not only to another way of seeing, but also to another way of looking at the work of Stéphane Mallarmé.

MALLARMÉ AND THE PHOTO-GRAPHIC PROJECT

In his 1896 "Le mystère dans les lettres," Mallarmé states that one should be "oublieuse même du titre qui parlerait trop haut" (*MOC* 2:234). Although my title for this book is one that Mallarmé might have classed among the too resounding, each of its reciprocally reflecting terms highlights the pivotal points of my discussion of his aesthetic. "Frameworks" refers simultaneously to myriad frames of aesthetic and epistemological reference informing Mallarmé's theory and practice, to the role of the pictorial arts, and finally, to a complex process of framing and composition as graphic aspects of Mallarmé's texts.[1] I have chosen the term "interdisciplinary" not only to refer to parallels with the different arts, but also to evoke correspondences with the hard sciences and "new laws" discernible in Mallarmé's conception of poetic signification and his discussions of representation. Although the "photo" and the "graphic" in my subtitle allude to the advent of photography and the impact that such technological and scientific advances and metaphors may have had on aesthetic discourses and on discussions of mimesis in particular, the "photo" and the "graphic" refer primarily to Mallarmé's verbal exploitation of analogies with light and graphics, and to the various levels on which such "aspects"—derived from the Latin noun *aspectus,* "appearance," and related to the verb *ad specere,* "to look at"—may function in his texts. Through "scientific" analogies with light and graphics, Mallarmé's texts articulate a reconceptualization of mimesis and accentuate their own preoccupation with a mimetic capacity that may seem to eschew the tradition of *ut pictura poesis* (as in a picture, so in poetry). And yet, even when explicitly comparing poetic language to arts other than painting, it is through paradoxical games of the "photo" and the "graphic" and a complex approach to framing processes that Mallarmé articulates and activates his aesthetic.

FRAMING THOUGHTS: *M'INTRODUIRE DANS TON HISTOIRE*[2]

The work of Stéphane Mallarmé (1842–1898) has long been considered the product of a poet who had no concern for the outside world, no use for technological development or the sciences, and little interest in the ups and downs of the art market. Although he was recognized as the mastermind and host of the famous Tuesday evening Paris salons, a regular meeting place for painters and writers as diverse as Emile Zola, Paul Valéry, and André Gide, the "mystery" of this author's production has riveted critics for over one hundred years.

Frameworks for Mallarmé provides insights into the interdisciplinary and interartistic frameworks of the poet's "hermetic" writings. The book defines the cultural and socioeconomic matrices that fostered his poetic choices, demonstrating that what Mallarmé terms "a crisis in literature" ("Crise de vers," *MOC* 2:204–13) was the result of economic, political, and technological forces transforming the landscape of artistic production—pictorial and verbal. It situates Mallarmé's poetics within an economic, political, and aesthetic framework to demonstrate why and *how* he strategically sought to eschew traditional "realistic" precepts of representation.

By highlighting artists' perceptions of the popular press and scientific inventions such as photography, *Frameworks* suggests how the possibility of an "exact" representation of nature, the "menace" of the mass reproduction and dissemination of art, and the French government's midcentury push for nonfictional representation, all transformed art and literary markets of the time. Although Mallarmé's writings on the effects of the modernization of the art market have, along with his art criticism, received scant attention, this study shows that by paradoxically exploiting such "modernization," the poet deftly positions his art as a tactically ingenious response to contemporary aesthetic debates over the faithful representation of nature—mimesis.

By tracing the significance of the pictorial arts for Mallarmé's thought and the consubstantiality of the visual and the textual in his writing, *Frameworks* explores the place of the pictorial arts and the history of the painting–poetry comparison to show how they are fundamental for Mallarmé's aesthetic thought—even for his thoughts on music and dance. The book not only reexamines the poetry and painting of the 1860s and 1870s against the debates over realism that polarized midcentury aesthetics, it provides a concrete analysis of the place and functioning of the visual in Mallarmé's work as it was to develop through the 1890s.

Although my analyses focus primarily on the place and function of interartistic and interdisciplinary parallels in Mallarmé's aesthetic thought and practice, one of the insistent underlying questions I address here is: Why, more than a century after the poet's death, has this type of aesthetic contextualization not been ventured before? As a preliminary response, I refer the reader to Mallarmé's phrase in my subheading, "M'introduire dans ton histoire," which, like much of Mallarmé's aesthetic thought and practice, has been somewhat (though not entirely) arbitrarily isolated from its context.[3]

Since critical endeavors most often seek to illuminate an aspect of a writer's production, they remain, perhaps by definition, adventures in fragmentation. In some respects, this is due to our own scholarly heritage. As heirs to nineteenth-century critical practices and the dissection and reconstitution that characterized nineteenth-century epistemological endeavors, the desire to isolate, analyze, and classify seems to come quite naturally. While the "naturalness" of such endeavors has now come under scrutiny, this mode of inquiry, particularly as regards critical practices in the United States, seems to have gained momentum from our current academic literary market. Academic market forces determined the critical approaches to Mallarmé's work and, from the mid-twentieth century, prompted studies that were either devoted to a single author or to a single aspect of that writer's work. Necessarily centering certain themes, structures, or analogies at the expense of others, whether focusing on the poet's technique (Malcolm Bowie, *Mallarmé and the Art of Being Difficult,* 1978), imagination (Jean-Pierre Richard, *L'univers imaginaire de Mallarmé,* 1961), his "religion" (Bertrand Marchal, *La religion de Mallarmé,* 1988), metaphors (Deborah A. K. Aish, *La métaphore dans l'oeuvre de Stéphane Mallarmé,* 1981), rhyme (Graham Robb, *Unlocking Mallarmé,* 1996), or single works by the poet such as *Un coup de dés* (Virginia La Charité, *The Dynamics of Space,* 1987), "Prose" (Marshall Olds, *Desire Seeking Expression,* 1983), or "Igitur" (Robert Greer Cohn, *Mallarmé's "Igitur,"* 1981), Mallarmé studies has, until very recently, remained in line with this critical trajectory. It is thus not surprising that discussed in biographical or in scholarly monograph form, until the late 1990s, Mallarmé's work was more often than not considered in isolation from the cultural and aesthetic contexts in which it was produced.

It almost seems disturbing now that Mallarmé has, for well over a century, remained a cult figure whose writing is still associated with uniqueness. That said, it is indisputable that over the past forty years Mallarmé studies has become an increasingly diverse domain. While the field was once limited to discrete textual analyses or anecdotal presentations of the artist's struggle with his medium, Mallarmé has become a figure whose work and theories are discussed in courses and books in disciplines as diverse as philosophy, art theory, theater studies, music, and dance. In part, the dissemination of Mallarmé's "word" must be attributed to the critical efforts, theories, and far-reaching readerships of poststructuralist thinkers such as Julia Kristeva, Roland Barthes, Jacques Derrida, and Michel Foucault. These writers, via their psychoanalytic, semiotic, deconstructive, and historical approaches to discourse, have underscored the complexity and the richness of this poet-critic's vision. Offering new readings of particular Mallarmé texts, they have been instrumental in initiating modern and postmodern perspectives on Mallarmé and in providing the theoretical apparatuses with which critics of the 1980s and 1990s approached the writer's processes. Their works have reached a public well outside the sphere of traditional Mallarmé studies and so, in many ways, has Mallarmé.

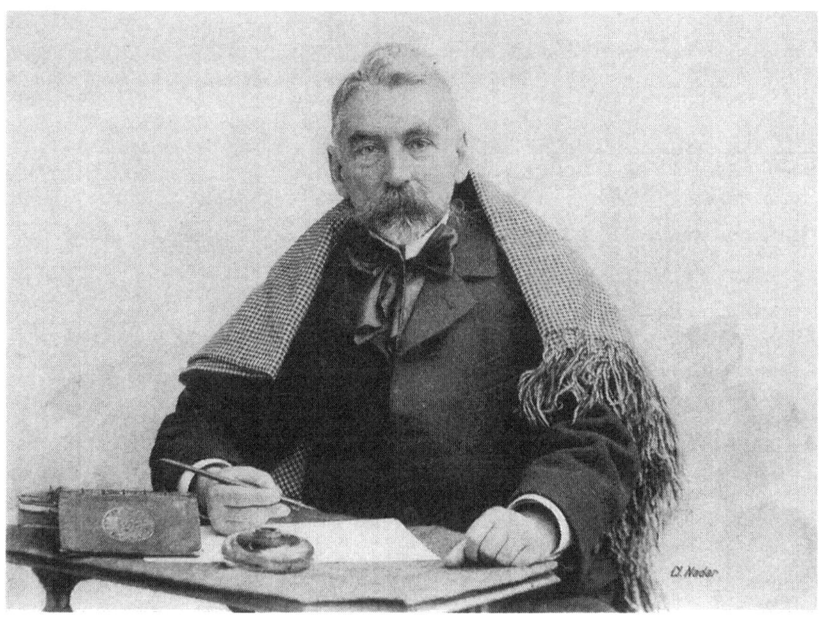

PLATE 1

Nadar, Mallarmé at his work table. Collection M. Edouard Dujardin.
Bibliothèque littéraire Jacques Doucet, Paris.

Significantly, the vulgarization of the vogue of theory and theoretical approaches to Mallarmé's work coincided in the United States with an ongoing constriction in academic publishing that, somewhat paradoxically, further disseminated and contextualized the poet's work. Most recently, manuscript-length works in the United States that treat Mallarmé have been characterized by more than merely the selection of an aspect, element, or theme in the poet-critic's work.[4] This trend in contemporary criticism, reinforced as well by the rise of cultural studies, may have been one of the major forces that propelled more open readings of Mallarmé. Often based on a model of juxtaposition, these books, which present a theme or structure and explore that model in a number of writers' works, have not only turned toward an examination of his textual processes, they have positioned Mallarmé's oeuvre within a variety of contexts. Constituting meaning and identity relationally, these juxtapositions have opened a window onto new inscriptions, transforming how we reconstruct our vision of Mallarmé's cultural production.[5]

The heightened sensitivity that marked critical endeavors from the 1960s on—sensitivity to the dynamics of discourse and the implications of one's position in discourse—had a clear impact on studies of Mallarmé. Nonetheless, while this type of self-conscious appraisal has become almost a generic practice, its relevance here is magnified less by a desire to mark my work as self-aware than by the conspicuous absence of critical attention to Mallarmé's own self-awareness. I am insisting here on what would now seem a somewhat obvious relationship between the writing subject and shifts in print culture in order to underscore the rather surprising dearth of readings that would note a kinship between market concerns for writers today and those of Mallarmé. This disregard for the commercial and industrial perspicacity of a Mallarmé who is nonetheless typically read as a highly self-conscious author is all the more striking when we consider that he was an astute commentator on his times. As the former writer and editor of a fashion magazine, *La dernière mode,* and as a published poet, freelance journalist, and cultural correspondent, Mallarmé literally and lucidly inscribed his awareness of transformations and trends in his own publishing market. Indeed, given that most of Mallarmé's work was initially published in the periodical press, it is almost astonishing that, until very recently, his journalistic activities did not prompt more critical inquiry that would view one of the most celebrated visionaries of the latter nineteenth and twentieth centuries from such a perspective—as a discerning writer in a burgeoning, modern, mass market. Even criticism of the 1970s and early 1980s seems to have distanced one of the most meticulous and self-conscious explorers of the self—the writing self and its act, one of the writers who delved deepest into poetic process and what verbal representation and signification may entail—from the taking of a self-conscious aesthetic stance not only in relation to the forces of a rapidly transforming art market, but also in relation to a cultural context, the epistemological and technological discourses of his era, and, oddly enough, aesthetic convention. And yet many of Mallarmé's texts do more than merely allude to these concerns; indeed, the place of the writer in the modern society of his time is an explicit preoccupation.

To complicate matters further, Mallarmé's association with obscurity and hermeticism, his departure from conventional poetics, made his work "inaccessible" to many critics and readers for decades. Even post-1998, with a flurry of books and a plethora of colloquia marking the centennial of his death, a moment when Mallarmé scholars the world over extolled the father of modern poetics as one who changed not only the faces of rhyme and verse, but also those of modern philosophy, music, and dance; even when faced with an ever increasing number of studies of Mallarmé's impact on contemporary writers, visual artists, and philosophers, and numerous works that propose to "unlock" or "unfold" Mallarmé,[6] his work is repeatedly described as too "diffi-

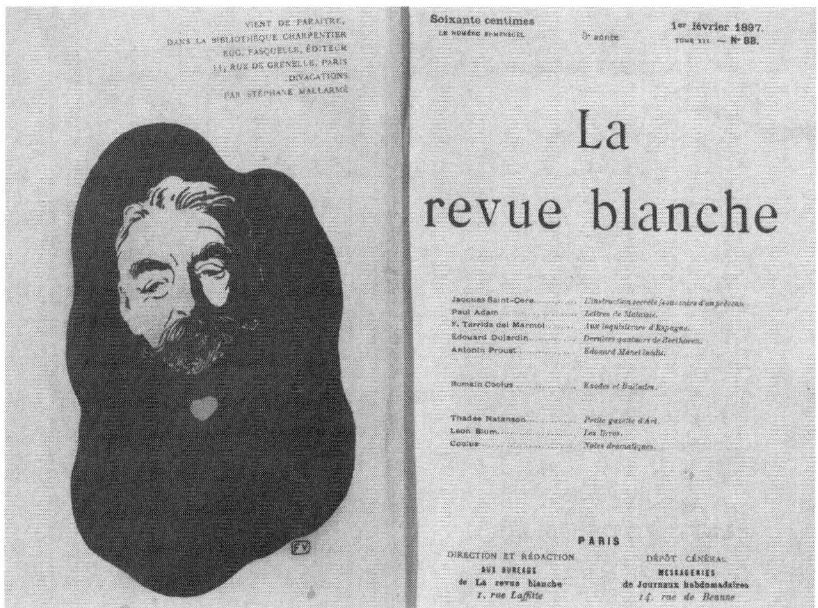

PLATE 2
Publication Annuoncement for Mallarmé's *Divagations* in *La Revue Blanche*.
Bibliothèque littéraire Jacques Doucet, Paris.

cult" to include in courses and even occasionally as "unreadable." The "difficulty" with which Mallarmé was and remains associated—one deftly illuminated by Malcolm Bowie, yet dismissed by Paul Benichou's 1995 *Selon Mallarmé* as a "je ne sais quoi"—is, however, now being productively addressed,
worldwide, from many theoretical and disciplinary directions.

My strategy in this book has been to approach Mallarmé's work from a
number of perspectives, systematically refusing to reduce the texts and the
generic hybridity of an author whose poetics is marked precisely by the desire
to inscribe the complexity of conceptual, material, and "modern" aesthetic
production. *Frameworks for Mallarmé* does not divorce Mallarmé's verse from his
prose, nor does it seek to include itself among the already abundant strictly
chronological introductions to the author's work. While I continually insist on
the richness and multivalence of many of the works, this book is intended to
appeal to readers of various levels and disciplines. The nonspecialist may glean
a better understanding of this poet's work, and, more generally, of how writers
in the nineteenth century might have responded to their aesthetic and cultural

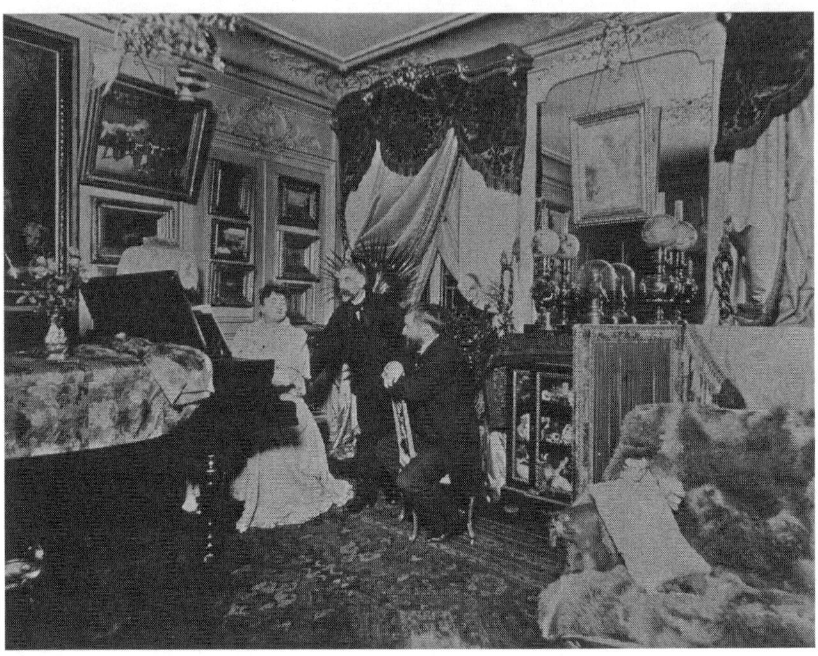

PLATE 3
Dornac, Mallarmé and Gervex with Méry Laurent, in her apartment.
Bibliothèque Jacques Doucet, Paris.

contexts. Nineteenth-century specialists and scholars who focus on the relationship between literature and the visual arts will find a reading that situates Mallarmé within the tradition of *ut pictura poesis* (the painting–poetry comparison) as well as within the cultural and technological unheavals of the late nineteenth century.

One noteworthy development in post-1998 Mallarmé studies that this book engages is a focus on the circumstantial and quotidian axis of the poet's oeuvre. Until recently, many of Mallarmé's texts were understudied or dismissed as "circumstantial" and therefore unworthy of serious scholarly attention.[7] Some commissioned texts were not included in the 1945 Gallimard/ Pléiade edition, his correspondence with Méry Laurent was sealed for one hundred years at the request of his family, and it was not until 2003 that Bertrand Marchal's two-volume *Oeuvres complètes* would gather, reframe, and resituate Mallarmé's writings in the context of their production and publication.[8] Why have so many critics neglected the circumstantial and the contextual in approaching Mallarmé? The fact that the most explicit and enlightening documents regarding this poet's conception of the role and functioning of art in his era have been marginalized is not solely an effect of our own market's demands. In fact, we rarely consider how our own tendency to isolate Mallarmé from the epistemology of his era, from many central and fundamental aesthetic traditions, may be more clearly seen from yet another perspective— the encoding of the texts and the writer's image by the writer himself.

In many ways, the "mystery" that has characterized Mallarmé's aesthetic production, and the aesthetic decontextualization that has isolated him from one of the most fundamental aesthetic principles of poetic and literary production, the *ut pictura poesis* comparison, may have been designed by the poet himself. The question, then, of a writer who worked at a time when literary markets were in dramatic transition might be posed otherwise: Might his own poetics have consciously contributed to his critical isolation? Might such a self-positioning be, much like our own, a response to market demands, in this case, demand for the rare? And finally, is it a coincidence that these texts have become such ideologically and aesthetically desirable commodities, or does their accrued desirability reflect the tactics of an extraordinarily astute speculator?

To address these issues, *Frameworks for Mallarmé* seeks to highlight some of the fundamental principles of Mallarmé's poetics, and to suggest hypotheses as to why Mallarmé's work has for so long remained so "mysterious." With such goals in mind, it may initially seem surprising that the study focuses primarily on the place and function of *ut pictura poesis*—at first glance so at odds with the poet's aesthetic. Even more surprising might be the effort to examine interdisciplinary parallels with the sciences—which seem far removed from the poet of "Brise marine" and "L'azur," a poet many readers of the canonized Mallarmé have come to know and revere. These aims, however, are much less divergent than they might appear.

Only recently have scholars begun to reassess the role of the sciences and the visual arts in Mallarmé's writing. By tracing the significance of the pictorial arts for Mallarmé's thought and the ways in which optical and photographic metaphors inform the visual and the textual in his writing, *Frameworks* responds to three distinct (yet not unrelated) historical categorizations of the poet's work. The first has understandably tended to crystallize around the importance of music. The second has largely ignored the significance of the scientific gaze, presuming—despite the poet's call for "depersonalization"—a rejection of positivism and a move toward metaphysics. This approach is in some respects responsible for the classification of Mallarmé as a poet who sought the "absolute," and, by extension, it can also be associated with a long tradition of viewing the father of modernity, one of the most fascinating poets and theoreticians of the nineteenth and twentieth centuries, as "impotent," "sterile," or as a "failure." The third tendency in criticism, now greatly on the decline, has either neglected or dismissed the fundamental role of visuality and the visual arts in framing the underlying framework—what Mallarmé terms the "échafaudage"—of this poet's aesthetic. As we will see, however, this third tendency is not all that surprising.

Mallarmé was determined to profit from all the arts. The metaphorical density of his texts, combined with a notoriously consistent practice of erasing his frameworks, strategically veils the painting–literature comparison to which his work responds. The dense palimpsest of interartistic and interdisciplinary analogy, as well as the combination of stratification and erasure that so productively multiplies dimension and effect in his poetic writing, destabilizes conventional poetic frames and shatters the looking glass of representation to push the outer limits of signification in the verbal arts. It would also seem to distance the poet completely from conventionally received notions of *ut pictura poesis* and the realistic biases associated with vulgarizations of this tradition.

Both Mallarmé's classification with music and his "uniqueness" have contributed to his critical isolation, a status that until recently tended to decontextualize him from the historical and epistemological moment, from the poets who influenced him most, and from the movement in which he began his career. To better elucidate the innovative poetics his texts present, chapters 1 and 2 culturally situate Mallarmé's poetic production in relation to mid-nineteenth-century aesthetics and epistemology. In chapter 1, "Frames of Reference I: *Une exquise crise, fondamentale,*" through a description of certain facets of the self-conscious development of the art scene in reaction to economic, political, and technological transformation, I delineate how a mid-century preoccupation with verisimilitude and the debates revolving around realism elucidate the Mallarméan oeuvre. The series of wide-angle shots presented in this chapter exposes the complex cultural matrix that informs Mallarmé's poetic choices. In particular, I discuss how economic and political pressures and scientific and technological developments provoked a reexamination of referentiality in art and a reinterrogation of the place of the *ut pictura poesis* analogy itself.

Although Mallarmé's writings on the effects of a modernization of the art market are largely ignored, as is his art criticism, in chapter 2, "Frames of Reference II: *Le futur vers se dégage,*" I show how and why, by paradoxically exploiting "modernization," Mallarmé adroitly positions his art as a tactical response to the aesthetic debates over the faithful representation of nature. Indeed, the latter section of the chapter demonstrates how the development of Mallarmé's "scientific" aesthetic responds to these issues while strategically seeming to refuse to address them as such. Here, I focus on Mallarmé's understanding of the functioning of cognition and the application of this knowledge to his poetics *in context*. Chapters 1 and 2 thus prepare the detailed presentation of Mallarmé's conception of psychic and textual image production traced in my reading of "Igitur."

Chapter 3, "Frames of Consciousness in 'Igitur': *Devant le papier l'artiste se fait*," is the cornerstone reading of the book; it provides a close analysis of an early kernel text, "Igitur," that rethinks Cartesian subjectivity and the cognitive processes involved in image perception and production. "Igitur" analyzes the place of the mirror and the mirroring function of both consciousness and art. It demonstrates how Mallarmé's textual production operates via analogy with contemporary visual models of psychic functioning to innovatively reenvision the optical biases associated with mimesis. It shows Mallarmé's conception of psychic creation as grounded in a dynamic model of virtual image production that, though positioned against and conceptualized through the visual, remains nonetheless figurative and fictive. My reading of "Igitur" also allows me to reconcile Mallarmé's "a-visual" conception of psychic image production with textual games of visual allusion and with what Leo Bersani describes as an "intention to create intentionality" (*The Death of Stéphane Mallarmé*, 19).

While critics often underscore the importance of the interrelationships between poetry, music, and painting in the nineteenth century, they rarely view the Horatian tradition or the concept of imitation as fundamental catalysts in the explorations that occurred between the visual and the verbal arts. In chapter 4, "Framed Works and Mallarmé: *The steadfast gaze of a vision restored to its simplest perfection*," via a detailed reading of one of Mallarmé's rarely studied English texts on Manet and the impressionists, I provide a very different picture of *ut pictura poesis,* methodically highlighting the degree to which Mallarmé's text demonstrates his awareness of its tenets and his dialogic engagement with trends in the pictorial arts. My discussion examines a series of interlocking subtexts that frame the article: *ut pictura poesis,* mimesis, and the effects of the advent of photography on both of them. I demonstrate how Mallarmé's piece comments on the evolution of modern art forms and explicitly links a reformulation of the faithful representation of nature in the pictorial arts to "new laws" and to parallel trends in the verbal arts. A close reading of the article on the impressionists illuminates the role his aesthetic "other" will play in the fashioning of his own poetic identity and vision.

Chapter 5, "Frame *Works* for Mallarmé: *Dans l'oubli fermé par le cadre se fixe, de scintillations,*" addresses the ways in which the poet explores and seeks to transgress conventional assumptions regarding verbal representation; it examines the use of analogies with the pictorial and graphic arts in the writer's verse poetry, texts on the pictorial arts, and his writings on dance. Here I analyze concrete examples of the multiple diegetic layers of Mallarmé's diagrammatic "photo-graphics," a complex use of light, graphics, and framing that grafts one set of representational relations onto another, paradoxically repositioning his writing within a reanimated tradition of *ut pictura poesis.*

Perhaps more than any other nineteenth-century innovation, photography captured the minds of the public and aestheticians of the mid- to late nineteenth century: while to some it represented a perfect mimesis that should be accepted on faith and faithfully copied, for others, the innovation presented a stimulus for *tekhné.* The currency of photographic effects generates innovation in the verbal arts, as a new, reanimated, and rejustified genre of *ut pictura poesis* develops.

Since *ut pictura poesis* has a long history of association with realism, a word that Baudelaire aptly describes as both "vague" and "élastique" ("*Madame Bovary* by Gustave Flaubert," *BOC* 2:80), critics have for the most part dismissed the comparison. However, the careful consideration of the underlying tenets of the sister art comparison presented in chapter 4 proves extremely productive in chapter 5 for readings of Mallarmé's work and analyses of his process. Mallarmé's reanimated mimesis actually uses conventions of mimesis and the *ut pictura poesis* comparison against themselves. Indeed, the traditional distinctions between the two arts become points of intersection forming a new species of *ut pictura poesis,* achieved through a complex use of light and graphics that rethinks verbal art's relationship to action via temporality.

At stake in the Mallarméan framework is a rethinking of the question of temporality via movement *in and of* space and time. Mallarmé's conscious rethinking of the faithful representation of nature as the faithful representation of *the nature of the sign* illuminates his conception of referential process in art. His model of perception and sensation is based on an analogy with natural law and the optical afterimage that he applies to textual creation, in a fascinating recuperation of the *ut pictura poesis* comparison. His acute awareness of the distinctions between verbal and visual signs and their relative representational capacities elucidates not only his use of the visual but his recourse to a series of analogies with music, the theater, and dance. In the latter sections of chapter 5, I examine how a delineation of the multiple levels of representation through interartistic analogy helps Mallarmé to dissimulate his fundamental aesthetic frameworks while simulating an experiential dynamic, one that has many affinities with the aspirations envisioned by the new painting of the impressionists he so admired.

In chapter 6, "Interartistic Frameworks: *Employez des comparaisons prises à tous les arts, mais la poésie les résume*," I show that even when explicitly comparing poetry to arts other than painting, the use of allusions to these other arts is permeated by a subtle, yet insistent, use of analogies with the graphic arts and visuality; Mallarmé articulates his comparisons with music, theater, and dance through games of light and graphics. This chapter concludes with readings of Mallarmé's verse, prose poetry, and critical writings that demonstrate how his recourse to different interartistic analogies serves to index a particular attribute of the poetic process. Such analogies insist on what I shall term the diagrammatic kinesis of a poetic language whose operations respond to the tradition of the painting–poetry comparison and "subsume" the attributes of all the arts.

The Coda, "Exposing Change: Quotidian Frameworks and Developing Movements," concludes the book with a consideration of the ways in which Mallarmé's aesthetics are integrated into daily writing practices, and, conversely, how daily life is accordingly appropriated and reshaped. I focus on the poet's oeuvre and his vision of the journalistic practices of his age to review how the writer's keen awareness of market issues, his readings of the hierarchical struggles between the fine and industrial arts, and his cunning incorporation of the daily and the spectacle of the modern life, may now critically mature as the work of an astute speculator. Mallarmé actively engaged the history of art, consumer culture, and technology. He was highly cognizant of the newly emerging markets he wished to play; his appraisals of the developing movements and the evolution of modern art forms reformulate and reactivate the *ut pictura poesis* doctrine, sounding a spectacular diagram of visual thinking and new laws.

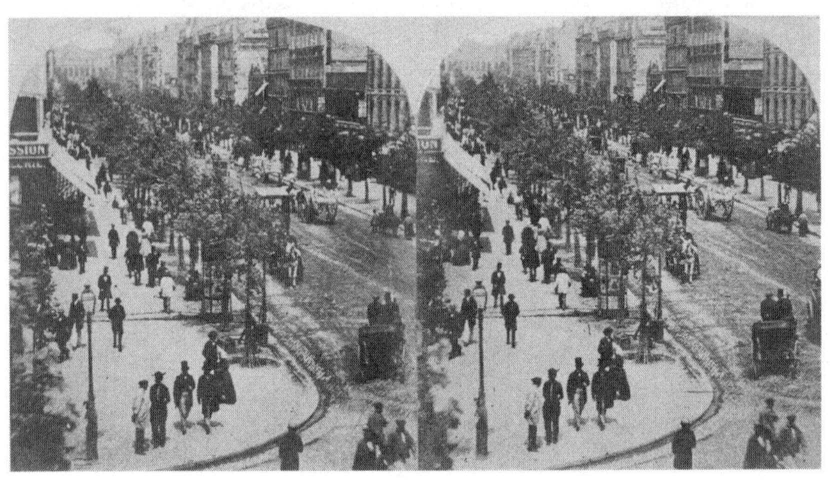

PLATE 4

Anonyme, Instantané parisien: Vue du boulevard de Strasbourg, vers 1860.
© Musée d'Orsay, Dist RMN/© Patrice Schmidt.

CHAPTER 1

Frames of Reference I

Une exquise crise, fondamentale

TOUT DEVIENT SUSPENS, DISPOSITION FRAGMENTAIRE[1]

SPEAKING WITH remarkable clarity as both poet and aesthetician, commas and colons chiseling each element of his enunciation, Stéphane Mallarmé in his 1885 text "Crise de vers" announces and contextually situates a crisis in literature:

> Notre phase, récente, sinon se ferme, prend arrêt ou peut-être conscience. . . .
>
> Même la presse . . . s'occupe du sujet, tout à coup, à date exacte.
>
> La littérature ici subit une exquise crise, fondamentale. (MOC 2:204)

Setting the stage in sentences that articulate the implications of their observations with formal resistance to their own narrative progression, in this passage Mallarmé foregrounds the medium of his art with halting acuity and intimates a self-interrogation on the part of an entire society's conception of verbal representation. For this halt, this coming to an awareness, refers not only to a crisis in literature. It also evokes a crisis in perception, as an era abruptly confronted with its own image becomes conscious of its modes of self-representation. What emerges is a specular and narcissistic crisis: A society's alienated image, projected and dissected before its own eyes, reveals the elements of its own construction(s).

In "Crise de vers," Mallarmé as both the observer of his times and the scriptor of the crisis presents an expanded version of the narcissistic crisis reflected in his earlier text, "Igitur."[2] Moving outward from that early close-up of the individual's spatiotemporal situation, the wide-angle frame of "Crise" exhibits not only Mallarmé's self-positioning as a writer, an observer, and a chronicler of his era, but also many aspects of the overdetermined cultural matrix with which he engaged. By highlighting the self-conscious developments of the aesthetic field and invoking their relations to economic, political, and technological transformations, "Crise" additionally links the formal innovations Mallarmé describes and enacts to a larger pattern of epistemological shift. In "Crise," which can be seen as a culmination of the thought process begun in the 1860s, Mallarmé suggests the degree to which his work exposes itself as highly conscious of its observatorial function and the concomitant systems of convention such observation assumes, its "take" on representation, and its place and functioning somewhere between the postromantic and the modern. But what is this "phase récente"?

Mallarmé's proclamation of a "finale d'un siècle," heralded as a news item ("fait d'actualité"), insists upon a historical break and performatively denotes that crisis in the shrieking assonance of the phrase, "*ici* une exqu*i*se cr*i*se." He hyperbolically frames this break—"pour la première fois, au cours de l'histoire littéraire d'aucun peuple," "jusqu'à présent," "toute la nouveauté" (207)—to display and contextualize a rupture in the history of representation, as an era distinguishes itself from the past and decrees itself "modern." In this essay, evoking the death of Victor Hugo and a new and modern conception of French verse, Mallarmé also invokes the press, profits, truth, science, and the materiality of language, all to announce that the revelatory poetic act involves a resynthesis of fragmented elements: "l'acte poétique consiste à voir soudain qu'une idée se fractionne en un nombre de motifs égaux par valeur et à les grouper" (209).

Mallarmé's enumeration of themes in "Crise" indicates that he envisions the crisis he declares in terms of discrete yet interrelated "fragments" of a cultural system in flux. While the culmination of this type of observation is actualized in his vision of the poetic act—how it should be "seen" and how its fractionated elements should be arranged—it proves worthwhile to take pause ("prendre arrêt") to examine how what he explicitly describes as a heterogeneous and constantly shifting system of economic, technological, and institutional relations forms and informs his observatorial and discursive practices, for many of the shifts in print and visual culture that characterize the nineteenth century cannot be extricated from epistemological transformations that prepare them, and which they, in turn, actualize and reproduce.

The notion of seeing things as their parts, fragmenting and isolating the elements of an alienated object of observation, infiltrates all areas of nineteenth-century knowledge, including this culture's conception of representation and its modes of self-representation. The rise and popularization of scientific thought and the late nineteenth-century aesthetic exploitation of fragmentation, in particular, are seen here ultimately as consequences of one another. For scientific thought implies first the Cartesian gaze, the separation of the subject from the object of knowledge, the poet from his poetry, the speaker from his era, and, second, a new epistemological way of looking and of looking at seeing. And while it could (and will) be argued that the subject–object distinction and the observer it presupposes were reexamined in the nineteenth century, they were nonetheless essential axioms in the atomistic world outlook of Mallarmé's era.

Paradoxically, the subject–object distinction that subtends nineteenth-century aspirations to mastery in myriad domains is one of the very first axioms subjected to its own objectifying gaze for scrutiny. The once-stable relationship grounded in the immobile pair viewer/viewed begins to shift, as discoveries in physics, optics, physiology, and chemistry, and technologies such as the diorama, the kaleidoscope, the phenakistoscope, the stereoscope, and, not least, photography, capture the integral instability of light waves and visual perception, shaking the authority of the model and metaphors of the camera obscura as a window onto nature and the natural processes of the eye and the mind.[3]

But it is not only the rise and currency of visual culture that destabilize the land- and cityscapes of the nineteenth century. Urbanization, industrialization, and the technological revolutions that give rise to journalism and photography, and also to railroads, crowds, and devices such as artificial lighting, the telephone, and the match, which with one movement could trigger a series of processes, all serve to modify the environment and society's perceptions of it. In his critical works "Paris, Capital of the Nineteenth Century" and "The Work of Art in the Age of Mechanical Reproduction," Walter Benjamin posits a crisis in art and perception catalyzed by technological changes and mass production geared toward consumption by the multitudes; he underlines the importance of photography as one of the developing forces in this transformation of perception.

> During long periods of history, the mode of human sense perception
> changes with humanity's entire mode of existence. The manner in
> which human sense perception is organized, the medium in which it is
> accomplished, is determined not only by nature but by historical cir-
> cumstances as well. ("The Work of Art," 222)

Alluding, well before Benjamin, to a crisis in perception and integrating the epistemological transformations occurring in "modern life," Mallarmé's practice, marked by an active search for analogies and technical advancements in poetry, is prompted by a cultural context that fosters analogical thinking among the disciplines, as well as the application and exchange of epistemological systems in analyzing perception and art. Might the complex interaction between Mallarmé's "phase récente" and his poetic language elucidate the logic underlying his aesthetic choices and the means he exploits to articulate them?

Mallarmé's writings are visibly conscious of the interrelations among the arts and their shifting positions in the society that produces and consumes them. In "Crise," the rise and popularization of scientific thought and the late nineteenth-century aesthetic exploitation of scientific observation and metaphors, fragmentation, and kinesis are seen as intimately related to a crisis in literature. And while Mallarmé's interest in representation, along with his obsession with specularity and the contingent problems of subjectivity and objectivity, will here be examined within the broader cultural context of his era, such a point of departure does not assume that the cultural history of Mallarmé's aesthetics is more important than the "how" or the "product." On the contrary, it endeavors to respect and appreciate the itinerary of Mallarmé's own path of development and his aesthetic choices: his "manner" and "medium," in Benjamin's terms. As early as the 1860s, more than twenty years before "Crise de vers," Mallarmé considered the writing process in material terms and envisioned the written work as a self-conscious artistic product that, by imposing itself within existing epistemological and aesthetic frameworks, reshapes a society's systems and definitions of representation. Indeed, a consideration of the complex interaction as philosophical, scientific, and aesthetic discourses overlap with mechanical techniques, institutional requirements, and socioeconomic forces is crucial to any account of Mallarmé's evolution as an observing and practicing writing subject who, like his aesthetic, presents at once a "historical product and the site of certain practices, techniques, institutions and procedures of subjectification" (Jonathan Crary, *Techniques of the Observer*, 5).

The discussion in the remaining sections of this chapter, presented as an array of snapshot views, reflects the emblematic descriptions, in "Crise," of verse, the literary market, and the poet's era: "tout devient suspens, disposition fragmentaire" (*MOC* 2:211). These views of a heterogeneous background taken from different angles explore shifts in print culture that imply changes in the status of the writer within capitalistic society. Such shifts, I suggest, are linked to more than the economics and technologies that alter the status of the art object and its producer; they also engage with the political institutions that legislate and occasionally censor their activities. Additionally, the pervasive discourses of scientificity and the scientific method are fundamental to an understanding of the field in which the writer's perception and aesthetic self-positioning will evolve. Indeed, much of Mallarmé's discussion of perception as visually encoded points to sites where aesthetics and epistemology intersect, informing the metaphoric relations between the arts and the sciences of his era and reshaping the relations between the arts. I argue here that it is precisely the progressive assimilation of a process of alienation, dissection, and reconstitution, particularly its role in the refashioning of the term "realism" and its corollary, "imitation," that gives rise to Mallarmé's internally performative, "photo-graphic" aesthetics.

TRIOMPHE, DÉSESPOIR . . . LE HAUT COMMERCE DE LETTRES[4]

During the reign of Louis-Philippe (1830–1848), as France entered the Industrial Revolution, nineteenth-century artists were thrown into a rapidly changing environment. Mallarmé's early childhood years were marked by an atmosphere of cultural explosion and political turbulence. His lifetime (1842–1898) spanned the rise and fall of five governments, two revolutions, a coup d'état, and major societal transformations catalyzed by economic development and supported by the successive governments of the reigning bourgeoisie.

The implications of the Industrial Revolution and the resulting economic and technological advances affected artistic and intellectual thought and production throughout the nineteenth century. Reactions to industrial development in France fluctuated between an intense enthusiasm for—and faith in—technology, and a wary distrust of its effects. Provoked by the unsettling rapidity of change in its everyday environment, the culture's consciousness of its historical moment was further heightened as the Enlightenment ideal of progress, feverishly pursued in all domains, generated dramatic transformations in artistic, literary, and journalistic production. The public not only experienced a reshaping of their world, they read about it.

A particularly prophetic statement by Alphonse de Lamartine, in an 1831 response to the editor of *La revue européenne*, projects the profound effects upon the literary world that technology was to catalyze:

> Ne voyez pas dans ces paroles un superbe dédain de ce qu'on appelle journalisme; loin de là. J'ai trop l'intelligence de mon époque pour répéter cet absurde non-sens, cette injurieuse ineptie contre la presse périodique, je comprends trop bien l'oeuvre dont la Providence l'a chargée; avant que ce siècle soit fermé, le *journalisme* sera toute la presse, toute la pensée humaine. Depuis cette multiplication prodigieuse que l'art a donnée à la parole, multiplication qui se multipliera mille fois encore, l'humanité écrira son livre jour par jour, heure par heure, page par page; la pensée se répandra dans le monde avec la rapidité de la lumière; aussitôt conçue, aussitôt écrite, aussitôt entendue, aux extrémités de la terre, elle courra d'un pôle à l'autre, subite, instantanée, brûlant encore de la chaleur de l'âme qui l'aura faite éclore, ce sera le règne du Verbe humain dans toute sa plénitude; elle n'aura pas le temps de mûrir, de s'accumuler sous la forme de livre; le livre arriverait trop tard; le seul livre possible dès aujourd'hui, c'est un journal. ("De la politique rationnelle," 128–29)

Preceding the great rise in periodical literature by only a few years, Lamartine's commentary not only anticipates the rapid expansion of the press under Louis-Philippe and the Second Empire, it also foresees a new conception of journalism.

The swift expansion of industry and the increase of capital that launched the revolution of the press dates to 1836, the year that Emile de Girardin initiated his innovative marketing measures for financing *La presse*. For the first time in France's history, newspapers would no longer be financed only by subscriptions, but by advertisers' announcements.[5] The result, as other papers followed suit, was a dramatic increase in readership. This rapid growth of the press and the development of more affordable printing methods did not, however, immediately revolutionize the book industry. Book publishers remained plagued by poor revenues and distribution problems that were then passed along in low payments to writers. Given these unfavorable conditions, many artists of the 1830s and 1840s began to publish in periodicals, which offered immediate payment and exposure.[6]

With the conditions of production in the literary market in dramatic transformation, the ideological functions of journalism and its role as creator and transmitter of information changed drastically. As Lamartine foresaw, the press would profoundly affect intellectual and literary life and thought. Particularly prophetic when applied to Mallarmé studies is Lamartine's assertion that "le seul livre possible dès aujourd'hui, c'est un journal." But the eerie accuracy of Lamartine's prophecy is even more compelling, for Mallarmé's "Livre," the culmination of his literary dream, the ultimate book, remained only a dream during the poet's lifetime:

> Voilà l'aveu de mon vice . . . non pas à faire cet ouvrage dans son ensemble . . . mais à en montrer un fragment d'exécuté, à en faire scintiller par une place l'authenticité glorieuse, en indiquant le reste tout entier. . . . Prouver par les portions que ce livre existe, et que j'ai connu ce que je n'aurai pu accomplir. ("A Verlaine," *MOC* 1:788)

From the Second Empire on, reforms in education and the relaxation of censorship in the 1860s reinforced capitalism's earlier financial support of the press. As sales in the periodical press increased, so did literacy rates within the general public.[7] The progressive "democratization" of the public, coupled with the rise of periodical literature, provoked uneasiness in the literary world and eventually precipitated changes in its structures. Indeed, as a growing number of writers' careers functioned around the sine qua non of publishing in the periodical press, the distinctions between journalistic and artistic life became increasingly blurred; consequently, the role of the writer changed profoundly.

As rapid technological and economic development continued through the Second Republic (1848–1851) and the subsequent imperial reign of Napoleon III, innovations in the printing industry eventually brought on a substantial increase in the production and publication of books, and technological progress eventually permitted mass production at lower prices.[8] Begun in the 1830s, the explosion in the literary marketplace of the 1860s and 1870s (which would continue through the mid-1880s) coincided with a dramatic change in the status of the literary art object and the status of the writer. Indeed, the second half of the century saw writing become a bourgeois *métier*—a mere trade—rather than a noble activity, as modifications in the public and in public education multiplied the ranks of debutant and professional novelists, poets, and critics.[9] Artists' ambivalence about the implications of a mass dissemination of their works and what Mallarmé in "Etalages" terms "l'extraordinaire surproduction actuelle" (*MOC* 2:222) was compounded by the tightening bonds between book publishing and the press. For while the rise of periodical literature and literary journalism made works and theories rapidly accessible, and indeed could determine the success or demise of literary works and careers, it at the same time exposed them both to criticism. No longer under the system of patronage, the writers of the latter half of the nineteenth century became advocates of and propagandists for their own work and their aesthetic vision—in short, for themselves. Moreover, as literature, once a luxury item, became an object of consumption, a complex dialectic was set in motion between literature as a market product governed by bourgeois tastes and a bourgeois public sphere created by the artists.[10]

Beginning early in the century, real, material demands of the market and changes in production modified art's self-image as well as artists' aesthetic decisions and choices. Many artists rejected the imposition of enforced conventions of creation and the menacing notion of what could become supply-and-demand market forces. The wary artist found himself in the contradictory situation of spurning the pressure to produce for the demands of the market and at the same time wanting to create a marketable product. Artistic responses varied. Literary reactions, in particular, ranged from a rarefaction and reification of literature that sought to maintain its aura of luxury and its value as art object, to the development of a new, active engagement that was essentially political and explicitly social in orientation. Often (and frequently in the same writers), both phenomena occurred simultaneously.

As mounting capital produced a new leisure-seeking and art-acquiring public, the number of art and technology exhibitions and reviews increased rapidly. The enlargement through journalism of the writer's role in commenting on daily life, analyzing frequent cultural events, and in the formation of a public of bourgeois consumers helped engender the figure of the poet-critic.[11] As writers felt compelled not only to justify their art, but to inform the public of the virtues of certain styles and works (whose aesthetics most often corresponded to their own), salons, art criticism, and the press began to serve as a laboratory not only for exchange among the arts, but also for exchange between the arts and the sciences, the latter often informing and "justifying" the former.

The tightening of links between, on the one hand, journalism, art, and literary criticism, and, on the other, technological developments and the hard sciences, proves instrumental in understanding the underlying tenets of Mallarmé's aesthetic pronouncements and his response as a late nineteenth-century writer coming to terms with a changing poetic identity. Contextualized, Mallarmé's poetic theory and language can be examined through the strategies he employs to adapt, reorient, and consequently subvert the dominant discourses and conventions brought to the fore and popularized through the press in the mid-nineteenth century. His "moment" is key to an understanding of how his choices, his manner and medium, respond to and establish the aesthetic and epistemological norms of his era.

UNE AMÈRE SENSATION D'EXIL. . . . QU'EST-CE DONC QUE LA PATRIE?[12]

Mallarmé's literary "career" began during the Second Empire, well after the strict censorship days of the 1850s had passed, and squarely within an explosion in literary production and publication affecting the novel and, particularly, poetry. This said, it must be understood that his direct models and masters were products of the July Monarchy and the Second Republic as well as the reign of Napoleon III. His early heroes were what Richard Terdiman refers to as the alienated "generation of 1848" ("1848, Class Struggles," 705).[13] According to Terdiman, this generation became highly conscious of the overwhelming contradiction between its self-image and its capitalist economic reality; the culturally constructed image of a republic of brotherhood and equality abruptly clashed with its economic reality when an iron-handed centralized government crushed the workers' rebellion in 1848. The outcome of the Revolution of 1848 marked, in part, an arousal of the consciousness of society's self-portrayal and the nature of representation as a construct.[14]

The dichotomy between political and social practice and the manner in which an epoch chooses to represent itself through discourse grew even more flagrant in the years following the Revolution of 1848. That year, Louis-Napoleon was elected as head of the Second Republic; however, after a coup d'état in 1851, the new government drastically tightened its rein on literary activity. The overt appearance of the mechanisms of the state apparatuses in these years, marked by strict censorship of journalism and literary production, and by consciously centralized education, not only blatantly contradicted the 1789 call for liberty but compounded the issues brought to the fore by technological forces in the artistic world. Highly conscious of the discourses of power and the mechanisms of ideology as determining forces, the intelligentsia quite simply became more determined.[15]

Mallarmé's first literary models lived under and reacted to the strictures of the Second Empire's early policies and represented their disillusionment and detachment from these forces as a rethinking of representation in general. Ross Chambers remarks that Louis-Napoleon's coup d'état of December 2, 1851, was the landmark of a new view of art's role and the artistic subject's conception of itself. Referring to the active and explicit role of literary figures in contemporary political events that characterized the earlier part of the century, Chambers borrows the expression "deterritorialized" to characterize a generation of writers subject to strict surveillance and highly conscious of their changing role and function in society. He describes the product of this self-consciousness culminating in the 1850s as a period that questioned the referential value of artistic signs:

> Deterritorialized art entered a period of confused self-interrogation concerning the referential value of artistic signs: what was art to be "about"? A formalist movement proclaimed the separatist doctrine of "art for art's sake," which had tempted Théophile Gautier since his preface to *Mademoiselle de Maupin* (1835), itself a response to the July Monarchy's authoritarian turn. It was to flourish in the Parnassian movement (Charles Leconte de Lisle, Théodore de Banville, José Maria de Heredia), which dominated French poetry in the latter half of the century, influencing Rimbaud and Mallarmé before the emergence of symbolism. ("1851, 2 December," 711)

Chambers suggests that despite the increase in the number of possibilities for publication and distribution, writers now subject to strict political censorship became all the more conscious of their activity; the role of the writer in the mid-nineteenth century began to diverge significantly from the active role of the social romantics. Chambers does not imply that these writers no longer alluded to political and historical events (especially in such genres as the novel), but rather that an insistent ambiguity concerning social reality marks these works; he describes the resulting literary phenomena as "forms of textuality which produce constant instability," and he proposes that such instability can be seen as "a response, with its own political force, to the imposition of order and control that characterized the dominant social discourses and practices of the Second Empire (1852–1870)" (712).

Particularly significant in the 1850s was the Riancey Amendment, which regulated and censored newspaper publications, promoting signed, non-fictional representation and thus demanding strict referentiality. The effect: Newspapers would be fined for publishing fictional writing. Not surprisingly, writers of that decade, subject to these guidelines and controls, responded to the suppression of their power to create new fictions and objected to the usurpation of their power to render the ideology of their time through art. These political restrictions, coupled with the social demands of the growing bourgeois public, essentially prepared the ground for a great deal of innovation. Whether in the self-conscious poet's shift toward the subjective in art or in the rallying behind the more objective "art for art's sake," individual writers, as well as the collectivity of writers, scrambled to situate their art and themselves in their historical context.

ARTIFICE QUE LA RÉALITÉ, BON À FIXER L'INTELLECT MOYEN
ENTRE LES MIRAGES D'UN FAIT; MAIS ELLE REPOSE PAR CELA
MÊME SUR QUELQUE UNIVERSELLE ENTENTE[16]

The progressive push for referentiality, reinforced by a bourgeois government and public, accumulated a bit more momentum than was expected. Rather than summoning a consensual entente in the domain of aesthetics as realism—whether pictorial or verbal—the concept resurrected a fragmented image as the term itself diffused. Quarrels over "realism" and "reality" in literature and the pictorial arts proliferated in journals of the 1850s; controversy over Gustave Courbet, the literary tracts of Jules Champfleury and Louis Edmond Duranty, as well as the notoriety of the literary trials of Charles Baudelaire and Gustave Flaubert (whose "realistic" texts were prosecuted for moral outrage), only compounded the problem.[17] Rather than promoting and clarifying the aesthetic norms of realism, these polemics illustrated the progressive denigration and vaporization of the terms "realism" and "realistic"—the diffusion of the "reality" problem.

The "realism problem" of the 1850s, rooted in the romantics' ambiguous promotion of nature, provoked a reinterrogation of the relations between representation and reality that would push the issue to its logical limits. Furthermore, the photograph and the dissemination of knowledge about the photographic process bore heavily on mimetic convention; in the pictorial arts, the implications of the photographic crystallized, immobilized, and posed in new terms the ancient questions of subjectivity, objectivity, realism, and truth in art. The rising importance and popularization of realism in painting and literature, compounded by technological development, resurrected one of the age-old conventions of representation: mimesis.[18]

However, both realism and mimesis are culturally and temporally charged conventions. As the problems triggered by the debates over realism and representation forced realism out from behind its veil, the term underwent the same careful analysis and dissection other cultural constructions of the period knew, and was revealed to be not simply a univocal concept, but a quite complicated and slippery word. The minute reexamination of "realism" would lead to revisionary definitions in both the literary and the pictorial realms.

Debates between the "academics" and the "modernists," which surfaced in the rise of romanticism in the 1830s and 1840s, had, at the onset, focused on whether to imitate ideal models or to paint "naturally." The moderns gained a great deal of popularity and created a following in painting and in literature; their ambiguous praise of "nature" and the "natural," originally structured in opposition to the academics' imitation of aesthetic models, soon provoked both confusion and, in some respects, the rise of realism. Was the artist to copy nature? As the highly sensationalized debates ensued on the relative virtues of imitation and exactitude, the romantic modernists progressively refined and, indeed, radicalized their positions. To temper the ambiguity of their insistence on the natural, modernists stressed the nature of the artistic agent's perception of the real or art's metaphysical properties.[19] Nevertheless, their early insistence on verisimilitude, illusions of "reality," and the "natural" provided the impetus for the various strains of realism that came to the fore in midcentury painting and literature. Similarly, the polemics between artists on the differences between painting and photography were highly publicized, and these discourses, polarized by the question of imitation and symptomatic of a fear concerning the future role of art and the function of the artist, infiltrated all artistic disciplines.

The tightening of the bonds between painting and literature, as both arts were affected by debates over realism and imitation, was particularly significant for Mallarmé's aesthetic thought. As contact and communication between the pictorial arts and literature were nourished by the rise of combined (literary and artistic) journals, the study and application of the methods and techniques of the two arts flourished. The inevitable comparisons that arose between painting and literature were defined in part historically, in part in terms of the contemporary sharing of knowledge, and finally, as a result of combating common enemies.

The painting–literature analogy, historically charged by the Horatian doctrine of *ut pictura poesis* (as in a painting, so in poetry), and the contingent convention of mimesis underlying the concept of realism on which it is based, took an interesting turn in later nineteenth-century French aesthetics. Mimesis and the term "realism" underwent analysis; the history of the Ingres/Delacroix debate had set the stage, and one of the effects of technology's capacity to reproduce natural scenes with exactitude was a move toward art forms that stressed the human, subjective side of creation. Finally, as scientific systems and historical methods put literary and artistic production and processes on their dissection tables, new discoveries about the action of the physical world and the nature of perception (especially optical perception) completely transformed the terms and conventions of the representation of reality in art.

Baudelaire's art and literary criticism document many of the issues that came to the fore at midcentury, as well as the kind of scrutiny to which they were subjected. Baudelaire's work also provides an example of one poet-critic's conscious attempt to analyze contemporary phenomena and to participate in the formation of the artistic values of his era. Without question one of the most important poets for Mallarmé's early poetic production, Baudelaire would also play a capital role in Mallarmé's later self-positioning as aesthete, journalist, and poet-critic.

NULLE ENSEIGNE NE VOUS RÉGALE DU SPECTACLE INTÉRIEUR,
CAR IL N'EST PAS MAINTENANT UN PEINTRE CAPABLE D'EN
DONNER UNE OMBRE TRISTE[20]

By its very nature, art criticism entails a dialogue with the public. The discursive subject, however, does not necessarily position himself on the public's level. Baudelaire, the art critic,[21] is the Baudelaire who may openly express and promote his aesthetic beliefs with the extraordinary conviction of a "master"; he sees it as his role and right to illuminate the public. Already in the *Salon de 1846* he consciously reminds the bourgeoisie of both his social significance and aesthetic superiority:

> Vous êtes la majorité,—nombre et intelligence; donc vous êtes la force, qui est la justice. Les uns savants, les autres propriétaires;—un jour radieux viendra où les savants seront propriétaires, et les propriétaires savants. . . . En attendant cette harmonie suprême, il est juste que ceux qui ne sont que propriétaires aspirent à devenir savants; car la science est une jouissance non moins grande que la propriété. Vous possédez le gouvernement de la cité, et cela est juste, car vous êtes la force. Mais il faut que vous soyez aptes à sentir la beauté. ("Aux bourgeois," *BOC* 2:415)

In his art and literary criticism Baudelaire takes issue with the push for nonfictional, "realistic" representation. His various discussions and *Salons* reveal that, at the outset, he clearly advocated Delacroix and romanticism and considered himself a modernist. By the 1850s, his stance is in direct opposition to authority's attempt to regulate representation; likewise, his texts show that he is overtly wary of the increasingly important role of technology in the arts. His tactic is to inform. Endeavoring to educate the public and artists alike, Baudelaire in his *Salon de 1859* (*BOC* 2:619–28) clearly stresses the subjective and the value of imagination—"la reine des facultés"—in art.

Deftly addressing the complex issue and ambiguity of the word "realism," Baudelaire makes explicit his desire to surpass visible nature in painting and in literature. He distinctly explains that his brand of "realism" encompasses and engages the imagination and the "reality" of the mind. The subjective perception of impressions of the objective world constitutes reality for Baudelaire: "Cependant, *if at all,* si Réalisme a un sens—Discussion sérieuse. Tout bon poète fut toujours *réaliste.* Équation entre impression et l'expression. Sincérité" ("Puisque réalisme il y a," *BOC* 2:58, emphasis in original). Turning the popularity of "realism" against itself, Baudelaire insists upon both stylization and imagination as essential functions in "realism" and in the creation of art. The reality of the artist's impression rendered in its appropriate form determines that which is "realistic" for Baudelaire. He thus dismisses the vulgarized conception of "realism" as nonfictional or as denoting the exact imitation of nature and treats the term as nothing more than a label for a convention that can be seen in more than one way, a catchall term. Baudelaire affirms that one can be a "realist" while simultaneously privileging connotative artifice as art; his vivid depictions of Parisian city life and the grotesque images of the streets are not to be seen as the imitation of nature divorced from the artist's mind and method.

In his 1857 article, "*Madame Bovary* par Gustave Flaubert," Baudelaire expresses his dissatisfaction with the misconceptions caused by the term "realism." He imagines Flaubert's thought process as follows:

> Et aussi, comme nos oreilles ont été harassées dans ces derniers temps par des bavardages d'école puérils, comme nous avons entendu parler d'un certain procédé littéraire appelé *réalisme,*—injure dégoûtante jetée à la face de tous les analystes, mot vague et élastique qui signifie pour le vulgaire, non pas une méthode nouvelle de création, mais une description minutieuse des accessoires,—nous profiterons de la confusion des esprits et de l'ignorance universelle. (*BOC* 2:80, emphasis in original)

Baudelaire sets out to clarify the common misconceptions of the word "réalisme." Rhetorically exploiting the insecurities of the dominant class, whose desire to become connoisseurs of art demonstrates their wish to possess knowledge, Baudelaire propagates his own view on the imitation of nature—the poet's nature. While he could easily have demonstrated the complexity of the word "mimesis" as a construct, which, like "réalisme," is both "vague" and "élastique," his strategy of attack is to discuss its principal tenet—the faithful imitation of nature. In the *Salon de 1859,* he again insists that the artist's intellect and perception are essential:

> Il est évident que, d'après les notions que je viens d'élucider tant bien que mal . . . l'immense classe des artistes, c'est-à-dire des hommes qui

> se sont voués à l'expression de l'art, peut se diviser en deux camps bien distincts: celui-ci, qui s'appelle lui-même *réaliste,* mot à double entente et dont le sens n'est pas bien déterminé, et que nous appellerons, pour mieux caractériser son erreur, un *positiviste,* dit: "Je veux représenter les choses telles qu'elles sont, ou bien qu'elles seraient, en supposant que je n'existe pas." L'univers sans l'homme. Et celui-là, l'imaginatif, dit: "Je veux illuminer les choses avec mon esprit et en projeter le reflet sur les autres esprits." (*BOC* 2:627, emphasis in original)

In this *Salon,* Baudelaire touches not only on the ridiculousness of the word "realism" and its vulgar slippage into positivism, but also on one of the principal arguments that has plagued the analogy between painting and literature, an argument that, since Plato and perhaps even today, gives a sort of primacy to visual representation. While Baudelaire could easily have attacked the vulgarization of realism on the grounds of the Aristotelian redemption of movement—the representation of animation and action as the faithful imitation of nature—he steers clear of the issue, and with reason. Into the Horatian prescription of *ut pictura poesis,* Baudelaire injects a fine dose of Aristotelian "making."[22] By insisting on the question of *which* nature (exterior or interior) one is to represent, he chooses the interior reality as experienced by the artist and rendered in formal medium and thus insists only on artifice:

> Dans ces derniers temps nous avons entendu dire de mille manières différentes: "Copiez la nature; ne copiez que la nature. Il n'y a pas de plus grande jouissance ni de plus beau triomphe qu'une copie excellente de la nature." Et cette doctrine, ennemie de l'art, prétendait être appliquée non seulement à la peinture, mais à tous les arts, même au roman, même à la poésie. (619–20)

Baudelaire valorizes the role of the agent and the essentiality of artifice. Through avoidance of the Aristotelian legitimization of movement, he eschews one key problem emerging from the pictorial arts; he was quite aware that the photograph was not only causing a stir due to its capacity to reproduce a natural scene, but that it was able—however "distortedly"—to capture and represent movement and atmospheric phenomena. Strategically evading the problem of respect for referentiality via imitation, he simply insists on man over machine and human nature over model.

As the poet critic rejects the constraints of the push for imitation of nature and attempts to create a voice for himself in the history of art, he asserts that both the imitation of nature as the public understands it and its

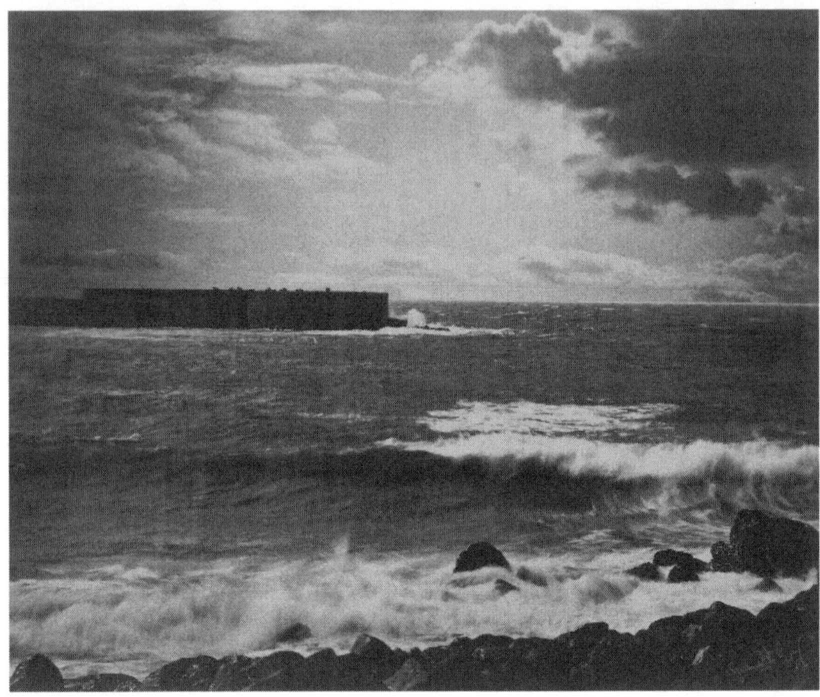

PLATE 5
Le Gary, Marine, La Grande Vague, Sète, 1851.
Paris, Musée d'Orsay.
© Photo RMN/© Hervé Lewandowski.

application to literature are anti-artistic. In the 1859 *Salon,* Baudelaire expresses his exasperation with his cultural environment. Addressing the bourgeois public's craving for the imitation of nature, he takes a few shots at the specific technological development of his time that was aggravating the contagious malady of the copy in the pictorial arts:

> Dans ces jours déplorables, une industrie nouvelle se produisit, qui ne
> contribua pas peu à confirmer la sottise dans sa foi et à ruiner ce qui
> pouvait rester de divin dans l'esprit français. . . . En matière de peinture
> et de statuaire, le *Credo* actuel des gens du monde, surtout en France
> (et je ne crois pas que qui que ce soit ose affirmer le contraire), est
> celui-ci: "Je crois à la nature et je ne crois qu'à la nature (il y a de
> bonnes raisons pour cela). Je crois que l'art est et ne peut être que la
> reproduction exacte de la nature. . . . Ainsi l'industrie qui nous don-

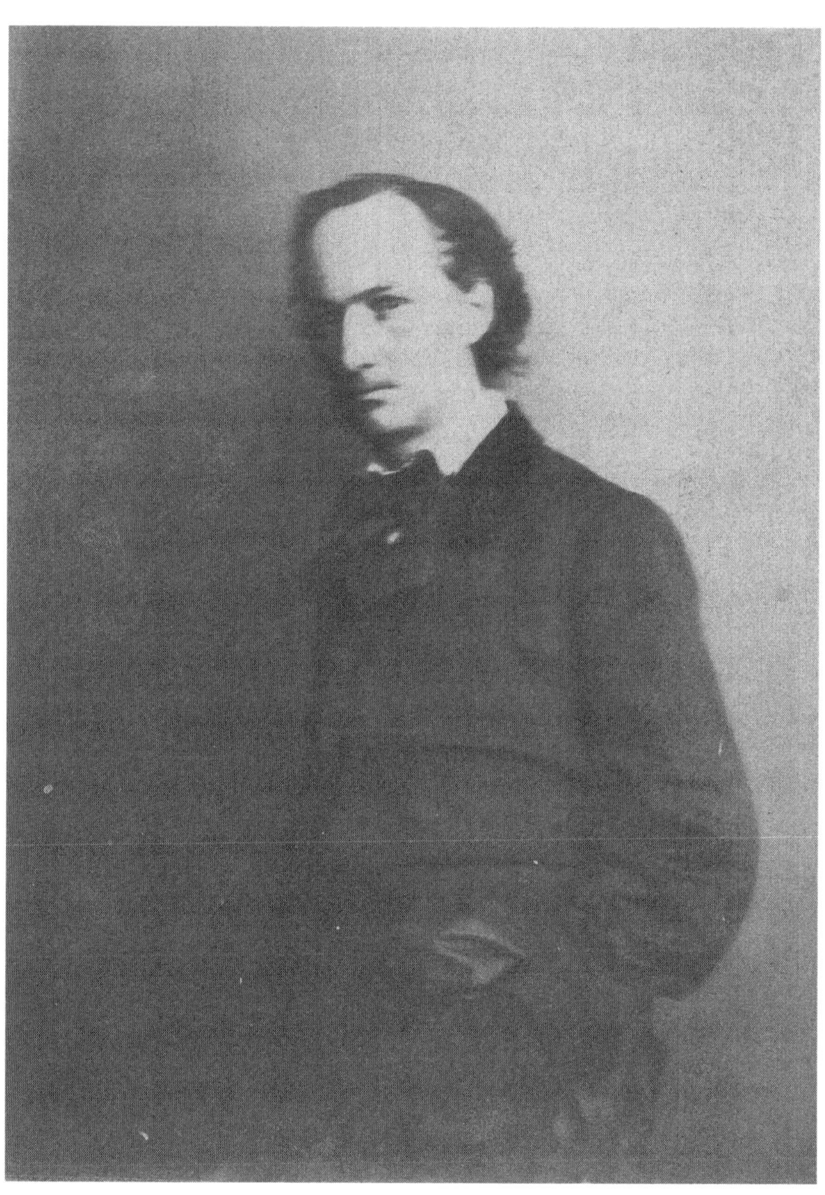

PLATE 6

Nadar, Portrait de Charles Baudelaire (1821–1867), poète.

Vers 1855.

Paris, Musée d'Orsay.

© Photo RMN/© Hervé Lewandowski.

> nerait un résultat identique à la nature serait l'art absolu." Un Dieu
> vengeur a exaucé les voeux de cette multitude. Daguerre fut son
> messie. Et alors elle se dit: "Puisque la photographie nous donne toute
> les garanties désirables d'exactitude (ils croient cela, les insensés!), l'art,
> c'est la photographie." A partir de ce moment, la société immonde se
> rua, comme un seul Narcisse, pour contempler sa triviale image sur le
> métal. (616–17, emphasis in original)

Striking home in his criticism of the society's taste, narcissism, and idiocy ("sottise"), Baudelaire distinguishes between art and industry; he makes it quite clear that the public doesn't know the difference. Positioning objectivity as contrary to art, Baudelaire consistently refers to photography as "une industrie" and states that this industry has been "le refuge de tous les peintres manqués" (618).[23] He concedes that photography has its place, namely in science, but he insists that it is a dangerous factor contributing to "l'appauvrissement du génie artistique français, déjà si rare" (618). Elaborating on this menace, he goes on to articulate very clearly the problem of art in a consumer market:

> Que l'artiste agisse sur le public, et que le public réagisse sur l'artiste,
> c'est une loi incontestable et irrésistible; d'ailleurs les faits, terribles
> témoins, sont faciles à étudier; on peut constater le désastre. De jour en
> jour l'art diminue le respect de lui-même, se prosterne devant la réalité
> extérieure, et le peintre devient de plus en plus enclin à peindre, non
> pas ce qu'il rêve, mais ce qu'il voit. (619)

In his definitions and evaluations of art, artifice, and excess, that which exceeds and artistically transforms the imitation of external nature is essential for artists and writers. Inspiration, then, which accounts for the reality of the mind and takes technique out of the realm of the ordinary, the reproducible, is of prime importance. Baudelaire's direct response to the modern threat to art explicitly stresses the subjective, the role of the agent in conceiving and forming the work of art of his era. But there are other innovations and literary strains germinating from this acutely conscious reevaluation of *which* nature to represent, if, in fact one should do so at all.

QUE CE BEAU MONUMENT L'ENFERME TOUT ENTIER[24]

In his discussion of Théophile Gautier, Baudelaire states that poetry has but one objective—itself: "La poésie ne peut pas, sous peine de mort ou de déchéance, s'assimiler à la science ou à la morale; elle n'a pas la Vérité pour objet, elle n'a qu'Elle-même" ("Théophile Gautier," *BOC* 2:113). This self-referentiality, taken up by poets under the banner of "art for art's sake," can be seen as both a reaction against and a direct product of the popularity of "realism" and referentiality. These poets, often associated with a transcendental "culte de la Beauté," nonetheless move toward the objective pole.

The poets called "Parnassian" here are those who participated in Catulle Mendès's first periodical symposium. *Le Parnasse contemporain,* organized in 1866 by Mendès and Louis-Xavier de Ricard, united a relatively divergent selection of poets. Though the group soon splintered into factions, the ideal behind the review was a collective response to social and political events that transformed not only art's self-consciousness, but the means for art's production—its "manner." A position overtly promoted by many of the participants of the review, the doctrine of "art for art's sake" promoted and propagandized art's separateness while proposing a new way of looking at art and its form. The move away from lyrical outbursts, from literature as useful or as an expression of the poet's thought, and toward a classical vision of form, marked a new way of perceiving the art object in an era when "realism," promoted by the state, by many critics, and by the bourgeois public, was prevalent. The *Parnasse* contributors were characterized by an aspiration to profit from the exchanges of the arts occurring during the period and an effort to create a separate reality for all the arts, simply saying art is "other."

Charles Leconte de Lisle, José Maria de Heredia, Théodore de Banville, and Théophile Gautier,[25] most often associated with the Parnassian movement, exemplify a mode of innovation in response to the issue of realism. As writers rejecting the utilitarian consumerism of their era and its implications, they shifted toward a concretization of literature as a molded medium with an existence and purpose of its own. By insisting on form, these writers produced poetic objects that call attention to the medium of their art. Exploiting properties typically associated with other arts and conventions of realism, their highly visual, formally rigorous texts appeal to sculpture and architecture in order to avoid the contingent problems of utility—demands on their art as language—as well as the forced imitation of a nature external to their work. Though these writers asserted that their art was distinct from "reality" and publicly denounced such notions as utility and progress in art, their descriptions are nonetheless extremely precise and objectified. In Gautier's *Emaux et Camées* and the sonnets of Leconte de Lisle, for example, while the poetic voice is the organizing force behind the poems, explicit subjectivity is removed. In a letter to Baudelaire, Victor Hugo astutely acknowledges the difference between the public pronouncements and tactical positions of partisans of "art for art's sake":

> Je n'ai jamais dit: L'Art pour l'Art; j'ai toujours dit: L'Art pour le Pro-
> grès. Au fond, c'est la même chose, et votre esprit est trop pénétrant
> pour ne pas le sentir. En avant! c'est le mot du Progrès; c'est aussi le cri
> de l'Art. (*BOC* 2:1129)

Recognizing the subtlety of "art for art's sake," Hugo exposes his awareness of the process of identification and differentiation in artistic process: "Que faites-vous?" he asks Baudelaire. "Vous marchez. Vous allez en avant. Vous dotez le ciel de l'art d'on ne sait quel rayon macabre. Vous créez un frisson nouveau." Acknowledging the generational contestation and competition that character-ized the self-positioning of literary vogues of the era, and affirming that any movement is innovation and thus progress, Hugo's interpretation of poetic innovation (which does not correspond to either Baudelaire's or the Parnas-sians' positions) insists that even in the explicit rejection of one's own cultural environment, the artist is responding to it: "Le poète ne peut pas aller seul, il faut que l'homme aussi se déplace. Les pas de L'Humanité sont donc les pas même de l'Art—Donc, gloire au Progrès." And adding the final touch to his evolutionary portrait, Hugo concludes his letter by putting Baudelaire in his rhetorical place: "Théophile Gautier est un grand poète, et vous le louez comme son jeune frère, et vous l'êtes" (1129).

CHAPTER 2

FRAMES OF REFERENCE II

Le futur vers se dégage

WHILE MALLARMÉ'S youthful poems and critical works are markedly Baudelairean, his correspondence reveals that he was simultaneously in close contact with the younger Parnassian poets. Many of these budding authors, Mallarmé included, were published in *Le Parnasse contemporain* (1866), alongside more established collaborators such as Baudelaire, Gautier, Banville, and Leconte de Lisle. Mallarmé clearly associated himself with the younger members of this new formalistic movement. In a letter to Henri Cazalis in 1864, he declared: "Nous sommes d'une école: nous vivons dans la mode" (*Corr* 1:118), and a year later, in 1865, he assured Eugène Lefébure that the latter, Villiers, and Mendès were among the young writers who composed his "famille spirituelle" (*MOC* 1:670).

Still far from the radically dense impersonal form and the syntactic fragmentation of his later manner, the poems Mallarmé published in 1866 indicate an evolution from the poetry of his youth and demonstrate his heightened insistence on form. In the same 1865 letter to Lefébure, Mallarmé alludes to his own conscious transformation of manner:

> J'étais renommé pour ne savoir pas m'arrêter. Or, depuis, n'ai-je
> pas, au contraire, exagéré plutôt l'amour de la condensation? . . .
> Qu'y a-t-il de plus différent que l'écolier d'alors, vrai et prime-
> sautier, avec le littérateur d'à présent, qui a horreur d'une chose
> dite sans être arrangée? (669)

Mallarmé's language and vision of art, like his contemporaries' views on the function of art, relate to cultural and social forces affecting aesthetics. In

1862 Mallarmé had already published several critical pieces that attest to his acute awareness of the issues affecting the modern writer. His polemical 1862 piece, "Hérésies artistiques: L'Art pour tous" (*MOC* 2:360–64), published in *L'artiste*, alludes to alterations in conditions of production for the poet.[1] This early critical publication announces the voice of a vigorously engaged, critical Mallarmé who is obviously well versed in the issues affecting modern aesthetics as defined by Baudelaire's criticism.[2] Mallarmé suggests in this essay that improvements in the means of literary production, the rapid commercialization and lowering of prices of literature, and the rise of a democratized public are not necessarily beneficial to the writer: "On multiplie les éditions à bon marché des poètes. . . . Croyez-vous que vous y gagnerez de la gloire, ô rêveurs, ô lyriques?" (*MOC* 2:363).

L'HOMME PEUT ÊTRE DÉMOCRATE,
L'ARTISTE SE DÉDOUBLE ET DOIT RESTER ARISTOCRATE[3]

Striking his pose early on in this 1862 piece, Mallarmé addresses the function of the artistic persona. Insisting on the mystery of the noble writing act, he states in "Hérésies artistiques": "Toute chose sacrée et qui veut demeurer sacrée s'enveloppe de mystère" (360). The apparent goal of promoting art as mysterious and sacred would, of course, be to safeguard literature from vulgarization:

> L'heure qui sonne est sérieuse: l'éducation se fait dans le peuple, de grandes doctrines vont se répandre. Faites que s'il est une vulgarisation, ce soit celle du bon, non celle de l'art. . . .
>
> O poètes, vous avez toujours été orgueilleux; soyez plus, devenez dédaigneux. (363–64)

Mallarmé insists that in this critical time marked by a menace to poetry, poets must assume a posture of condescension with regard to their public. One of his most obvious means to this end is the exploitation of religious vocabulary, a well-documented strategy of the Parnassians. The logical corollary of such a pose is that art and its image should thus be constructed in a fashion that maintains not only its cult value, but its market value as well. Mallarmé clearly recognizes that, in a consumer market, this amounts to one and the same thing: the higher the price, the higher the cult value.

> Et maintenant cette foule qui vous *achète* pour votre bon marché vous comprend-elle? Déjà profanés par l'enseignement, une dernière bar-

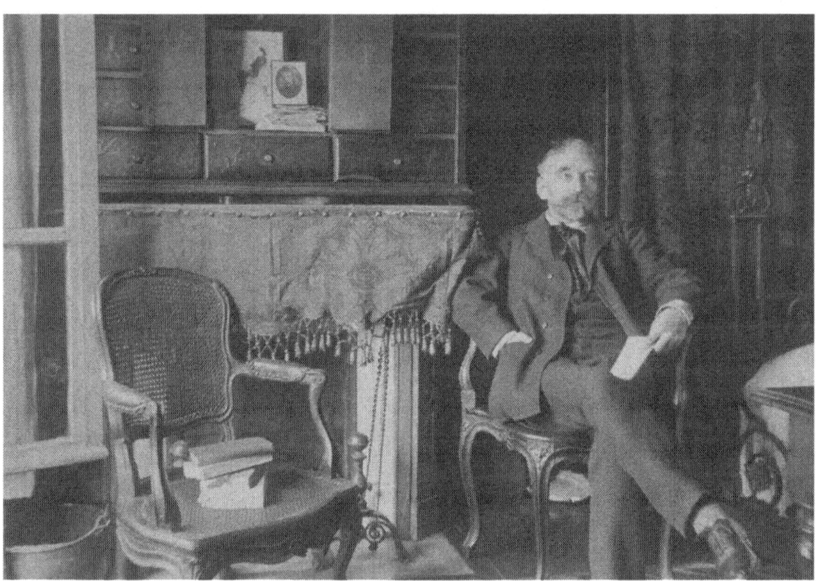

PLATE 7
Dornac, Stéphane Mallarmé, poet. Series "Nos Contemporains chez eux."
Bibliothèque littéraire Jacques Doucet, Paris.

rière vous tenait au dessus de ses désirs,—celle des sept francs à tirer
de la bourse,—et vous culbutez cette barrière, imprudents! O vos
propres ennemis, pourquoi (plus encore par vos doctrines que par le
prix de vos livres, qui ne dépend pas de vous seuls) encenser et
prêcher vous-mêmes cette impiété, la vulgarisation de l'art! (363,
emphasis in original)

Mallarmé expresses his frustration with the lowering of prices of books
and castigates the writers themselves as their own worst enemies. He also
firmly denounces the popularization of "doctrines" of art and explains that the
public should be informed as to how to perceive literature as art and the artist
as a lofty figure:

Il est à propos de dire ici que certains écrivains . . . ont tort de deman-
der compte à la foule de l'ineptie de son goût et de la nullité de son
imagination. Outre "qu'injurier la foule, c'est s'encanailler soi-même,"

> comme dit justement Charles Baudelaire. . . . Rappelons-nous que le
> poète (qu'il rythme, chante, peigne, sculpte) n'est pas le niveau au-
> dessous duquel rampent les autres hommes; c'est la foule qui est le
> niveau, et il plane. (362)

Without explicitly addressing specifics of any of the "doctrines" to which he
alludes, and certainly not the issue of imitation, or the push for referential literature lurking in the margins, Mallarmé distinguishes himself from Baudelaire
and proposes to instruct the public to accept poetry as an art that must be
practiced by trained artists and one that must not be tailor-made to vulgar
market demands or explained away. To reinforce the thesis that despite poetry's
use of the common medium of language, it should be experienced as an art
form, Mallarmé again draws analogies between poetry and the other arts:

> C'est que, la musique étant pour tous un art, la peinture un art, le statu-
> aire un art,—et la poésie n'en étant plus un (en effet chacun rougirait de
> *l'ignorer*, et je ne sais personne qui ait à rougir de n'être pas expert en
> art), on abandonne musique, peinture et statuaire aux *gens du métier*, et
> comme l'on tient à sembler instruit, on apprend la poésie. (361, empha-
> sis in original)

In his comparisons with the other arts, Mallarmé insists that the poet manipulates language as a sculptor would model a piece, or as a painter might arrange
color, light, and lines on canvas. The use of the analogy with music renders this
argument more forceful. He suggests that the signs on the page must no longer
be considered as words to tell the public a story, but as opaque elements of a
structure: "Nous sommes pris d'un religieux étonnement à la vue de ces pro-
cessions macabres de signes sévères, chastes, inconnus" (360). By comparing
poetry to music, Mallarmé already alludes to the slippage in poetry that renders the poet's use of language "mysterious"—words as nonimitative triggers.

HORS ET À L'INSU DE L'AFFICHAGE, DU COMPTOIR AFFAISSÉ SOUS LES EXEMPLAIRES OU DE PLACIERS EXASPÉRÉS[4]

The progressive hermeticism for which Mallarmé is known has traditionally
been used to depict him as either creatively frustrated and sterile, or as a poet-
priest devoted to a poetics dissociated from any real-world context and intelli-
gible to initiates only. This might be explained by the poet's own ambiguous
statements on the position of the poet:

> je crois que la poésie est faite pour le faste et les pompes suprêmes
> d'une société constituée où aurait sa place la gloire dont les gens sem-
> blent avoir perdu la notion. L'attitude du poëte dans une époque
> comme celle-ci, où il est en grève devant la société, est de mettre de
> côté tous les moyens viciés qui peuvent s'offrir à lui. Tout ce qu'on
> peut lui proposer est inférieur à sa conception et à son travail secret.
> ("Sur l'évolution littéraire," *MOC* 2:700)

Assertions such as this one and rhetorical techniques such as the repeti-tion of religious vocabulary, which promotes the image of a poet-priest and a sacred position for the artist and the work of art, can, however, be seen in another light. Taken literally, the previous citation proposes the necessity of a society that would be "constituted," a created society in which poetry would hold a glorious place. It does not seem altogether extraordinary, then, that a poet might wish to advocate a sacralization of his domain and *métier*. The cita-tion also posits the poet's "attitude" as a stance in the adversarial epoch in which he lives. Society is portrayed both as the force against which the artist struggles and the entity that must be reconstituted by the work of the poet.

Mallarmé practices what he preaches; he assumes the image of a poised poetic persona with a role in society, one that must be constituted in writing: "car méditer, sans traces, devient évanescent" ("L'action restreinte," *MOC* 2:215). His positioning of himself as poet-critic far from the crowd makes the authoritative distinction clear. A close reading of his discourses on the figure of the artist, his art criticism, and his correspondence reveals that many of the commonplace notions surrounding Mallarmé's legacy, the legacy of his pose, and his aesthetic promotion of obscurity are not only reductive but quite often read out of context.

Mallarmé, whose career revolved largely around teaching, was deeply involved in activities of the press. In addition to publishing poems and literary and art criticism in more than twenty different journals in France (one of them his own), Mallarmé acted as a regular cultural correspondent and occa-sional critic for several journals abroad.[5] With the role and function of the poet in rapid flux, Mallarmé actively engaged in the new functions of poet-journal-ist and poet-critic while maintaining and promoting the myth of the ivory-tower poet.

Despite a number of highly provocative critical pieces that seem to dis-miss and mock the press, all of Mallarmé's (non-posthumous) original pub-lished works first appeared in periodical form. Whether one chooses to accept the myth of the "total book" or to view the book as "virtual,"[6] the fact remains that Mallarmé's book, the *Oeuvres complètes,* is by and large a compilation of works published in the periodical press long before they had time to culminate in "le livre."

Under the imperial government of Napoleon III, Mallarmé had by the age of twenty already published ten pieces, and he would go on to publish twenty-one more before the fall of the empire in 1870. This substantial evidence repudiates Mallarmé's "ivory-tower," "poet-priest," and "sterile" image. The romantic image of the writer as an ideal or sacred figure was quite prevalent, and this facade, which Mallarmé and many other poets coming of age with *Parnasse* wished to project and to promote, was in fact largely cultivated and disseminated by the authors themselves—in the periodical press!

In reality, very few writers of Mallarmé's era were not published in, affiliated with, or involved in the editing of periodicals. Despite comments often taken out of context, such as "Il faut, si l'on fait de la littérature, parler autrement que les journaux" (*Corr* 3:67), which was actually written in *praise* of the appearance of a new type of specialized literary journal, Mallarmé remained intensely connected to the journalistic world: His correspondence of the 1870s documents that he was constantly seeking journalistic work, and, in the 1880s, he was one of the major supporters of *La revue indépendante*.[7] Mallarmé acted as critic, journalist, and advocate of the arts in journals and literary reviews and openly took stands on issues of taste, judgment, and the pricing of art. Further, pieces such as the "Etalages," "L'action restreinte," and "Le livre, instrument spirituel," reveal him as a particularly astute chronicler of the press and the literary market. Serving as informer and former of the new reading public, Mallarmé took part in the social and the speculative sides of his profession,[8] and, as a journalist, literally propagandized the figure of the poet and the vision of poetry he hoped to propagate. As noted earlier, Mallarmé's youthful article appears decidedly elitist; calling attention to the dangers of a mass dissemination of literature and of a dominant and undiscriminating bourgeois public, it invokes a different conception of literature. Given the context in which it was written, such a stance is quite comprehensible.

Mallarmé's "depersonalization" and other means exploited in his poetic language are intimately associated with the recreation of his authorial persona and the figure of the poet; all three constructions—poetic language, poetic-critical voice, and image—react to the context out of which they develop: "Agir . . . signifia, visiteur, je te comprends, philosophiquement, produire sur beaucoup un mouvement qui te donne en retour l'émoi que tu en fus le principe, donc existes" ("L'action restreinte," *MOC* 2:214). Projecting a poetic persona and product that are alienated from the world is quite sensible as a marketing strategy; such a pose is consistent with a belief that the artist and the art object should be constructed to maintain their market and cult values, and it seems in line with Mallarmé's ultimate aesthetic convictions. In short, his explicit (and often neglected) discussions of commercial forces attest to his keen awareness not only of the mechanism of poetics but also of the cultural transformations and issues affecting all the arts. This does not, however, imply that Mallarmé's work will position itself as antireferential, or that his work can be dismissed as "difficult for difficulty's sake."

Commonly referred to as "obscurity," Mallarmé's progressive flirtation with syntactic difficulty and his insistence on medium have mostly been considered as aspirations toward words devoid of meaning or words of infinite meaning, and only infrequently as conscious artistic stances taken in relation to forces in the artistic and epistemological realms by a poet who is acutely aware of "beauty's transformations." Claims of a disengaged poet with no relation to the outside world and artistic convention not only contradict most of what Mallarmé had to say about his world, nature, and art, but misunderstand the cleverness of his pose and the intense rigor and positioning of his analogical aesthetic production: "Comme le Poëte a sa divulgation, de même il vit; . . . selon un pacte avec la Beauté qu'il se chargea d'apercevoir de son nécessaire et compréhensif regard, et dont il connaît les transformations" ("Etalages," *MOC* 2:223).

Mallarmé's "strike" against society, the evolution of his artistic stance, which shifted from high elitism to what has been perceived as persistent hermeticism, can be understood through the position he forged within artistic convention and his relationship to the other disciplines. Indeed, the interdisciplinary techniques and metaphors that figure in Mallarmé's distortions and deferrals of referentiality reflect his positions on subjectivity, objectivity, imitation, and movement, as well as how his speculative aesthetic is integrated into quotidian writing practices.

NUL VESTIGE D'UNE PHILOSOPHIE . . . NE TRANSPARAÎTRA[9]

One key to what in "Igitur," discussed in chapter 3, will figure as the "grimoire"—Mallarmé's arcanum—is that he analogically relates subjective process to the functioning of language. As will be noted in "Igitur," psychic, linguistic, and textual creation are grounded in a dynamic model of "virtual" image production whose functioning diagrams that of the optical afterimage. This is significant not only for the writing of a fictional persona through language, but also for the progressive sculpting of a poetics of identification and differentiation. His art, like his persona, strategically differentiates itself within the history of poetics. The difficulty and obscurity of Mallarmé's language are not ends in themselves. Rather, the logic of Mallarmé's ambiguity can be seen as a tactical interdisciplinary response to the aesthetic debate over imitation, subjectivity, and objectivity—a response that ingeniously shifts the "reality" of the problem.

"Et laisse-moi finir par une recette que j'ai inventée et que je pratique[:] 'Il faut toujours couper le commencement et la fin de ce qu'on écrit.'" ("A Cazalis," *MOC* 1:657). Adapting and applying innovations in conceptual thought about artistic creation, Mallarmé concocts a "secret recipe" that restructures art's relationship to nature and the nature of cognition. He exploits and reactivates insights gained through a contemporary rethinking of the "great doctrines" from which he distinguishes his art. While Mallarmé's aesthetic studies examine the representational premises and techniques of all the arts, he affirms in his letter to Cazalis that these internal and external frameworks should not be explicit: "L'art suprême, ici, consiste à laisser voir . . . qu'on est en extase, sans avoir montré comment on s'élevait vers ces cimes" (657). The "framework," whether theoretical or practical, should not be apparent.

> Eviter quelque réalité d'échafaudage demeurer autour de cette architecture spontanée et magique, n'y implique pas le manque de puissants calculs et subtils, mais on les ignore, eux-mêmes se font mystérieux exprès. Le chant jaillit de source innée, antérieur à un concept, si purement que refléter, au dehors, mille rythmes d'images. Quel génie pour être un poète; quelle foudre d'instinct renfermer, simplement la vie, vierge, en sa synthèse et illuminant tout. L'armature intellectuelle du poème se dissimule et tient—a lieu—dans l'espace qui isole les strophes et parmi le blanc du papier: significatif silence qu'il n'est pas moins beau de composer que les vers. ("Sur la philosophie dans la poésie," *MOC* 2:659)

Particularly significant for Mallarmé's aesthetic thought and for his conception of the processes taking place "amidst the white of the paper" were the tightening bonds between the pictorial arts and literature, as mechanistic and naturalistic thought infiltrated their domain; the issue of the "faithful imitation of nature" in the arts was further complicated as scientific and historical methods attempted to systematize artistic production and process *as natural*. As we will see, the result of this naturalization is that image production in the two arts is described as analogous. The effects of modernization reshape *ut pictura poesis* and the discourses of realism through a rethinking of the problem of the real in terms of cognitive perception. Mallarmé's innovative poetics of provocation exploits and then annihilates the traditional subjectivity–objectivity dichotomy posed by the imitation problem. Appropriating the scientific method's way of looking at cognition, Mallarmé's interdisciplinary analogies reconstruct a novel way of imitating the nature of image perception: subjectivity objectified.

The reinterrogation of referentiality in art that sprang up early in the century, as camps divided and grouped themselves around either the (academic) imitation of models or that of nature (as a pretext for revealing the truth of the artist), aggravated by the threat of infinite mechanical reproduction and epistemological osmosis, forced artists to rethink traditions such as the role of reality in representation and, along with it, the question of aesthetic choice. What was to be worthy of representation? Mallarmé's "obscurity" can be understood as a response to the imitation quandary through innovative choice of manner and medium—a scientifically motivated response to an issue it never acknowledges as a question: As in a picture, so in poetry?

UN LIEU SE PRÉSENTE[10]

In nineteenth-century poetry and painting alike, a shift occurred concerning the definitions of the subjective, the objective, the natural, and the nature of reality. These factors prepared the aesthetic ground for the subsequent rise of nineteenth-century literary and artistic movements that questioned not only mimesis and *what* to represent, but conventional techniques of *how* to represent. It is this sea change in underlying aesthetic assumptions of the mid- to later nineteenth-century aesthetics, a "critical hour for the human race" ("The Impressionists and Edouard Manet," *MOC* 2:468), that Mallarmé notes in his art and literary criticism.[11] Not insignificantly, in his critical pieces that look at the developing movements in painting, the "subject matter" is in fact shown to be the "nature" of the sign, both created and creating through its inscription.

By concentrating on how language evokes rather than what it evokes, Mallarmé seemingly eludes the question of the imitation of nature. Barbara Johnson notes that, by emphasizing the medium rather than the message,

> Mallarmé's critical theory brings to Western letters a productive hypersensitivity to the functioning of language as such rather than as a mere equivalent for an extralinguistic meaning. . . . It is not that language does not refer ("suggest," or "allude," as he puts it), but that there is something about language that makes it more like a prism than like a

> window. As soon as one writes, one disappears behind the initiatives
> that words themselves begin to take. ("1885, June," 800)

This language, which is "more like a prism than a window," could easily characterize Mallarmé's verse as well. In his poems, one finds substantives denoting concrete objects from daily life (such as gold, fans, violins, mirrors, desks, pens, paper, lamps, and body parts), and references to nature (the sky, flowers, stars, lakes, swans, and stars), as well as more abstract signifiers of affective states and temporality. These signifiers do have signifieds. However, through syntactic placement, they are strategically conceived and positioned to refer not only to an outside referent but also to each other: reflecting among themselves, words insist on what they are doing in the poem. On a theoretical level, Mallarmé proposes: "ce à quoi nous devons viser surtout est que, dans le poème, les mots . . . se reflètent les uns sur les autres jusqu'à paraître ne plus avoir leur couleur propre, mais n'être que les transitions d'une gamme" ("A Coppée," *MOC* 1:709).

Instead of merely aspiring to describe or relate by means of the sequential progression of a narrative in his texts, Mallarmé focuses on the power of words to institute another genre of mobility; words echo each other irrespective of the sequential narrative unfolding and its progression via the ordinary syntactic order associated with verbal art. His renowned fragmentation—often effected as and effecting a layering lexical reflection—suspends the temporal linear movement of the text to defer referentiality. This distortion of conventional syntax, layered with the activation of another kind of movement, positions his texts as a direct response to aesthetic conventions of his century. Mallarmé's poetics can be seen as a logical outcome or perhaps even a compromise between aesthetic visions and values determining referentiality in art. The word "compromise" here refers to a complex oscillation, present in Mallarmé's poetics and his theory alike, between the arbitrary and the internally and externally motivated signifier. This oscillation adapts and appropriates aspects of modern life, scientific ideas about human perception, and a diagram of visual processing to reconfigure artistic medium and manner. Indeed, Mallarmé's poetics emerges out of his very serious engagement with aesthetic vision and value, an engagement with the demands of form, contemporary epistemological models of the nature of language, and society's expectations.

Insistence on medium and manner, as demonstrated by Mallarmé's emphasis on the materiality of language through extreme arrangement, does not occur in an intellectual vacuum. In fact, an insistence on movement had been one of the major thrusts of the romantic positions in art criticism since the beginning of the century. A radicalization of this incorporation of mobility is exactly what was happening in the 1870s and 1880s in the pictorial arts, as ways of understanding visual processing—the effects of light and color, especially conceptions of the afterimage—linked optical modes of perception to psychic ones.[12]

Popularized conceptual frameworks of perception were quickly related and applied to systems of representation, both pictorial and verbal. Developments diffused into the artistic world by scientific discourse and disseminated in the debates over imitation and reality in art are incorporated into Mallarmé's works as a tricky reverse aesthetic strategy that applies a reconception of a newly justifiable "reality."

Aside from new knowledge about structures of optical perception, as the discovery of the light spectrum and the mass diffusion of accounts of its molecular functioning were applied to optical and psychic process, the real external environment of the nineteenth century was also changing. Benjamin shows that the rise of technical and mechanical devices proved to be a force that modified human sensory perception. What he describes as the haptic shock experience ("On Some Motifs in Baudelaire," 174–75), that is, the increase in the number of developments that through one movement could provoke a series of processes, expanded during the nineteenth century. Some of these inventions were the match, the telephone, lithography, and, of course, photography. Furthermore, the popularity and frequency of salons in the nineteenth century, the proliferating art criticism, the advent of photographic *cartes de visite*, and the widespread use of photographs in painting, all attested to the rampant expansion and transformations of the pictorial image in nineteenth-century society. This explosion in visual culture, including the rise in the distribution of an illustrated press—whose formatting and ads conjoined the visual and the verbal, and whose very texts were described by Mallarmé as "notation fragmentée" ("Le livre, instrument spirituel," *MOC* 2:226) and "activés par la pression de l'instant" ("Le mystère dans les lettres," *MOC* 2:231)—created an environment that was constantly modifying specular experience, an environment that was also, in fact, "more like a prism than a window."

EVOQUER, DANS UNE OMBRE EXPRÈS, L'OBJET TU[13]

Already in the mid-1860s, when "Hérodiade" was taking shape, Mallarmé's poetics asserts itself as nonimitative of objects. In an 1864 letter, he clearly explains that his seemingly obscure poetry aspires to diagrammatically replicate what occurs as the senses are triggered by language:

> j'invente une langue qui doit nécessairement jaillir d'une poétique très nouvelle, que je pourrais définir en ces deux mots: *Peindre, non la chose, mais l'effet qu'elle produit.*
>
> Le vers ne doit donc pas, là, se composer de mots, mais d'intentions, et toutes les paroles s'effacer devant la sensation. ("A Cazalis," *MOC* 1:663).

The objective of his poetics is not, then, to produce a carbon copy of nature, but to represent a new conception of the nature of the mobile mind.

Mallarmé had already been interested in the relationship between the physiological and psychic experience in the earliest days of his career. Writing in 1862 about "Vere novo,"[14] he states: "C'est un genre assez nouveau que cette poésie, où les effets matériels, du sang, des nerfs sont analysés et mêlés aux effets moraux, de l'esprit, de l'âme" ("A Cazalis," *MOC* 1:639). It is clear in the allusions Mallarmé makes to his creative processes from the mid–1860s on that he is already experimenting with the relationships between language and psychophysical process.[15] He is well on the way to considering the material word in its capacity to stimulate sensation and the thought process, on the way to a poetics that seeks to trigger cognition through a new conception of perception in relation to sensation and psychic functioning. In 1865, Mallarmé alludes to this phenomenon:

> j'ai pris un sujet effrayant, dont les sensations, quand elle sont vives, sont amenées jusqu'à l'atrocité, et si elles flottent, ont l'attitude étrange du mystère. . . . J'ai du reste, là, trouvé une façon intime et singulière de peindre et de noter des impressions très fugitives. Ajoute, pour plus de terreur, que toutes ces *impressions* se suivent comme dans une symphonie, et que je suis souvent des journées entières à me demander si celle-ci peut accompagner celle-là, quelle est leur parenté et leur effet. ("A Cazalis," *MOC* 1:666, emphasis in original)

Here, the distance between the physical world and its dynamic effects on the mind comes into play. The influence of systematic scientific analysis of sensory phenomena related to artistic creation, rooted in the earliest romantic efforts to seize the physical laws of visual and auditory stimulation and already in high gear during the 1860s, would continue throughout the century. Mallarmé's dense arrangement of activators and his provocative use of fragmentation and unconventional syntax are foreshadowed in the 1860s, when, in "Igitur" and other writings, he begins to link the objective world to subjective phenomena—a development that coincides with the emergence of impressionist painting in reaction to realism.

Many of Mallarmé's aesthetic identifications grow apparent in his circumstantial writings of the 1870s. The most explicit documents attesting to his expertise in the pictorial arts are probably his writings on the impressionists. In his 1874 defense of Manet's art, he dealt with the role of the jury, and in his rarely read 1876 article on the impressionists and Manet, which will be discussed in chapter 4, he shows that he was well versed in the major aesthetic issues of the visual arts and clearly knew how to manipulate these issues.

While highly vocal enemies of scientific thought and of photography pronounced their threat to art and valorized the subjective gaze, which they thought the photograph could not achieve, others, including painters such as Camille Corot, were assessing and appropriating photography's innovative properties as a means of observing "reality" (material and human) and applying the insights of this observation to representation. Photography became a means of both recuperating and reversing conventions of realism.

The progressive infiltration of the theories of light, color, chemical process, optical and sensory functioning, and photography as a mechanical means of pictorial reproduction of nature not only wrought havoc on academic convention, but furnished the impetus for a reinterrogation of subject–object relations in the world and in art. The advent and pouring forth of a pictorial image fixed by, and often fixing, the action of light had vast implications for the late nineteenth-century reconception of representation—despite its stigmatization and the conspicuous absence of its consideration in many artistic and critical texts.

The photographic process revealed much more about "reality" and optical "truth" than even its practitioners could have predicted. The aberrations of a still-imperfect photographic process captured the movement of light rays and produced blurred images. The photograph also revealed that conventional horizon lines, background, and foreground lighting were incorrect when captured by the lens, that horses' legs in movement were quite different than when assimilated by the eye and mind. Black and white had an infinite number of tones in between, yet when arrested by the lens in artificial light and subjected to immature chemical processing, these tones disappeared and became sharply contrasted. The optical "veracity" of the object was dependent on the degree of light and the lens to which it was exposed. The "photo," the

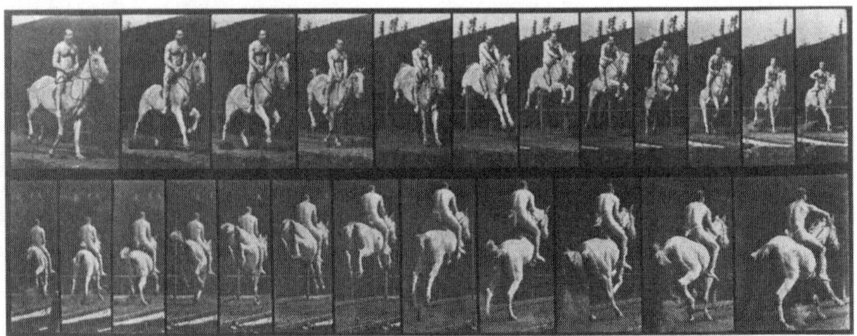

PLATE 8
Muybridge, Saut d'obstacle, vue de face et de dos, 1887.
Paris, Musée d'Orsay.
© Photo RMN–©Droits reserves.

phenomenon of light and its relations to optical processes of perception, sparked reexaminations of the nature of "optical truth," "image processing," and "realism"—new conceptions of the perception of "reality" based on scientific principles.

The photographic image also revealed that a city scene does not necessarily have an orderly foreground, background, and center, but that objects and buildings, and people's heads, legs, and arms, get cropped out. Centering was a matter of choice. These unconventional images already existed in painting, but the photograph brought them to the fore en masse, disseminating a new way of looking and seeing that encompassed focusing, cropping, and illuminating.

Similar tendencies were already present in literary and critical discourse early in the century; the popularization of the photograph and science only served to reinforce them. The desire to pin down the scientific laws governing the analogous production of sound and light waves and their effects on consciousness (which precedes even Baudelaire's famous "Correspondances"—in the work of Diderot, for example) pointed the way to an understanding of the natural laws governing their principles. The effects of the photographic image and process on art, the rethinking of how reality appears to the lens, was but one step away from the theorization of how reality appears to the eye and the mind. This dissection of perception as process provides some interesting new ways of examining Mallarmé's aesthetic theory and process, not only intellectually but practically.

*OUI, JE CROIS L'ÉCRITURE UN INDICE. . . . TOUTEFOIS, L'ÉCRIVAIN
DE PROFESSION . . . LUI, RECOPIE OU VOIT D'ABORD EN LE MIROIR
DE SA PENSÉE, PUIS TRANSCRIT DANS UNE ÉCRITURE UNE FOIS FAITE
POUR TOUJOURS, COMME INVARIABLE. L'EFFET IMMÉDIAT DE SES
ÉMOTIONS N'EST DONC PAS VISIBLE EN SON MANUSCRIT*[16]

Arising out of mid-century sources, Mallarmé's poetics is not a product of a late nineteenth-century disgust for scientific thought, nor does he discount or deny the sensory. On the contrary, he systematically approaches both the scientific and the sensory as subject to analysis. In "Color as Cognition in Symbolist Verse," Françoise Meltzer notes:

> The nineteenth century extended seventeenth-century empiricism. . . . The logical corollary . . . is that all sensory experience is regarded as suspect. Newtonian physics had rationalized the laws of the universe in reducing its properties to anatomical structures and laws of motion. . . . Those areas of perception which had remained unquantifiable were dispelled as illusion or attributed to the necessary limitations of the human mind. The theories of John Locke . . . are the classic philosophic expression of the disjunction between sensory experience and knowledge which, in its nineteenth-century versions, would lead to the symbolist revolt. (253)

Despite the intellectual transformations resulting from the infiltration of scientific thought, the sensory remained a vital area of concern throughout the century. Part of Mallarmé's particular "symbolist revolt," a legacy of the romantic preoccupation with the self and the artistic agent, entails systematic analysis of sensory perception and its representation. The sensory, regarded as a system with its own movements and processes grounded in mechanistic theory and based on natural law, was already in the 1860s linked, in Mallarmé's thought, to language, fiction, and "l'esprit humain" ("Notes sur le langage," *MOC* 1:503–5).

Subjective experience became a realm of study in and of itself. Perception as process was analogically associated with recent developments in chemistry, physics, psychology, and physiology, and was quickly related to the new technological knowledge gained in the realms of light, chromatics, the elemental sciences, and optics. Scientific discourse applied to the sensory seemed only a short and logical step away from the relations of optical and auditory systems to the physical universe. As the subjective was cultivated more and more for observation in writing and painting, methodical systems of representation (including language) were praised and seen as pseudotechnical processes based on the metaphor of the machine and/or on natural law (e.g., in the works of Emile Zola and Honoré de Balzac); the effects of science and mechanistic discourse diffused into studies and discourses of the mind and psychic impression, facilitating and justifying a naturalization of the aesthetic—and not only conventional aesthetics.

Given their common desire to understand psychic and artistic phenomena, it is perhaps not surprising that Hippolyte Taine and Mallarmé were not only working at the same time, but coming to very similar conclusions. Taine began to publish various critical articles in the 1850s, and his lectures at the Ecole des Beaux Arts were published as written texts in the 1860s. Mallarmé's correspondence documents that he, Lefébure, Des Essarts, and Cazalis were reading and discussing Taine's theories in 1864 and 1865. It is obvious, however, that by the time Mallarmé received the first (documented) text, sent by Lefébure in 1864, he was already acquainted with Taine's ideas:

> Merci encore pour vos articles de Taine. Je ne les ai pas lus. Ce que je reproche à Taine, c'est de prétendre qu'un artiste n'est que l'homme porté à sa suprême puissance, tandis que je crois, moi, qu'on peut parfaitement avoir un tempérament humain très distinct du tempérament littéraire. . . . je trouve que Taine ne voit que l'impression comme source des oeuvres d'Art, et pas assez la réflexion. Devant le papier, l'artiste *se fait.* ("A Lefébure," *MOC* 1:669, emphasis in original)

While Mallarmé's and Taine's views differ on certain issues, they also converge on many points. In fact, the conceptual similarities of their theories of cognition could be considered uncanny had they not been the product of a more global epistemological movement that sought to formulate the human relationship to nature through science. Although Taine's thesis proposal on "sensations and perception" was rejected in 1854, he continued to try to understand the relations between sensations, perception, and art. Before developing his totalizing theory explaining the entire environment of the artist (which leaves little room for the personal reflection Mallarmé insists upon), Taine sought to view man as a construct of his senses, with the goal of formulating a mechanistic theory of knowledge. He published the culmination of this side of his thought in his 1870 treatise *De l'intelligence,* positing a model of the self as the sum of sensory input and motor responses:

> Il n'y a rien de réel dans le moi, sauf la file de ses événements. . . . ces
> événements, divers d'aspect, sont les mêmes en nature et se ramènent
> tous à la sensation. . . . la sensation elle . . . même . . . se réduit à un
> groupe de mouvements moléculaires. (7)

Taine continues to discuss the body, "le corps n'étant que des mobiles moteurs, il n'y a rien de réel en eux que leurs mouvements; à cela se ramènent tous les éléments physiques" (8). These thoughts bear a striking resemblance to the notes Mallarmé was writing on Descartes at the same time and to many of the notions formulated in the text "Igitur," particularly his rereading of the Cartesian *moi* as a fictional projection. Taine states: "De même que la substance spirituelle est un fantôme créé par la conscience, de même la substance matérielle est un fantôme créé par les sens" (8). The insistence on movement should be noted, for, despite his deterministic side, Taine is positing, as did Mallarmé, the thought process as a dynamic series of "molecular movements."

Taine's study of cognition further explained the physiological process of thought as modeled on the resurrection and recollection of images associated with optical and retinal functioning. Mallarmé's conception of meaning as created and constituted in the absence of the word or physical index is quite similar. "Igitur" is explicitly addressed to the reader's mind: *"Ce Conte s'adresse à l'Intelligence du lecteur qui met les choses en scène, elle-même"* (*MOC* 1:475, emphasis in original). Here, Mallarmé focuses on the desired effect on the reader, who, precisely, can lean on the words when he "stages" things in his turn. Both Taine and Mallarmé posit a link between the physiological, the linguistic, and the psychic; both consider the mind's production as being stimulated by the outside world, inherently fictional, and as a process of recollective movement created in the absence of the object. In fact, Taine's definition of image perception theorized the phenomena or impressions to which Mallarmé alludes in discussions of "Hérodiade." In his treatise on the workings of the mind, Taine states:

> Quand l'image de la forme aperçue tend à renaître, elle entraîne avec
> elle les images de ses différents accompagnements. Mais ces accompag-
> nements, étant différents, ne peuvent renaître ensemble; . . . les images
> resteront à l'état naissant et composeront ce qu'on nomme en langage
> ordinaire une impression. Cette impression peut être forte sans cesser
> d'être vague; sous l'image incomplète règne une sourde agitation, et
> comme un fourmillement de velléités, qui d'ordinaire se terminent par
> un geste expressif, une métaphore, un résumé sensible. Tel est notre état

> ordinaire vis-à-vis des choses que nous avons plusieurs fois expérimen-
> tées. (148–49)

In his theorizations of sensation and perception in life and art, Taine naturalized image functioning and provided a link between nature and representation.[17] By explicitly systematizing image perception as a natural phenomenon, he provided a conceptual model for the "reality" of apparently imaginative and inherently fictive representation. Taine's observations on how the mind processes thought, how images are perceived and conceived, made the functioning of pictorial and linguistic signs a "reality" in both art and nature. Of course, these intuitive correspondences between nature and the senses in relation to art had already been alluded to in art criticism early in the century. Knowledge about the functioning of light and sound waves and the perception of color became central issues for the "moderns," who, while promoting the imitation of nature, progressively moved toward privileging the nature of the agent's perception. The texts of poet-critics such as Balzac, Gautier, Baudelaire, and Hugo often reflected just such a tendency.

A passage from Baudelaire's prose poem "Le confiteor de l'artiste" describes the artist's dilemma as a "duel" with his medium as he seeks to represent the subjective experience of nature's beauty and is vanquished. The artist laments: "Car il est de certaines sensations délicieuses dont le vague n'exclut pas l'intensité." The syncretic effect of sensations that are at the same time intense and vague is that which the artistic mind aspires to fix but which escapes concretization due to its "caractère mouvant," the fact that it is "mal défini," "flou," and "confus." Baudelaire even evokes the phenomenological confusion brought on by the sensory perception of nature: "toutes ces choses pensent par moi, ou je pense par elles" (*BOC* 1:278–79).

Mallarmé's earliest writings discuss these relations between the material external world and the psychic effects of language and words alluded to by Baudelaire and his predecessors and theorized by Taine. While Mallarmé's symbolist heirs would reject much of scientific positivism and the language of progress, Mallarmé remained very much a product of an *esprit de système* and optimistic about the conscious and methodical—if unexpected, unconventional, or "new"—application of epistemological models to poetics. As he states in "Prose": "Car j'installe, par la science / L'hymne des coeurs spirituels / En l'oeuvre de ma patience" (*MOC* 1:28). Embedded in this lucidity and "patience," one finds Mallarmé's principal reservation about Taine's theorization of artistic production: Taine's inability to conceive of the writer as aware of his surrounding epistemological moment and environment and able to take them into account.[18] Although Mallarmé's speculative strategies proved Taine wrong in this regard, their principles on perception clearly ran parallel, and there were other concurrences that provide an interesting approach to the "realist" quarrel over imitation. Taine maintains that art is not a literal imitation and that "dans l'oeuvre littéraire comme dans l'oeuvre pittoresque," art is a transcription that respects "les rapports et les dépendances mutuelles des parties . . . c'est-à-dire leur logique" (*Philosophie,* 28–29). The shift from a strict imitation of nature to an insistence on choice, the act of systematically isolating and illuminating an essential aspect of the object, is as important to Taine's theory as it is to Mallarmé's practice. In Taine's words:

> Nous avons cru d'abord que son but [celui de l'art] est *d'imiter l'apparence sensible.* Puis, séparant l'imitation matérielle de l'imitation intelligente, nous avons trouvé que, ce qu'il veut reproduire dans l'apparence sensible, ce sont les *rapports des parties.* Enfin, remarquant que les rapports peuvent et doivent être altérés pour conduire l'art à son faîte, nous avons établi que, si l'on étudie les rapports des parties, c'est *pour y faire dominer un caractère essentiel.* (*Philosophie,* 38, emphasis added)

Mallarmé's aesthetic was not a product of lofty and unattainable ideals but rather a highly technical, well-informed doctrine that effectively engaged, appropriated, and assimilated artistic conventions firmly grounded in a literary tradition that insisted on process. The result is a highly effective poetic language that rarely strays from his aesthetic predications. Rather than a poetics of exclusion or difficulty for difficulty's sake, Mallarmé's "obscurity" activates a cunning aesthetic statement.

> *SI, TOUT DE MÊME, N'INQUIÉTAIT JE NE SAIS QUEL MIROITEMENT,*
> *EN DESSOUS, PEU SÉPARABLE DE LA SURFACE CONCÉDÉE À*
> *LA RÉTINE—IL ATTIRE LE SOUPÇON*[19]

In his many attempts to elevate literature and demarcate its domain from common narration and communicative writing, Mallarmé, it would appear, intends to "exile the republic." In his break with the lyricism and didacticism that characterized the romantic poets, Mallarmé seems to adhere to "mystery in literature" as a slogan intimating a poetics for initiates only. Nonetheless, his 1896 essay "Le mystère dans les lettres" serves much more as a statement on the nature of literature and representation than as a claim for pure hermeticism or exclusivity.

Published well past what some consider Mallarmé's high elitist period, "Le mystère," which certainly perpetuates the common nineteenth-century topos of the misunderstood poet who disdains the public, in fact contains a far more nuanced message: it espouses a clever theoretical and practical *art poétique* in response to the conspicuously absent issue of imitation. Indeed, Mallarmé stirs up conventions of "realist" representation with a technique that is nothing less than a paradoxical integration of new perspectives on optical image perception and cognition.

For Mallarmé, art should not be obscure just for the sake of obscurity. Rather, it should be a dynamic cognitive adventure, an exercise for those willing to tax the brain as well as the pocket. It should thus be constructed in a fashion that maintains its cult value in a consumer market (an idea already present in the essays of the 1860s and 1870s). The idea of "mystery" in literature does not, however, necessarily imply that the essay's main objective is exclusion. While his defense of mystery clearly opposes art and common communication, he illustrates that "obscurity"—his disruptions of conventional narrative description and its temporal movement—is in fact a mechanism for another genre of meaning production. Mallarmé may be proposing an art that is no longer didactic or an expression of the self, but in this essay he is definitely telling the crowd what literature is, what it does, and how it is experienced.

In "Le mystère dans les lettres," the blatant double meaning of "lettres," signifying "letters" and "literature," demonstrates Mallarmé's attempt to concretize the thought processes involved in literature and signification: the perception of letters and their created images as a dynamic process. From the inherent opposition he embeds within the mystery of works of art and their revelation, it becomes clear that the essay is actually a rigorous commentary on literary representation. Mallarmé deliberately weaves a web of polysemy around the word "mystère" as both arcane and revelatory. This polysemy surfaces with a bit of intuition—or, as he puts it, a thunderbolt of logic. In fact, these very processes he proposes to institute elucidate his maintenance of mystery in literature, unveiling how he envisions representation and imitation through a new conceptual way of looking at textual perception and the thought process. Mallarmé's poetics sets its sights on stimuli strictly structured so as to be perceived by human consciousness. As a corollary, Mallarmé would and did affirm that reading, like textual creation, is an exercise that imprints and imposes meanings—in between the words. Let us here return to appearances.

Mallarmé's first move in "Le mystère dans les lettres" is to establish a (Baudelairean) discursive position that distinguishes the artist from the crowd, as well as from his critics. He then turns to a discussion of art and its relationship to the general public:

> Tout écrit, extérieurement à son trésor, doit, par égard envers ceux
> dont il emprunte, après tout, pour un objet autre, le langage, présenter,
> avec les mots, un sens même indifférent: on gagne de détourner l'oisif,
> charmé que rien ne l'y concerne, à première vue. (*MOC* 2:229)

While he seems at first to suggest that there should be a certain submission to,
or respect for, the public's expectations—after all, it is their words that are
used—Mallarmé dismisses the thought, and implies that since the work transforms the crowd's language into an object that does not necessarily relate to
them, both the poet and the people may be charmed to go their separate ways:
"Salut, exact, de part et d'autre—" (229). Except, he adds, that this is only their
first impression. After an initial glance, the lingering experience may lead to
something more.

Turning his attention to those who are not immediately revolted, Mallarmé describes the reactions of those "malins" (229) who, suspicious that
something lies within the depths of the work of art, express this intuition and
cognitive frustration by simply crying "ténèbres!" (230). Mallarmé asserts that it
is the sheer existence of mystery that the crowd seems to resist, and yet this
resistance is automatically equated with a lack of light:

> Il doit y avoir quelque chose d'occulte au fond de tous, je crois décidé-
> ment à quelque chose d'abscons, signifiant fermé et caché, qui habite le
> commun: car, sitôt cette masse jetée vers quelque trace que c'est une
> réalité, existant, par exemple, sur une feuille de papier, dans tel écrit—
> pas en soi—cela qui est obscur: elle s'agite, ouragan jaloux d'attribuer
> les ténèbres à quoi que ce soit, profusément, flagramment. (230)

In other words, if the poet were to present a trace of the mysterious process of
a "reality" rather than copying it, the crowd would break out into unfounded
criticism of his "obscurity." The crowd's resistance to the phenomena created
on and by the paper, this "something" that is vague but inhabits the commonplace, corresponds perfectly to scientific expectations; for Mallarmé sought to
provoke in poetry the psychic effects of image perception as theorized in the
nineteenth century. He chose to render in his art an emblematic aspect of the
nature of representation itself, the simultaneously intense and vague afterimage-like impressions provoked in the mind. Paradoxically, this is a quite conventional take on imitation; Mallarmé focuses on, stylizes, embodies, and
embellishes one essential aspect of the nature of a visible object—literature.

Mallarmé playfully pities the "poor vilified poet" who, having been misunderstood, must submit to unfounded angry criticism, and, here addressing the

critics, he enters into his distinction between the literary and the nonliterary. According to Mallarmé, the criticism that *other* critics (not poet-critics) practice has no literary relevance; theirs is an undertaking that "does not count, literarily," because it involves merely showing the banal, outward aspects of rather than the underlying mechanisms that generate and govern their existence:

> Quant à une entreprise, qui ne compte pas littérairement—
> La leur—
> D'exhiber les choses à un imperturbable premier plan, en camelots, activés par la pression de l'instant, d'accord—écrire, dans le cas, pourquoi, indûment, sauf pour étaler la banalité; plutôt que tendre le nuage, précieux, flottant sur l'intime gouffre de chaque pensée. (231)

Distinguishing between common communication and literature, a formed, contemplated art that, although it may also be activated by the pressure of the moment, spreads the precious mist that floats, cloudlike, about the secret abyss of every thought, Mallarmé moves on to formulate his definition of what literature is, why it is mystery, and why, as I maintain, it is not for mystery's sake.

Mallarmé first establishes the mysterious impressions evoked by the symphony, which he states found its origin in the "répertoire de la nature et du ciel" (232). The stimulation of intellectual processes he describes recalls the oscillation between Platonic appearances, ideas, and forms. The liberation of the thought process, a sudden or gradual stimulation of the human powers of cognitive association, is described by Mallarmé as akin to the revelatory quality of a repertory originating in nature. He views this expository composition that stimulates the thought process as analogous to literary writing, but he insists that at some point in the musical piece, a motif emerges. Synthesis occurs ("un sujet se dégage").

> La Musique, à sa date, est venue balayer cela—
> Au cours, seulement, du morceau, à travers des voiles feints, ceux encore quant à nous-mêmes, un sujet se dégage de leur successive stagnance amassée et dissoute avec art. (231)

Mallarmé exploits the analogy with music to facilitate expression of an evocative memory process of reconstitution. Reversing the problematic Platonic notion of imitation in poetics as twice removed from the "truth," Mallarmé proposes to refabricate an aspect of "reality": the "truth" and mobility of the process of signification (in the absence of the visible or spoken word). Just as in the era's understanding of retinal afterimages and optical reconstitution, or in Taine's allusion to "molecular movements," the dynamic is one of fragmentation and resynthesis.

It is precisely this mysterious dynamic of mental stimulation that Mallarmé claims for his explanation of visible written signs: "Je sais, on veut à la Musique, limiter le Mystère; quand l'écrit y prétend" (232). Music is invoked to index an animated experiential phenomenon that does not communicate conventional discursive meaning, nor, according to aesthetic discussions of the era does it imitate.[20] Mallarmé insists on music's ability to create resonance via auditory stimulation, an echoing in the imagination that is akin to the effect of the written word: both music and writing, then, imply a distinction from the spoken word:

> L'écrit, envol tacite d'abstraction, reprend ses droits en face de la chute
> des sons nus: tous deux, Musique et lui, intimant une préalable disjonc-
> tion, celle de la parole, certainement par effroi de fournir au bavardage.
> (232)

The type of mental stimulation that Mallarmé claims as the domain of the written word induces a liberation of perception. But, as we remarked, Mallarmé does insist that "un sujet se dégage" (231). While mystery, or obscurity, has the effect of expanding consciousness and liberating meaning, this heightened perception, a textually induced mobile lucidity, is in some way reconstructed in the mind. While it seems a question of constant activity, triggered by the perceptions of the reader's inductive mind, these impressions are structured by a semantic, syntactic, literary, or even social context.

In the discussion of syntax that follows in the essay, Mallarmé addresses the systematic arrangement of words and the way in which this deliberate poetic technique maximizes the resonance of words and multiplies and organizes their possible significations. Though the following quotation contains grammatical terms, arrangement does not entail a mere contortion of grammar, but rather a creative effort toward a particular placement of words—syntax:

> Quel pivot, j'entends, dans ces contrastes, à l'intelligibilité? il
> faut une garantie—
> La Syntaxe—
> . . . Un parler, le français, retient une élégance à paraître en
> négligé et le passé témoigne de cette qualité, qui s'établit d'abord,
> comme don de race foncièrement exquis: mais notre littérature dépasse
> le "genre," correspondance ou mémoires. Les abrupts, hauts jeux d'aile,

> se mireront, aussi: qui les mène, perçoit une extraordinaire appropria-
> tion de la structure, limpide, aux primitives foudres de la logique. Un
> balbutiement, que semble la phrase, ici refoulé dans l'emploi d'inci-
> dentes multiplie, se compose et s'enlève en quelque équilibre supéri-
> eur, à balancement prévu d'inversions. (232–33)

Mallarmé describes French literature as manifesting a fluttering mobility that may seem at first to stammer, to hold back, but then multiplies and takes on order or meaning through the guarantee of syntax. His explanation of the "mystery" in letters insists on a dynamic hesitation preceding cognitive ordering. It is precisely this ability of language to strip itself of conventional meaning that provokes a renewed flurry of association and enables the reading process—unveiling the process of signification, itself based on a conception of psychic phenomena. He theorizes this very mechanism as essential to both the work of art and human thought. The mystery lies ultimately not in the exclusion of the reader but in the reader's sensory and cognitive engagement.

Mallarmé clarifies the result of the practice of reading rarefied literary language. While it may initially provoke a series of mysterious impressions, it has salient affinities with what we term "cognition" and with nineteenth-century epistemological metaphors for psychic figuration that, significantly, were articulated through the discourse of optical perception. Although it may not be methodical or deductive, reading is the gathering and reassembling of associations in a manner analogous to the retina's fragmentation, gathering, and reconstitution of light. In this essay, Mallarmé explains how his apparent "ténèbres" (230) actually illuminate a poetic language that aspires, through strictly structured graphic stimuli, to provoke this process.

For Mallarmé, reading conjoins a conscious effort and an unconscious chain-reaction process, "an exercise" of triggers and responses; it is the atmosphere, the "in-between" of the process that he chooses to frame and stage. To vanquish chance word by word does not entail an attempt to represent mimetic physical reality pictorially, but to concentrate on the written word as a site of impression that simulates and stimulates impressions. Heightened emphasis on the function of the word insists on the scene of signification itself:

> Lire—
>
> Cette pratique—
>
> Appuyer, selon la page, au blanc, qui l'inaugure son ingénuité,
> à soi, oublieuse même du titre qui parlerait trop haut: et, quand
> s'aligna, dans une brisure, la moindre, disséminée, le hasard vaincu mot

par mot, indéfectiblement le blanc revient, tout à l'heure gratuit, certain maintenant, pour conclure que rien au-delà et authentiquer le silence. (234)

This view of reading as a quest whose journey takes place in between the words is essential to Mallarmé's discussion of mystery; he embodies it in his poetic language by representing what goes on beyond the first "impression" of the text. In this essay, Mallarmé proclaims that literature illustrates the mystery of letters. He stresses the mystery of signification—of what we know as linguistic signs—as well as the "blank" as sign. Since the reading process for Mallarmé is a systematic reading of "indices" that create meaning in the interstices, his pointing toward a period anterior and posterior to comprehension alleviates the imitation problem while posing the cognitive one. The illustration of the oscillation from sign as arbitrary to meaningful to motivated and back, that white space between and in the margins, functions as does the atmosphere of air and transparency he so often praised in his art criticism. How he concretizes it is another question. Mallarmé paradoxically exploits visual triggers, light, and graphics, and turns conventional pictorial vividness against itself, diagramming a visually conceived capacity for movement.

Literature, for Mallarmé, should not remain a "mystery for mystery's sake." The mystery that the crowd so often intuitively resists is the mystery of signs. In the beginning of the essay, Mallarmé says, "on gagne de détourner l'oisif, charmé que rien ne l'y concerne, à première vu" (229). Nonetheless, rather than a treatise on exclusion, "Le mystère dans les lettres" is an essay that artfully and fashionably explains the mystery that is literature, the letter, and the crowd. "La littérature ici subit une exquise crise, fondamentale."

CHAPTER 3

FRAMES OF CONSCIOUSNESS IN "IGITUR"

Devant le papier, l'artiste se fait

"DEVANT LE PAPIER, l'artiste *se fait*."[1] Embedded in the poet's 1865 correspondence, this jewel-like "maxim" crystallizes Mallarmé's aesthetic principles. Concretizing a complex process of distance, dissection, and reconstitution, the maxim both envisions and embodies a visual model of psychic functioning that will be reflected throughout the writer's theory and practice. Its logic provides the critical paradigm for this chapter's reading of "Igitur," an early kernel text that rethinks Cartesian subjectivity, the cognitive processes involved in poetic technique, and the logic behind Stéphane Mallarmé's aesthetic self-positioning.

Conspicuously self-reflexive, the maxim not only suggests a general interpretive paradigm, but also announces a specific method for its own exegesis. The "devant" of "devant le papier," the most complex facet, reflects a series of specular processes informing the poet's vision of artistic creation.[2] In his rigorous exploration of the medium and processes of the artistic event, Mallarmé delved into the most remote aspects of the psychic and cognitive operations at work in aesthetic creation. The word "devant" connotes distance and the alienated objective gaze that accompanies an intense, hyperlucid separation of the subject from its object of study. Throughout his career, Mallarmé increasingly cultivated this objectification by exploiting a mode of inquiry modeled on the scientific method characteristic of his epistemological moment.

CAR J'INSTALLE, PAR LA SCIENCE,
L'HYMNE DES COEURS SPIRITUELS
EN L'OEUVRE DE MA PATIENCE[3]

During the latter half of the nineteenth century, attempts to apply scientific methods of analysis to literary criticism and creation became common currency.[4] Whereas Mallarmé has not typically been associated with scientific method, and while Mallarmé studies are characterized by generalized assertions that link the poet to a symbolist rejection of positivism, his aesthetics attest to a progressive recuperation of the scientific gaze that was all-pervasive as a cultural discourse of his time. In the words of his contemporary, Emile Zola: "Vouloir introduire la méthode scientifique paraît d'une ignorance, d'une vanité de barbare. Ce n'est pas nous qui introduisons cette méthode, elle s'y est bien introduite toute seule" (*Le roman expérimental,* 232).

Mallarmé methodically interrogates the generative operations of image creation and artistic conception. His effort to arrive at an objective vision of the creative act entails an in-depth study of the processes and products of art as systems of autonomous elements that are constantly in process, incessantly interacting with one another. What I call Mallarmé's "photo-graphics" suggests just such a game of constant motion and reflection, a kinetic "play" that analogizes and reenacts his underlying and mobile conception of the logic of psychic and textual image production.

As the detailed readings throughout this chapter will demonstrate, Mallarmé grounds his poetics in an optical model of image perception that is inextricably linked to his study and dissection of subjective functioning. The subjective experience of the mind, like the artistic process, is distanced and examined as in a mirror. The "papier" is both metaphor and mirror of the void on which he was to impose form and out of which he was to create his aesthetic and his artistic self: "l'artiste *se fait.*" Emphasized, the verb "se faire" highlights the reflexive nature of this process of self-creation.

The abundance of mirrors in Mallarmé's oeuvre exhibits his intense interest in subjective experience examined as exteriorized reflection. This reflection exposes a series of analogies between subjective phenomena and the functioning and perception of light spectra:[5] thought, likened to waves of light reflected in a mirror, returns to the observing subject as an object whose distribution is observable. Strikingly similar to the product and process of photography, which offer graphic re-presentations of photic (light or light-related) phenomena (light tracing itself), the verbal inscription of this alienated vision of subjective experience articulates a model of image conception and perception that is analogically applied in the creation of the text.

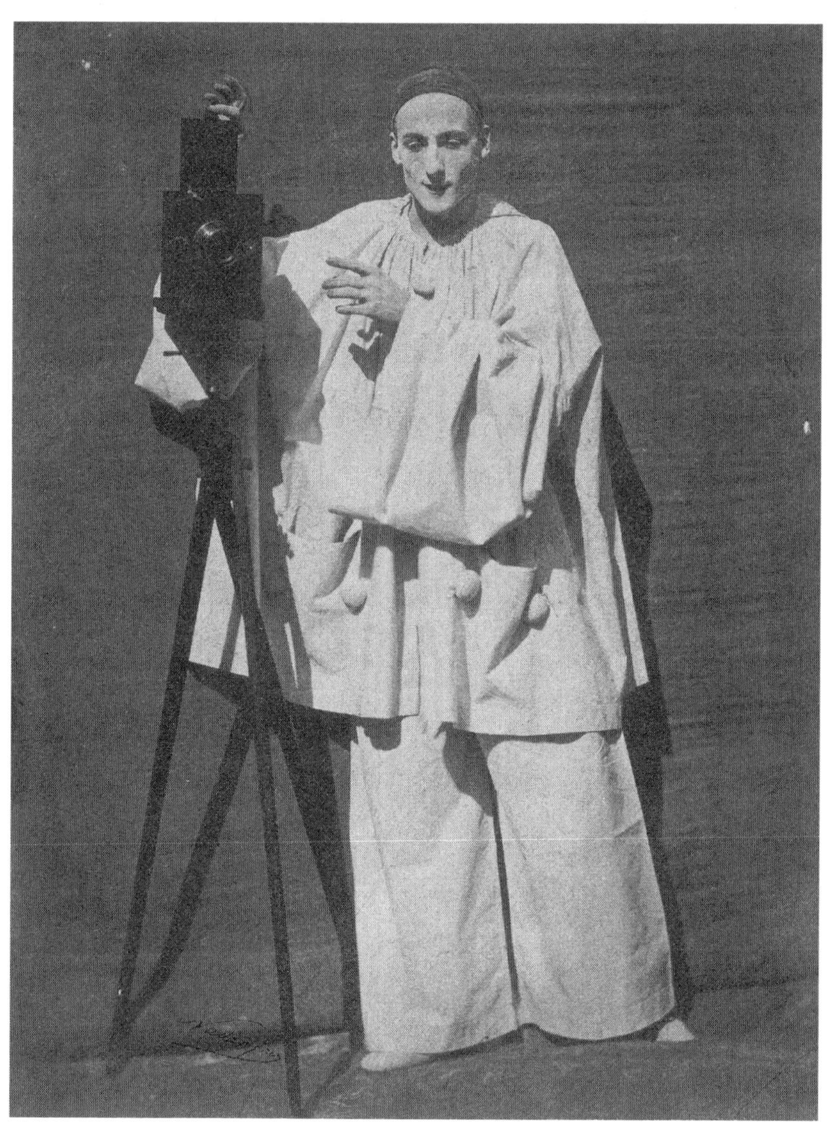

PLATE 9
Nadar, Le Mime Debureau: Pierrot photographe, 1854–55.
Paris, Musée d'Orsay.
©Photo RMN/© Hervé Lewandowski.

> *NOUS N'AVONS PAS COMPRIS DESCARTES. . . .*
> *LA FICTION LUI SEMBLE ÊTRE LE PROCÉDÉ MÊME DE L'ESPRIT HUMAIN*[6]

Mallarmé's examination of the practical means of implementation of this poetic "vision" is evidenced in his intense study of how words and language function, a science of poetic language. His notes from 1869 document that as early as the 1860s Mallarmé was already experimenting with a science of language.[7] He explicitly situates his project for "un étrange petit livre . . . à la façon des Pères" in the wake of

> la grande et longue période de Descartes
>> Puis, en général: du La Bruyère et du Fénelon avec un parfum
> de Baudelaire.
>> Enfin du moi, et du langage mathématique. ("Notes sur le
> langage," *MOC* 1:504–5)

Positioning himself as the heir to a tradition that is literary as well as scientific, the author's notes explain that the objective of such a study would be to show that "nous n'avons pas compris Descartes" (505). Suggesting that the significance of Cartesian discourse lies less in the *cogito* than in the fact that it is grounded in fiction and language, these "Notes" summarize a rereading of Descartes that is fundamental to an understanding of how Mallarmé envisions the relations between the self, cognition, fiction, and language.

> Toute méthode est une fiction, et bonne pour la démonstration. Le langage lui est apparu l'instrument de la fiction: il suivra la méthode du Langage. (la déterminer) Le langage se réfléchissant.
>> Enfin la fiction lui semble être le procédé même de l'esprit humain—c'est elle qui met en jeu toute méthode, et l'homme est réduit à la volonté. (504)

Mallarmé focuses first on the links that Descartes establishes between science, method, and fiction.[8] He zooms in on Descartes's notion of the fiction of the subject and the composition of the subject as fabrication. Moving logically from an assertion that any discourse on a method is a fiction precisely because that discourse involves the use of linguistic signs, the reflexivity of language ("Le langage se réfléchissant") foregrounds Mallarmé's awareness that the self-conscious scientific gaze cannot be divorced from the language of the mind that conceives it. Precisely, he asserts that language is the "instrument" of the fiction, the method, and the self; linguistic "fiction" emerges as "the very process of the human mind," the impetus to all method, reducing man to will.

The plan for this "strange little book" (drafted while Mallarmé was still hoping to write his doctoral thesis) further substantiates the importance he placed on the conjunction of science and language:

> La Science ayant dans le Langage trouvé une confirmation d'elle-même, doit maintenant devenir une *confirmation* du Langage. . . .
> Cette idée de la Science appliquée au Langage, maintenant que le Langage a eu conscience de lui et de ses moyens, reste féconde.[9]

These early notes that link subjective experience and a science of language to the production of an artistic subjectivity already attest to the dissection and reconstitution inherent in the "spectral" workings of the creative act as it is presented Mallarmé's work. Each occasion on which he put himself before the white page can be read as yet another test and reaffirmation of his hypothetical contention that "devant le papier, l'artiste *se fait*" (*MOC* 1:669). The lucid objectification of the writing act seen through the prism of his specular maxim casts light on some of the most densely constructed and paradoxical productions of literary "indirection"[10] known to the French canon.

Mallarmé's texts, especially his later texts, are often seen as "difficult," "obscure," and sometimes "unreadable." Yet each word, each chiseled image, provokes an analogical process of reflection and mobility that is anything but haphazard and demonstrates this poet's particular phenomenology of perception. Mallarmé's implicit (and occasionally explicit) theorization of reader response is, according to the writer himself, in part the result of his openly professed isolation of, and insistence upon, the materiality of words and their signifying operations.

Returning to his 1896 "Le mystère dans les lettres," we note that Mallarmé uses allusions to visual phenomena to illustrate the functioning of words, their signifying operations, and the mystery of his own art. Privileging kinesis, the text's analogy with optical perception insists that words trigger a slidelike spectacle of animated, a-visual afterlight that co-*mneme*-orates[11] effects of the verbal signifying event in the theater-like "cave" ("grotte") of the mind:

> —Les mots, d'eux-mêmes, s'exaltent à mainte facette reconnue la plus rare ou valant pour l'esprit, centre de suspens vibratoire; qui les perçoit indépendamment de la suite ordinaire, projetés, en parois de grotte, tant que dure leur mobilité ou principe, . . . prompts tous, avant

> extinction, à une réciprocité de feux distante ou présentée de biais
> comme contingence. (*MOC* 2:233)

Words, of their own accord, are elevated. Their exalted and rarest facets are immediately registered by the mind, a center of vibratory suspension. Here, Mallarmé clearly states that the functioning of words analogically and diagramatically replicates a model of image perception and cognitive functioning that differs distinctly from those associated with conventional narrative arrangement—"la suite ordinaire." The multiple reflections, the refracting facets of his mobile words, are received by "l'esprit," where they are suspended in a shimmering refraction. Prior to synthesis, the mind perceives these fragments (the facets of words) independently of rationalized, logical, temporal order. In this passage, Mallarmé reanimates an *ut pictura poesis* that is metaphorized through the discourse of visual perception and optical processing. Textually staging how this poetic performance may be placed in relation to the visual arts, he thematizes and enacts a movement that is not conventionally associated with verbal representation. He exhibits how the instituting of a synchronic movement systematically overlays the diachronic "suite ordinaire" of the text. Paradoxically, he enacts this movement through narrative suspensions that function like the "pregnant moments" associated with painting—the only capacity for movement traditionally associated with the pictorial arts.[12] In sum, Mallarmé here shares with the reader three major epistemological figures[13] that inform his understanding of psychic and textual image production:

1. a mechanistic conception of cognitive processing based on fragmentation and mobility.
2. a vision of verbal mimesis that is grounded in a science of language,[14] itself inextricably linked to an understanding of psychic operations as being akin to optical perception and the experience of the afterimage.
3. *ut pictura poesis,*[15] or the tradition of verbal representation's relation to the visual arts.

By evoking the cave and the Platonic discourse that surrounds it, Mallarmé allows the reader to glimpse how his poetics may be placed in relation to the visual arts and, more specifically, in relation to an aesthetic history that has tended to polarize painting and poetry, situating them in an adversarial power struggle for sensorial and/or cognitive supremacy. He conceptually refashions Plato's cave, adorning it with mirrors that go beyond a mere modernization of imperfect representations of the idea, transforming it into a hall of mirrors. The figures in Mallarmé's 1896 cave of the mind are radically reconceived as dynamic word–image hybrids.

This conception of psychic figuration is not exclusively a mode developed late in Mallarmé's aesthetic career. On the contrary, as this chapter's study of the posthumously published "Igitur" will show, as early as the 1860s and 1870s, in his "Notes" and his story of Igitur's room ("chambre") of the mind, Mallarmé presents images as signs that are akin to verbal signs. As he does in the 1896 essay, in "Igitur" Mallarmé already seems to be developing a mechanistic conception of the mind as both darkroom and camera. Perhaps revealingly, the Greek root of "chambre," the room of the mind where Igitur's drama occurs, is *kamera,* implying the formulation of a perceptual and cognitive model whose mechanisms are, in turn, akin to *virtually optical* and photographic processing.[16]

Throughout his oeuvre, Mallarmé seeks to reenact his conception of the raw processes of subjective functioning and image perception. In his 1885 "Crise de vers," we recall, he defines the poetic act as a moment of "seeing" that ideas function and "se fractionne[nt]," like light, into fragments that must be "grouped" or framed (*MOC* 2:209). This focus on action within psychic and verbal image production,[17] along with the marginalization of the temporal logic associated with conventions of verbal narrative, radically distinguish Mallarmé's poetic frameworks from those of his predecessors. This writer's overdetermined hypersensitivity to his medium does not merely call attention to the poetic event and its construction. It also reflects back on its "maker" and the position that the maker will take in relation to aesthetic history, convention, and his own epistemological moment. "Igitur" provides a synthetic example of how the logically structured fragments of Mallarmé's poetic vision come to light and "l'artiste *se fait.*" For the text—its framing of subjectivity, the frames of consciousness it will stage, and the visual analogies exploited to motivate both the events and the language of the story—seems to enact, well before the poet's mature exposition in "Le mystère dans les lettres," a highly systematic aesthetic self-positioning and a modern, scientific, and technological diagram of the camera and its "photo-graphs" (graphic representations of virtual light). It is a major step in the development of Mallarmé's "photo-graphic" process.

TRACES OF "IGITUR"

An incomplete dramatic short story published by Dr. Bonniot in 1925, "Igitur" is one of the few unfinished texts that were spared annihilation after Mallarmé requested that all his notes and incomplete texts be destroyed following his death.[18] The story recounts and represents one major event: the hero Igitur's encounter with his "self." This encounter, and the attempt to master the experience and represent it, are highly significant for Mallarmé's exploration of artistic creation, signification, and the processes of the poet. The text is also revealing in terms of the evolution of his aesthetic thought, for the genesis of "Igitur" spans most of Mallarmé's adult intellectual life.[19] As Bonniot comments, "il vécut trente ans avec ce rêve" (*MOC* 1945:429).

The earliest traces of "Igitur," drafts that were apparently written between 1867 and 1870, followed a period often described as the moment of Mallarmé's metaphysical crisis—a time marked by artistic sterility, anguish, and the poet's experience of the "void." Mallarmé himself referred to "Igitur" as a kind of homeopathic remedy, stating that if he could write it, he would be "cured."[20] Rather than speculating on the biographical origins of Mallarmé's malaise, I will focus on how this text's production and its discussion of the self illuminate not only Mallarmé's vision of verbal representation, but his aspirations for a distinctive art and a literary "self" in the later nineteenth century. Indeed, "Igitur" is a seminal text that illustrates, represents, and theorizes some of the questions most asked by Mallarmists of the late twentieth and early twenty-first centuries. It elucidates how Mallarmé's vision of language in the 1860s prepares his later production, and it rethinks psychic image production and poetic convention—most specifically, the frontiers of genre and the boundaries of visual and verbal representation.

While Mallarmé never intended to publish "Igitur" in its present form, it remains a document that lucidly relates individual narcissism to a conception of cognitive process and simultaneously allegorizes and actualizes the poet's response to a history of poetics that has tended to privilege the visual. Nonetheless, for many critics, "Igitur" continues to represent the failure of a literary ideal;[21] the fact of its incompletion is often viewed as evidence of an ambition that ended in failure or even "catastrophe."[22] Rather than viewing "Igitur" as an attempt at an impossible ideal, I shall consider how through an intricate exposure and framing of its own processes and assumptions, the text not only works through the poetic ideal that Mallarmé envisioned, but actually *figures* the means for its attainment. Mallarmé never threw the dice of "Igitur"—he chose not to publish it—and, for me, this is precisely its interest. It is my contention that aside from the representative difficulties of such a hybrid and abstract text, as well as the discouraging response to his initial reading of it to his friends Villiers de L'Isle-Adam and Catulle Mendès, Mallarmé's refusal to finish or publish any of the more polished sections of this text can be very pragmatically explained. For a poet who would pronounce that one should always erase one's intellectual framework ("échafaudage"), the processes explored in "Igitur" might have provided too obvious an exposition of the author's poetic aspirations. Of course, for the critic, it is precisely because the "framework" has not been erased that this text, like Mallarmé's "Notes" of the same period, presents a precious opportunity for insight into the early stages of his text, his processes, and his career.

While many critics have addressed the issue of subjectivity in this text, the ways in which its discussion of subjectivity relates to cognition, perception, verbal and visual signification, and especially aesthetic convention, certainly merit further discussion. In fact, the text's exposition of a rethinking of temporality as movement in verbal art—its replacement by a complex approach to "framing processes" and the relations between the visual and the verbal[23]—may just provide that sought-after negative from which the poet developed his (in)famously complex speculative aesthetic.

Bertrand Marchal's presentation of the manuscript in the recent Gallimard/Pléiade edition restores (when possible) the manuscript to its original order (state of draft versus notes versus relatively polished draft). This reconstruction is, paradoxically, a deconstruction, since it destabilizes the rationalized order presented by Dr. Bonniot in G. Jean-Aubry's 1945 edition of the *Oeuvres complètes*. While I retain all notation and cite page references from Marchal's edition, for the purposes of clarity here, I too will momentarily restore the narrative order, presenting the movement of this "conte dramatique" (which was probably originally conceived as a three-act drama) with the five "morceaux" (which I will call "acts") in the order established by Bonniot. As alluded to earlier, Marchal's choice to reformat the manuscript and to describe, in detail, the dossiers in which it was found, represents a major step toward more accurate readings of the text. However, Bonniot's ordering in the 1945 edition is not entirely unjustified. As Marchal's work confirms, the manuscript of "Igitur" does present an outline of the text that enumerates four principal sections: (1) "Le Minuit," (2) "L'escalier," (3) "Le coup de dés," and (4) "Le sommeil sur les cendres, après la bougie soufflée." (There is a fifth section, "Vie d'Igitur," whose placement is controversial.) It is this outline that the 1945 edition attempts to reconstruct and this order of action that I will retrace in the brief plot summary that follows.

The drama opens with Act I, entitled "Le Minuit." Igitur does not appear in this section. Personified, Midnight, which can be seen as both the setting of the story and Igitur's double, is the only entity discussed. Act II, entitled "L'escalier" in Mallarmé's outline, appears on the title page of the act with the heading: "Il quitte la chambre et se perd dans les escaliers." Recounting the hero's journey down an allegorical staircase, the narrative focuses on the sensory impressions he experiences during the descent. "Vie d'Igitur" was placed by Dr. Bonniot as an Act III. While Marchal insists on the difficulty of placing the "Vie d'Igitur" among the other four sections, he does accept that the original plan for a three-act division was probably replaced by Mallarmé with a five-act drama. "Vie d'Igitur" begins with a monologue in which Igitur describes his struggle to create an identity and the difficulties of relationally situating oneself with respect to one's ancestors. Its second segment presents a third-person narration of Igitur's life, his ennui, and his dramatic confrontation with a mirror. "Vie d'Igitur" concludes with an affirmation of Igitur's existence: "il est!" (*MOC* 1: 499). Act IV, "Le coup de dés" takes place among the tombs of Igitur's ancestors. Realizing that the creation of his self, the taking of an identity, was nothing but a fictive act, a necessary "folie" (477), Igitur shakes a set of dice before joining the already departed of his race; he lays down among the "cendres, atômes de ces ancêtres" (477), closes his book, and blows out a candle. Act V, which only exists as a sketch, presents Igitur resting among his ancestors. To one side of him remains an empty vial ("fiole") whose contents, as the narrator explains, he has already imbibed.

CONJUNCTIONS
"IGITUR": THE WORD, THE HERO, AND THE TEXT

"Igitur," which doubles as the title of the story and the name of its hero, is an extremely significant word choice. The Latin word *igitur* is a lead-in, a coordinating conjunction meaning "therefore" or "consequently"—in French, "donc."[24] This conjunction, which by its grammatical function defies closure, emblematizes the willed destruction or suspension of the self—the "donc" objectified and personified—and the psychic, linguistic, and aesthetic principles at the base of its conception.

In Act I of "Igitur," the question of the conjunctive function appears as a philosophical interrogation, as well as a ludic experiment with a rhetorical convention: the limit and value of the conjunction as a means to achieve a literary ideal—"un joyau nul de rêverie" (483). What value could be crystallized in a "nullified jewel" described as "une riche et inutile survivance"? One answer may lie in its value as shared representation, an attempt to test the limits and multiply the effects of language on cognition through the prism of the text. For, according to the text, the jewel has no apparent function "sinon que sur la complexité marine et stellaire d'une orfèvrerie se lisait le hasard infinis [*sic*] des conjonctions" (483). The word *igitur* as a title thus crystallizes the processes of a text that investigates the interactive operations of the word and cognition. How this conjunctive interaction emblematizes Mallarmé's vision of language, referentiality, and signification is suggested by the tragic protagonist's name, which in the text is not succeeded by what would grammatically and logically follow a conjunction; instead it is personified and stands alone in suspension as an absolute contingency: "consequently."

This absolute "consequently," both the title and hero of this adventure of the mind, emphasizes the speculative tenor of the text. How does one exist as a "donc"? How does a story entitled "therefore" exist, if not as the metaphor of suspension and of "becoming" itself? The title of this dramatic tale evokes, allegorizes, and personifies a suspension of referentiality that has multiple implications. By calling attention to its own material existence, it represents and objectifies itself. Simultaneously, however, the choice and exploration of a conjunction question the very possibility of objectifying and representing a deferral of closure. This attempt to coincidentally sustain suspense and objectify the movement and the triggering (signifying) function of the word metaphorizes the story of the hero Igitur on a microcosmic level. In other words, the interrogation of the possibility of representing movement in stasis on the linguistic level parallels the objectification of subjectivity in/as process that the narrative aspires to expose. This aspiration to seize and sustain an infinite and prismatic triggering of analogical process is apparent not only in the choice of "Igitur" as a name for his hero (and the text), but also in one of the most celebrated notes Mallarmé penciled when envisaging the text: *"Ce Conte s'adresse à l'Intelligence du lecteur qui met les choses en scène, elle-même"* (475, emphasis in original).

AN EARLY THROW OF THE DICE?

"Ce Conte s'adresse à l'Intelligence du lecteur qui met les choses en scène, elle-même." This declaration, best known for its placement by Dr. Bonniot as the epigraph to "Igitur," links the "conte" to theatrical representation via the suggestion of a mise-en-scène. By addressing the story to the "Intelligence" of the reader—with a capital "I"—the reader's consciousness "itself," the theater of the mind, is interpellated. Invoking the dynamic representational processes of the reader's mind and mediation (contingency), Mallarmé has not only given the work over to chance, he has also revealed a great deal about how he envisions the performative "nature" of the verbal and psychic representation the tale will thematize.

The format of "Igitur"—a work with prescribed scenic gestures divided into five acts—has been attributed to the enormous influence of *Hamlet* on the poet.[25] Yet, this recourse to the theatrical analogy to recount the drama of the mind can also be explained by Mallarmé's lifelong preoccupation with the performative possibilities and potential of poetic signification. To be *between* "to be or not to be" becomes not only a question of identity or suicide in the narrative's subject matter, but also a question of how signification occurs, how it informs Mallarmé's own aesthetic identity and his understanding of aesthetic *choice.* For while the intertextual existential question invokes the complex relations of subjective experience itself, it also interrogates the role of the writing subject with respect to aesthetic creation, aesthetic "others," and convention. The seeds of a logic behind Mallarmé's progressive rarefaction of his words and texts are already apparent. The choice of the theater can be seen as one early response to this interrogation of verbal signification. Although the story's subject matter entails a discussion of an individual's acquisition of a self, the exteriorization and performance implied by the mise-en-scène suggest an insistence on an objectivity that eliminates many of the trappings of the romantic hero and, simultaneously, many of the traps of the verbal artist.[26]

The "Ancienne étude," an introduction that appears as the first text in the "Igitur" manuscript, presents a stage setting that frames the context in which the protagonist will function. This context, recounted in both the future and future perfect tenses, establishes Igitur's existence in relation to his ancestors and posits a quest for a more perfect future:

> Lui-même, à la fin, quand les bruits auront disparu, tirera une preuve
> de quelque chose de grand (pas d'astres? le hasard annulé?) de ce
> simple fait qu'il peut causer l'ombre en soufflant sur la lumière—
> ... Igitur, tout enfant, lit son devoir à ses ancêtres. (473)[27]

The dilemma of *igitur,* that absolute conjunction, is situated in the very first line, where the eponymous hero exerts his force against the breath of his ancestors: "Quand les souffles de ses ancêtres veulent souffler la bougie, (grâce à laquelle peut-être subsistent les Caractères du grimoire)—il dit 'Pas encore!'" (473). This can be read as Igitur's attempt to maintain a certain amount of light (from the "bougie" and from the past), or as the moment when this conjunction, the hero, vindicates his own voice rather than allowing himself to be eclipsed by the voices of his literary and philosophical predecessors.

A dense plot summary following the "Ancienne étude" and the list of acts exposes the thesis of the story and the protagonist's adventure.[28] The time setting, established as the stroke of midnight, is followed by: "Igitur descend les escaliers, de l'esprit humain, va au fond des choses: en 'absolu' qu'il est. Tombeaux—cendres, (pas sentiment, ni esprit) neutralité" (474). The first comma sets up the sentence structure as an invitation to a polysemic reading. "De l'esprit humain" can be read in two ways: the steps can be the steps *of* the human mind, or they may be read as an exit *from* the human mind. In either case, it is a descent and not a transcendence. We are not dealing with an ascendant romantic idealism, but rather with a progressive exploration of alienation, informed by what appears to be a radical *esprit de système* turning its objective gaze on the mind *as* system. The hero, who acts out the drama of his name, descends the steps of/from the human mind, thereby experiencing a parenthetical moment of suspension of consciousness: "(pas sentiment, ni esprit)." The alienation and suspension of the self, which foreshadows what I refer to as a series of "photo-graphic" confrontations with mirrors later in the text, also acts as prelude, prefiguration, and metaphor for the hero's suicide in the final act. Igitur thus personifies and experiences a liminal moment, an *entre deux*. This suspension of consciousness, an exit from or into the mind, reiterates the resistance to closure signaled by his name, and simultaneously explores his position as a personified conjunction: Igitur *finds himself alienated,* unable "to exist" as a unified meaning, except as a fabrication.

"Igitur" recounts and explores the production of the illusion of existence by challenging the Cartesian separation of the subject from the object of knowledge—in this case, the subject itself. By paradoxically casting light on his own exploitation of this separation, Mallarmé throws doubt on the subject as object of knowledge. The experience of subjectivity alienated and objectified for examination, an exteriorization that conventionally precedes its reintegration and reappropriation, ironically nullifies itself in the experiment.[29] Igitur, the hero, explores the very process of acquisition of an "I" as the *becoming* of a fictive self. Replicating the phenomenon of *igitur* the word, the hero's adventure examines how Igitur, the subject, experiences materiality, signification, and meaning—in context.

Directly following is the passage, "il récite la prédiction et fait le geste" (474). "Prédiction" is related to the ancestors of his race and to the commonly accepted theories of the mind, consciousness, representation, and chance contained in the "grimoire" found on the table in the room of Igitur's mind. The word "grimoire," etymologically related to "grammaire," a book of Latin grammar unintelligible to the vulgar, conjures up and elucidates the mystery of *igitur* as word, hero, and text. For while "grimoire" means an unintelligible book of magic used by sorcerers, it also suggests grammar, a set of rules that systematically describe the constituent elements of a language and how to read it. "Igitur" is an extraordinarily synthetic incorporation of the logic that subtends Mallarmé's science of language and his aesthetic; an emblematic term, it systematically embodies the constituent elements of the word, the protagonist, and the text.

UNE EXTRAORDINAIRE APPROPRIATION DE LA STRUCTURE . . . LOGIQUE[30]

"Igitur" is not a conventionally anecdotal story whose "suite ordinaire" facilitates the act of reading. The work itself, unfinished and at times fragmentary, even in the more polished sections, gives the impression that the words have been concentrated. While a plot and certain thematic structures guide our reading, the piece resists assimilation, reduction, and its own linear trajectory. The text's incongruity, its "difficulty," stems from juxtaposed words and images that, reflecting on one another, divert attention from the anecdote to themselves, creating a self-reflexivity (ultimately the subject matter of the story) that is linguistically metaphorized and initially creates an "other" coherence. The words do not simply recount a conventional tale with the temporal movement traditionally associated with verbal mimesis. Concentrated, chosen, and highlighted, the words intermittently catalyze another movement through semantic and semiotic links that play out their integral instability in relation to one another.

As we have seen, Mallarmé later illustrated and justified this phenomenon in his discussion of the integral "mystery" of literature: "Les abrupts, haut jeux d'aile, se mireront, aussi: qui les mène, perçoit une extraordinaire appropriation de la structure, limpide, aux primitives foudres de la logique" ("Le mystère dans les lettres," *MOC* 2:233). Similarly, as we will see, it is this "abrupt, exalted play" of words, creating suspension, reflection, and mobility, that contributes to an impression of fragmentation within "Igitur."[31] The progressive institution of "limpid" structures (that "other" logic) from these densely compressed words and images in motion is further complicated by the play of allusion to literary sources. The evocation of convention and the text's simultaneous deviation from convention—its modernity—are constantly stressed. This presentation of the psychic perception and processing of words as mobile (analogous to optical perception and processing, yet a-visual and silent) calls attention to the text's own reproduction of the process it diagrammatically mimes. Textual discontinuity, like visual discontinuity, represents a "new" gaze, one that valorizes the fragmentary. Vision, once regarded as the fundamental means of orientation of perception and self-perception, is fragmented here and called into question; a new way of looking (and of looking at light) is presented through fragmentation.

Paradoxically, the fragmentation of the dissecting scientific gaze and its corollary positivism yield no definitive absolute other than the positively inevitable contingency of fragmentation itself. A closer look at the above passage from "Le mystère dans les lettres" reveals what Lucienne Frappier-Mazur has described as a characteristically Mallarméan "leveling of writing and its theme" ("Narcisse travesti," 47). The selection and cropping of the verbal text, the "abrupt" plays of the writer's pen that "se mireront," function visually and syntactically as the commas fragment the text, suspending the reading while a choice of semantic possibilities kinetically overlays the ordinary sequence ("suite ordinaire") of the temporal unfolding of the text. The explicit theorization of the writerly act and logic (inspired by the structure of those "primitives foudres de la logique") calls up the same mechanistic conception of the mind as camera that subtends the snapshot operations of the "cave" passage of this same essay. This conception of the mind as simultaneously dark room and purely perceptual camera suggests an understanding of psychic processing as being akin to the optical processing of fragmented photic phenomena. Prior to their rationalized reconstitution, the light waves are perceived according to another logic.[32]

In Igitur's story, the thematization of the subject's experience—visual, auditory, and subconscious perception, as well as cognition—presents not only the narrative of the subject's differentiation as he becomes an "I," but an allegory for the relational figuration entailed in verbal representation. There is, in "Igitur," an attempt to perform linguistically the generative stages of the fictions—of the word, the hero, and the text. As we will see in the following pages, the degree to which the self-reflexive text aspires to thematize, to inextricably superimpose, and simultaneously to develop all three of these narratives (fictions) supports my contention that the text itself may be considered as a metaphorical darkroom: a significant site of developmental processing that elucidates how Mallarmé envisions figuration itself. In fact, not only does the drama begin in darkness, but also, the two most polished sections of the "Igitur" manuscript, "Le Minuit" and "Il quitte la chambre et se perd dans les escaliers" (which correspond to numbers 1 and 2 in Mallarmé's outline) expose precisely this relationship between the development of images and the conception of a self. Both of the latter seem to operate (as do the two textual segments) as re-collections and reconstitutions—spectral representations—of characteristically fragmented distributions of two physical systems: the psyche and the text.

THE DARK ROOM: "LE MINUIT" AND "LA CHAMBRE"

In what was projected as the first act of "Igitur," the title, "Le Minuit," sets the scene and establishes the atmosphere. Midnight is personified and evoked as simultaneously absent and present. At once beginning and end, this absolute hour suggests both life and death. It is also a prelude. It foreshadows Igitur's encounter with the mirror in the "Vie d'Igitur," it anticipates the creation of a subjectivity through the willed de(con)struction of the self,[33] and, more important, it actualizes Mallarmé's new poetics. While the salient features of the poetics of the "animated chamber" are already manifest in "Le Minuit," a glance at how the poet would later theorize his ideal in the 1885 "Crise de vers" strikingly demonstrates the conceptual continuity of Mallarmé's aesthetics:

> L'oeuvre pure implique la disparition élocutoire du poëte, qui cède l'initiative aux mots, par le heurt de leur inégalité mobilisés; ils s'allument de reflets réciproques comme une virtuelle traînée de feux sur des pierreries, remplaçant la respiration perceptible en l'ancien souffle lyrique. (*MOC* 2:211)

The "elocutionary disappearance" of the poet, an axiom of the aesthetic of depersonalization for which Mallarmé has become so well known, as well as the theoretical concession to chance implied by the poet's surrender to the contingency of words ("le poëte, qui cède l'initiative aux mots"), are already inscribed in the dark room of "Le Minuit." This act in the drama exhibits not only particular words that "light up with reciprocal reflections," it also thematizes a "virtual trail of sparks flashing over precious stones," as the poet exposes cognitive functioning as a virtual animation whose operations are akin to contemporary models of optical perception. And finally, in "Le Minuit" the framing of mobility via the institution of a nonlinear instability is precisely what replaces conventions of description characteristic of lyric verse. The replacement of "la respiration perceptible en l'ancien souffle lyrique" that Mallarmé announces in the 1885 essay "Crise de vers" is already actualized in "Le Minuit."[34] Long before "Crise," "Le Minuit" worked out the logic of how matrices of reflection and light might analogically operate as a-visual diagrams of afterimages that silently destabilize the conventions of the "old lyric breath."

"Le Minuit" crystallizes the struggle of the hero Igitur and actualizes the new poetics. Itself a point of conjuncture, Midnight is neither day nor night but "mi-nuit," somewhere in between and both. Its presence, like Igitur's, is affirmed even as its absence is evoked. The traces of Midnight are depicted as experientially recognizable through virtual sensory experience: "Certainement subsiste une présence de Minuit. L'heure n'a pas disparu par un miroir, ne s'est pas enfouie en tentures, évoquant un ameublement par sa vacante sonorité" (*MOC* 1:483).

Midnight is thus not only recognized by its "vacant" sonority but in visual terms as well. It is perceived in the mirror as a "lueur virtuelle" (484).[35] This affirmation of a virtual glimmer of light as *present* is destabilized by the multiple meanings of the adjective that modifies it. Indeed, "virtuelle," a term from mechanics and physics, might suggest that the light is potential rather than actual—in other words, a fictive product that has no real effect. This would undermine any real existence of light in the darkness here. At the same time, however, in physics, the "foyer virtuel" of a mirror or lens is the point determined by the meeting of geometrical extensions of light rays. A virtual image of light would then be one from which rays of reflected or refracted light appear to diverge. This would in turn support an experiential phenomenon akin to the sensory experience of light. By alluding to the way in which presence is experienced by the mirror of the mind, "virtuelle" identifies the psychic effects of Midnight's virtual presence as akin, but not equivalent, to the sensorial impact of sonority and a visual effect of light projected in and from the mirror.

The discussion of Midnight's presence as a subjective experience is further supported by the subject of the enunciation's recollection of his sensation, his memory of this hour:

> Je me rappelle que son or allait feindre en l'absence un joyau nul de
> rêverie, riche et inutile survivance, sinon que sur la complexité marine
> et stellaire d'une orfèvrerie se lisait le hasard infini des conjonctions.
> (483)

Although the narrator has entered into a description of his subjective experience—the effects of midnight on his "self" or the midnight of his self—he describes the experience not only as the reflection of a physically nullified jewel but as a repetitive musical effect, perhaps an effect of the pendulum,[36] that surfaces visually in his memory.[37] The feigned "joyau nul de rêverie" is described at the end of the passage as both a "lueur virtuelle, produite par sa propre apparition en le miroitement de l'obscurité" and "le feu pur du diamant de l'horloge, seule survivance et joyau de la Nuit éternelle, l'heure se formule en cet écho" (484). Midnight is thus present as a memory. Triggered in its turn by the memory of auditory and optical experience, Midnight as memory finds expression as a fictive, "virtual" representation of light projected in the obscurity of the mirror of the mind. It would seem that like the eye or the camera, the mind presented here does not register images directly, but rather collects and reconstitutes fragmented emissions akin to light rays. Present to the senses and existing as would visual effects of light projected in and by the mirror, the reflecting facets of this early "joyau nul de rêverie" prefigure not only "Crise de vers," but also the "mots projetés, en parois de grotte" evoked in the 1896 "Le mystère dans les lettres," where the facets of words are perceived by the mind, that "centre de suspens vibratoire" (*MOC* 2:233). Foregrounded in "Le Minuit," the importance of light, which plays on an analogy with optics and optical processing, overshadows the musical analogy as the dominant metaphor evoked by the concept of Midnight: "Et du Minuit demeure la présence en *la vision* d'une chambre" (*MOC* 1:483, emphasis added). Although aspiring to the unrepresentable or even the unspeakable, the term "vision" here, evoking both seeing and knowing,[38] highlights the fundamental place of the visual epistemology informing, encoding, and articulating the endeavor. Moving, then, from the implicit depiction of the operations of the mind and cognition as akin to optical or even photographic processing, we might ask how such a vision of cognition as collection and reconstitution informs the poetics in which it is expressed.

The evocations of the diamond and gold in the passage suggest perfection, the poetic goal. They additionally pattern the narrative with pauses, creating suspense via matrices of metaphorical reflection among words and phonemes alluding to light and reflection. As in a picture, so in poetry? Certainly, but it is not only the reference to visual objects or phenomena that is of interest here. For the (ekphrastic) effects of the "virtual trail of sparks" and the "reciprocal reflections" function via networks of virtual sonority as well.

One example of how this poetic goal is achieved is evidenced in the juxtaposition of the words "son" and "or." The possessive adjective "son" also evokes its French homonym "son" (sound), and suggests the chiming of the clock in the room, the sounds of poetry, music, the heartbeat, and perhaps that universal hymn to which Mallarmé often refers. "Or" (gold) evokes light and that precious, pure substance that the alchemists and poets sought to create. Juxtaposed, however—"son or"—the two words can be heard as "sonore" (sonorous). Not incidentally, "or" is also a conjunction that marks the transitional moment of a thought process.[39] In this particular example, Mallarmé's insistence on the effects of sonority functions to multiply and reinforce the metonymic mobility of the reflecting semes in suspension (metaphorized by the conjunction).

The sparkling light of the stars on the sea, the gold of "son or," as well as the facets of the "joyau," the "feu" of the diamond, and the "miroitement" and "lueur" of the "apparition" in the mirror, link a series of textual associations triggered through the repetition of images of light reflecting one on the other. This repetition is reinforced by games of sonority, which, like the triggering of analogical effect by "son or," create semantic hesitation that destabilizes the text and exponentially multiplies its potential for cognitive effect. The constant association of sonority and visual effects of light seems to insist upon sonorous effect as an analogy for the metonymic movement of the thought process, itself akin to the movement of light waves and their perception. While this atomistic movement of thought as it reflects upon itself is emphasized by sonority, thought and the self are explicitly presented in "Igitur" as light illuminating itself: "un vague frémissement de pensée, lumineuse brisure . . . du retour de ses ondes" (483). Music sets the scene for and via light, and not the other way around.

SELF-DEVELOPMENT:

FABRICATION AND THE PHOTO-GRAPHIC MIRROR

Midnight is present to the senses. —Or is it? The subjective experience associated with this vacant sonority (or word) is crystallized visually as a memory: here a feigned product of *virtual* optical and sonorous effect. The fabrication of memory is metaphorized as a mirror in the chamber where the action of the drama begins. Consciousness is represented as a dark room in which, metaphorized as light, the fabricating movement of thought and image perception is paradoxically "seized." An exposition *en abyme,* the poet's detailed diagrammatic display of Midnight's effects on subjectivity parallels the description of the subject's reflexive gaze upon his self and how this sensory experience of the self is processed:

> Et du Minuit demeure la présence en la vision d'une chambre du temps où le mystérieux ameublement arrête un vague frémissement de pensée, lumineuse brisure . . . du retour de ses ondes et de leur élargissement premier, cependant que s'immobilise (dans une mouvante limite), la place antérieure de la chute de l'heure en un calme narcotique de *moi* pur longtemps rêvé; mais dont le temps est résolu en des tentures sur lesquelles s'est arrêté, les complétant de sa splendeur, le frémissment amorti, dans l'oubli, comme une chevelure languissante,

> autour du visage éclairé de mystère, aux yeux nuls pareils au miroir, de
> l'hôte, dénué de toute signification que de présence. (483, emphasis in
> original)

The "*moi* pur" suggests more than the metaphysical state that the previous poetic reading allegorizes: The chiming of the clock, the attempt to translate this "universal hymn," corresponds to heightened physical, psychic, and metaphysical self-presence, linking the physical and psychic in a bizarre mirror image of light that captures and then reflects back a refracted and decomposed vision of the self as light and of the body as a mere reflection of matter. In this moment of hyperacuity, the hero experiences a "vague frémissement de pensée" that becomes immobile, is alienated in the "yeux nuls au miroir, de l'hôte, dénué de toute signification que de présence." The decomposed illusion of self is expressed in clauses graphically and syntactically fragmented by commas. The temporary suspension of the narrative movement, however, is overlaid with another kind of movement: The fractionating commas provoke a semantic hesitation (or "vibratory suspension") that destabilizes the linear development of the text and any unified image of Midnight as memory, Midnight as vision, or Midnight as the self. The subject of the observation (the Midnight-self) and the subject of the story give way to a philosophical reflection on the optical reflection of materiality. The moment is thus one in which the "pure self" is simultaneously perceived and alienated *in* and *as* a reflection whose process of fabrication is likened to that of visual perception.

The experience of optical reflection so described seems to anticipate Roland Barthes's discussion, in *La chambre claire,* of the alienation inherent in the photograph (28–33). His analysis of the photographic image's inextricable link to presence and death is particularly applicable. According to Barthes, the photograph's re-presentation of an image always entails recognition of a past in the presence of the visual artifact or trace. The photographic experience is regarded by Barthes as one of intense presence that carries with it a knowledge, a record, and an awareness of loss and the past.[40]

Not insignificantly, the ambiguity of "C'est le rêve pur d'un Minuit, en soi disparu" (484), which follows in the text, explores just this type of alienating distance. This is particularly noteworthy because the pure dream of a Midnight, already suggested as Igitur's double, disappears into itself just as the hero Igitur descends the stairs and attempts to disappear into his own "persona." The second act of the text suggests this phenomenon by the verb "se perdre" in its title: "Il quitte la chambre et se perd dans les escaliers." The "rêve pur" of a Midnight "en soi disparu" refers to the hero's descent into the tombs of neutrality discussed earlier, and at the same time it parallels Igitur's attempt to figure his alienated self as a persona, to arrive at an objective distance from his self and to experience it from a perspective of internalized alienation. Indeed, as the hero prepares to descend from the "chambre," Act I closes with the following first-person confirmation of the hypothesis linking Igitur and Midnight: "Adieu, Nuit, que je fus, ton propre sépulcre" (484).

In the most polished draft of what was planned as the second act Igitur announces: "je vais m'oublier à travers lui, et me dissoudre en moi" (487). He thus describes the first steps (downward into "les escaliers") of a process of self-alienation. The "se perd" suggests the endeavor of the "je" to experience itself as "other." To liquidate the master "je" and impersonally examine the "moi" entails the cultivation of a self-induced split that allows the hero to explore and map the operations of his self from an objective perspective—one that is nonetheless a position within.

The allusion to a descent from the "chambre" implies an examination of the physical sensory experience of the self by an alien perspective. This hypothesis is supported by the insistence on the hero's heightened state of sensory and physical awareness. These first steps of the process are progressively radicalized and appear to lead up to the final section of the "Vie d'Igitur," where, as in the passage in "Le Minuit," the persona projected into the mirror is intuited only for an instant before the fiction of the imagination gives way to an image of pure corporeality and self-loss. This dialectic between the phenomena of virtual light and materiality is already foreshadowed through Igitur's double in this ambiguous, self-reflexive passage from "Le Minuit":

> C'est le rêve pur d'un Minuit, en soi disparu, et dont la Clarté reconnue, qui seule demeure au sein de son accomplissement plongé dans l'ombre, résume sa stérilité sur la pâleur d'un livre ouvert que présente la table; page et décor ordinaires de la Nuit, sinon que subsiste encore le silence d'une antique . . . parole proférée par lui, en lequel, revenu, ce Minuit évoque son ombre finie et nulle par ces mots: J'étais l'heure qui doit me rendre pur. (484)

Like Midnight's virtual reflection in the mirror of the mind's room, the only thing that remains after the subject's descent into the profound darkness of the self is the "Clarté." The light, or thought, that attempts to elucidate and examine itself reveals nothing but traces of reflected light. This is strikingly similar to the photograph, which would in principle seem to re-present that on which the camera turns its gaze, but in actuality presents nothing but a distribution of light—a trace. Igitur's "moi" as object of its own desire loses its status as subject and therefore substantially disappears. The recognition of the subject, like Midnight, as simply a "lueur virtuelle," a fictive existence as light whose only remaining trace is that of an afterlight ("Clarté") existing in the darkness of the mind's room, is said to recapitulate or sum up ("résume") its sterility on the whiteness of the page. The insistence on Midnight as Igitur's double, discussed previously in terms of semantic suspension, is rendered even stronger by the ambiguity of "C'est le rêve pur d'un Minuit, en soi disparu." The "soi" could simply be read as the pure dream of one Midnight, in opposition to other midnights; "en soi disparu" could be read as the dream's disappearance into itself or, more generally as the disappearance of any midnight (or self) into itself: Midnight's, Igitur's, the narrator's, or all of these. What is interesting is that the recognized "Clarté," the only light in the darkness of the room, picks up on the "joyau nul de rêverie" of Midnight's "lueur virtuelle" in the mirror. This "Clarté" is then related to the self—any self—as an image of light remaining in darkness that is intimately associated with its verbal summation (its name).

In "Igitur," the poetic struggle is repeatedly reflected and crystallized[41] via the image of what I call a "photo-graphic" mirror. Each of the first two acts develops a particular aspect of the specular experience, akin to the encounters with the mirror in the "Vie d'Igitur." In Igitur's attempt to alienate that conception of a self in the mirror,[42] the hyperlucid gaze, a registration of the process of perception that projects and dissects the self in the mirror—an attempt to visualize the self and its processes—reveals not the unified self he seeks to dissect and examine, but the optical reflection of the sheer physical body.

What we see in this description of Igitur's desire to alienate, study, and then create his own identity—his own place among the ashes of his ancestors—is a double movement of narcissistic desire. Igitur's investment of psychic energy in himself and the place he would like to claim for his "moi" is representative of the life drive, the positive side of the Janus-faced narcissism represented in the story. However, the very fact of its representation, of its reflection first in the mirror of Igitur's room and then in the framework of the text, is symptomatic of an attempt to reify a concept (the self) that can only exist when it functions. To encase and expose the self, or even a discussion of the self, within the spectrum of the representative frame is to write "le frémissement amorti" (483).

"Igitur," then, recounts the story of Igitur, a fantasmatic creation of Mallarmé's whose role is to act out the drama of his race—the drama of narcissism. The ancestors, mathematicians, and thinkers already evoked by the tale are once again questioned and perhaps even parodied in this age-old play that the hero seems condemned to repeat.

> Depuis lontemps morte, une antique idée se mire telle à [la] clarté de la chimère en laquelle a agonisé son rêve [et] se reconnaît à l'immémorial geste vacant avec lequel elle s'invite, pour terminer l'antagonisme de ce songe polaire, à se rendre, avec la clarté chimérique et le texte refermé, au Chaos de l'ombre avorté et de la parole qui absolut Minuit. (484)

The psychic drama of self-exploration, an attempt to replay the immemorial scene of the Cartesian *cogito,* is described as a "chimère" an "immémorial geste vacant." For the objectified image eventually dissolves into its constituent material elements, nullifying the fictive or virtual "rêve pur" constructed around it. It is in fact the "Clarté," the light thrown on the subject itself as object, that ultimately reveals the sterility of the subject.

"Vie d'Igitur," although it is one of the less-polished segments of the manuscript, illuminates the identity issues underlying the discussion and distinction of self in the text, as well as the working out of an aesthetic. Our opening maxim returns here through a series of parallels and ambiguities revolving around the mirror and narrative voice—that is, visual and verbal representation.

The first segment in "Vie d'Igitur" is a paragraph recounted in the first person. It opens with Igitur describing his past struggles with time and identity. The dilemma of identity, reminiscent of a passage from the "Ancienne étude" previously cited, is in the "Vie d'Igitur" somewhat more explicit: "Écoutez, ma race, avant de souffler ma bougie—le compte que j'ai à vous rendre de ma vie" (479). If we recall that the candle reflected in the mirror remains the only light and the sole trace of Midnight (Igitur's double) in the dark room of his mind, the passage reinforces the notion that Igitur's maintenance and creation of his own identity are explored and affirmed in the specular relation to the mirror. A second specular relationship—that between Igitur and his ancestors—is also implied by the opening "Écoutez," which suggests a dialogue.[43] Identity, and the substantiation of a self, are intimately associated not only with the mirror but with the verbal creative act ("le compte" and "le conte") as well. As Igitur describes his dilemma of identity, the allusion to specular relationships as creative acts involving mirrors is textually carried two reflexive steps further. Igitur's self is described as a fabric he weaves of precious atoms in an effort to affirm his existence in the face of his ancestors. Not only did Mallarmé often write in front of a mirror, but the parallel between the writer's specular experience and the experience of Igitur is rendered even more explicit by this densely woven fabric of precious atoms.[44] The parallel of subjective and textual density is presented as an effect of creating in front of the mirror—the effect of an objectifying gaze. But the obvious allusion to the mirroring text suggests that in the creation of the text-as-mirror, the artist reaffirms his own existence: "Devant le papier, l'artiste *se fait*"—in dialogic relation to his ancestors. What might this mean for how Igitur takes his position in relation to the ancestors of his race? And, more important, which reflection is superior? The visible mirror or the visible, verbal mirror of the text alluded to in the fabric?

> J'ai toujours vécu mon âme fixé sur l'horloge. Certes, j'ai tout fait pour que le temps qu'elle sonna *restât* présent dans la chambre . . . et comme j'étais obligé pour ne pas douter de moi de m'asseoir en face de cette glace, j'ai recueilli précieusement les moindres atômes du temps dans des étoffes sans cesse épaissies. —L'horloge m'a fait souvent grand bien. (498, emphasis in original)

Igitur's lamentation offers a striking example of Mallarmé's interest in the functioning of temporality in verbal art. Best known for its insistence on the metaphors of embroidery and lace, the passage certainly comments the significance of such allusions for the Mallarméan textual fabric. However, I would like to suggest that a less commonly noted aspect of the text—time—may play a more fundamental role in the passage and in Mallarmé's poetic texture. I am referring to the "horloge" to suggest the degree to which a very cognizant rethinking of temporality in verbal art weaves itself through all the levels of Mallarmé's work.

Igitur explains that in order not to doubt his own existence, he was obliged to sit in front of a mirror, to confront the reflection of his existence as reflection, and to gather all of its atoms to fabricate an existence. As in the passage from "Le Minuit," where thought and time are immobilized, the hero announces that time has played a significant role in how he envisions his self. In fact, it is apparent that Igitur's recourse to the mirror was provoked, in part, by his preoccupation with diachronic time. His desire to stay time ("que le temps . . . *restât*"), to frame his image in the mirror, catalyzes and frames his fabrication of himself and his aesthetic.

With Igitur's aspiration to make time "stay," Mallarmé takes another tack to the temporality issue and the capacity for movement in verbal art.

Although not explicitly developed further in the passage, the achievement of such a feat is suggested in the last line, which concludes with a very Mallarméan grain of salt: "L'horloge me fait souvent grand bien." The "great good" of the clock, I would suggest, elucidates how Mallarmé's verbal texts institute movement through the use of analogy. Indeed, the linking of mirror, fabrics, and atoms of time suggests a focus on time that emblematizes a reenvisioning of the movement one may incorporate in poetry and a very cognizant repositioning of the verbal within the framework of *ut pictura poesis.*

Such an optimistic conception of the power and will to self and self-knowledge is once again exposed in the third segment of the "Vie d'Igitur." It presents a detailed description of Igitur's encounter with his image in the mirror:

> quand je rouvrais les yeux au fond du miroir, je voyais le personnage d'horreur, le fantôme de l'horreur absorber peu à peu ce qui restait de sentiment et de douleur dans la glace, nourrir son horreur des suprêmes frissons des chimères et de l'instabilité des tentures, et se former en raréfiant la glace jusqu'à une pureté inouïe, jusqu'à ce qu'il se détachât, permanent, de la glace absolument pure, comme pris dans son froid. (499)

The more Igitur attempts to own his totalized identity, the more he must confront his own nullified, vacant image: a "donc." Subjectivity as a concept is recognized as an act that is always under construction and performed in context. With the realization that this identity is no more than a fiction, Igitur (the hero and the work) emerges in this third segment ("Il est!" 499), where temporality is explicitly articulated as an element in the process of identity formation.

COMING TO TERMS: "LE COUP DE DÉS" AND "SES ANCÊTRES"

Following his allusions to the complex relations of the subject to himself and his context comes the climactic moment of the narrative and the philosophical summit of the piece, a heroic moment: Igitur's throwing of the dice, which precedes his laying himself to rest on the ashes of his ancestors in Act V. Act IV, "Le coup de dés," appears to be a commentary on the psychic and literary experience that precedes it and allows the work and the poet to transcend the encounter with both the void and the absolute. The act, notes Haskell Block, "is a prelude to his death, yet the throwing of the dice is no suicidal gesture, but a heroic opposition of the Infinite to the Absurd implicit in chance. . . . It is

Igitur who closes the book and blows out the candle" (*Mallarmé and the Symbolist Drama,* 40). The narrative voice assures the reader that Igitur has come to terms with the necessarily illusory dimension of the fabrication of the idea of the self and the self as idea: "Alors il conçoit qu'il y a, certes, folie à l'admettre absolument: mais . . . par le fait de cette folie, le hazard étant nié, cette folie était nécessaire" (*MOC* 2:477).[45] As Marchal notes, it is here that

> La conscience d'Igitur n'a plus rien alors d'une conscience individuelle. . . . A ce point où la conscience individuelle rejoint l'inconscient universel, Igitur mérite son nom, dans la mesure où il n'est plus le sujet psychologique ou cartésien de l'Acte, mais devient l'instrument logique d'un acte qui relève d'une causalité tout objective, si bien qu'à la limite, il s'accomplit tout seul: *Mais L'Acte s'accomplit.* Or, c'est à ce moment où l'Acte s'accomplit tout seul, ou dans son sillage immédiat, que paradoxalement, resurgit le moi, dans une formule qui ressemble à un Cogito ironique. (*Lecture de Mallarmé,* 263–64, emphasis in original)

The existential quest to see and represent the self by textually replicating this act of perception is thus seen as a futile but necessary "folie." This can, of course, be read as the allegory of the poet's artistic quest: the representation of the repetitive desire to act out the tragedy of subjectivity in and through literature. The representation of the tragedy of narcissism as reflected in the mirror in Igitur's room parallels the narcissistic struggle of the poet-philosopher's identity problem when faced with his past and context.

"Igitur" is a literary creation that deconstructs the self *as a concept* and simultaneously applies such knowledge to verbal representation. It is a text that not only dissects the illusion of meaning attributed to materiality (and thus itself), but one that traces the construction of Mallarmé's vision of subjective functioning in relation to the functioning of images and of language. This complex study of subjectivity as a concept, seemingly resolutely theoretical and esoteric, pragmatically works out the logic of how the mind perceives words and images (analogically) and creates meaning (metonymically), in a specular process whose textual figuration is informed by a vision of the optical processing and perception of light as dynamic. Mallarmé diagrams this visual analogy in his poetics via series of aesthetic choices based on a rigorous science of psychic and linguistic functioning that aspires to objectivity and another genre of referentiality. The position Mallarmé takes with respect to artistic creation, one of depersonalization, is just that: the taking of a subject-position within the framework of the aesthetic context. The narcissistic struggle elucidates his conception of how one assumes a position by strategic choice and differentiation. From a study of the artistic subject, to the textual implications and applications of this process, the knowledge of how subjectivity functions is evidenced first in the willed creation of a poetic self reflecting certain ideological and aesthetic positions. Igitur's separation from his self, the knowledge gained by his methodical study and the drinking of the "goutte de néant" (478) in the final act prefigures, parallels, and logically elucidates certain paradoxes of Mallarmé's aesthetic practice and its others, as well as what he would later, in "Crise de vers," theorize as the "disparition élocutoire du poète" (*MOC* 2:211).

Marchal remarks that the poetic act supposes "un héroïsme ou une ascèse du sujet, qui doit se dépersonnaliser *absolument,* comme le fait Igitur" (265) and relates this apotheosis, as does Leo Bersani, to Mallarmé's famous "je suis parfaitement mort." In what Bersani calls Igitur's perception of "the process of self-specularization" (*The Death of Stéphane Mallarmé,* 63), Mallarmé parodies Descartes's intuition of existence and represents a crisis in self-perception. The parallel between the poet-hero and the hero of the story who seeks to vindicate his voice in the face of his ancestors is explored in the mirror of the story and the mirror of the text—precisely the experience alluded to in the "devant" of "Devant le papier, l'artiste *se fait.*"

Seen through a mid-nineteenth-century scientific lens, Igitur's mirror appears a literary analogue of nineteenth-century photography. The desire to seize the subject and its processes in the "photo-graphic" mirror—subjectivity objectified—is not only a modernized version of the myth of Narcissus that refigures Descartes's fictive subject and prefigures how the subject takes its position within what Lacan will call the Symbolic, it is also a manner of capitalizing on the objectification and impersonality typically associated with the photograph in order to vanquish "le hasard" word by word: "C'est t'apprendre que je suis maintenant impersonnel et non plus Stéphane que tu as connu, — mais une aptitude qu'a l'Univers spirituel à se voir et à se développer, à travers ce qui fut moi" ("A Cazalis," *MOC* 1:714).

As suggested in this chapter's opening maxim, Mallarmé was fascinated by the actual processes, (intellectual, literary, and psychic) of both poetry *and the poet*—what Julia Kristeva calls "signifiance": "précisément cet engendrement illimité et jamais clos, ce fonctionnement sans arrêt des pulsions vers, dans et à travers le language, vers, et dans et à travers l'échange et ses protagonistes: le sujet et ses institutions" (*La révolution du langage poétique,* 15). Mallarmé's self-positioning as a writing subject necessarily incorporates the institutions and discourses of his context.

Mallarmé's speculative formulation of poetic process moves away from the romantic self to a writing process of alienation that he explores and objectifies in "Igitur." This ontological study leads to a more generalized conception of the self and a deeper understanding of his own processes at work. It is through the knowledge gained in this representation of individual narcissism that Mallarmé appears to work out the logic of the cognitive process he perceives as governing his aesthetic choices. However, this literary self-positioning itself requires a reconfiguration of the poet's differential relationship to his contemporaries and literary predecessors.[46]

Mallarmé's suppression of the self, his willed impersonality, and the linguistic strategies employed in his "philosophical suicide" have affinities not only with photography and with the work of the Parnassian writers of the nineteenth century who cultivated impersonality and refracted subject positions,[47] but also with temporally more remote seventeenth-century classical writers who wrote from the depersonalized position of a strategically constructed first-person literary voice. In fact, Mallarmé's philosophical suicide, the self-engendering process of the writing subject, is not very different from other social ethics and intellectual constructions of the self that preceded it and are perpetuated in its production—a process already present in the "ancêtres" of Igitur, the hero, and the literary ancestors of Mallarmé, the poet.[48]

Mallarmé's discourse and writing processes, although perhaps more explicitly philosophical and literary than social, are linked to a tradition of a social and linguistic struggle to attain literary heroism that survives in the Parnassians, the symbolist drama, and "Igitur." The poetic hero emerging from Mallarmé's "conte" is a dramatic one. The use of the virtual theater allows Mallarmé to create his hero, Igitur, fictionally, and to create a poet-hero through a fictional drama much like what Freud describes as the satisfaction of desire in daydreams. In attempting to explore the self, to transgress and transcend individual psychic awareness and consciousness, Mallarmé envisions his poetic and intellectual method.

"Igitur," "wherefore," or, more commonly, "consequently" ("donc"), presents a thematization of conjunction that exposes and semantically and syntactically actualizes the ultimate story of suspension as a composition *en abyme.* "Igitur" bears witness to Mallarmé's extraordinary vision as he shifts away from the effusive romantic persona and detailed narrative description not only to portray its heir within the frame of the mirror (rather than nature), but to expose the very role and functioning of the verbal within the framework of *ut pictura poesis.* From the close-up exposition of individual narcissism (dis-)played via an afterimage-like dissection and reconstitution in the photo-graphic mirror *as other,* to the discussion of Igitur's societal narcissism, articulated as a subjective self-situating in relation to his ancestors' breath and the mirror *as others,* the text progressively delineates verbal art's own narcissistic experience "devant le papier," positioning itself in relation to *its* other: the pictorial. While strategically he may refuse to address his aesthetic others as such, this poet-critic's vision of textual fabrication can in no way be seen as oblivious of the aesthetic frames of reference to which his ontic models of image conception, perception, and production respond. Indeed, as his writings of the 1870s show, he is highly conscious of his pose and of how his photo-graphic aesthetic should be poised amid the cultural, socioeconomic, and technological movements destabilizing the landscape of artistic production—pictorial and verbal.

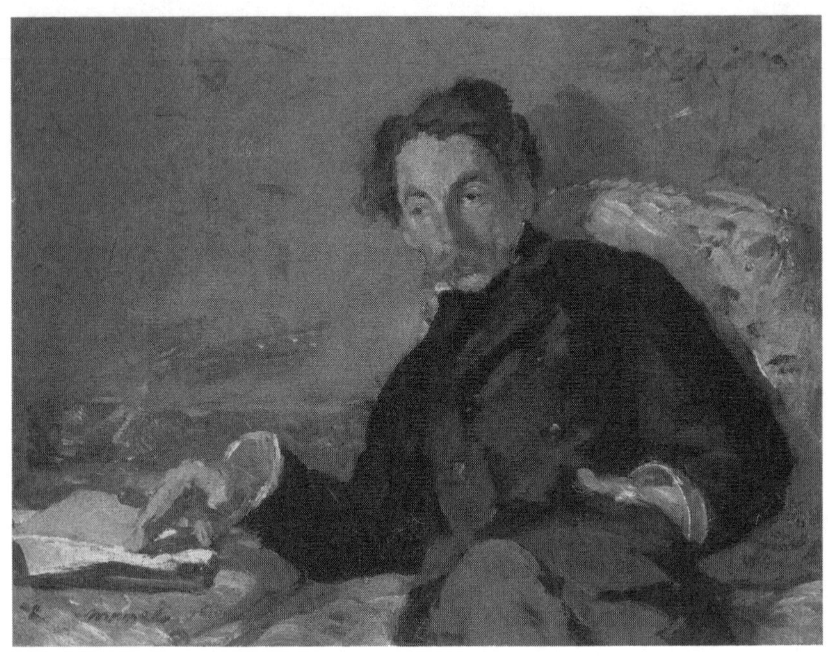

PLATE 10

Manet, Stéphane Mallarmé, poète, 1876.
Huile sur toile.
Paris, Musée d'Orsay.
© Photo RMN–© Hervé Lewandowski.

CHAPTER 4

Framed Works and Mallarmé

The steadfast gaze of a vision restored to its simplest perfection

"'IT IS THROUGH HER that when rudely thrown at the close of an epoch of dreams in the front of reality, I have taken from it only that which properly belongs to my art, an original and exact perception which distinguishes for itself the things it perceives with the steadfast gaze of a vision restored to its simplest perfection.'"[1] Speaking in the first person—as a painter—Mallarmé thus concludes one of his most extraordinary and clearly articulated pieces of art criticism. This key citation raises the main issues that will concern us in this chapter as we explore Mallarmé's recuperation and modernization of the principles of *ut pictura poesis*.

POET-CRITIC OF THE MODERN

As an active participant in literary and journalistic circles, Mallarmé was intimately acquainted with the aesthetic premises of the pictorial arts and visual conventions of representation. Aside from the constant intellectual exchange he derived from his weekly *mardiste* interactions with artists of virtually all disciplines,[2] Mallarmé, engaged in several interdisciplinary projects, was an international cultural correspondent as well as a critic of art and literature.[3] His early preoccupations with the theater ("Hérodiade," "Igitur," and *L'après-midi d'un faune*), his pieces on music and dance, and his collaboration on several illustrated texts, as well as his critical works on the pictorial and decorative arts published in various literary journals, all attest to his capacity to assimilate innovations from all areas of artistic production.

Mallarmé's contributions to the aesthetic debates of the period are an obvious source of potential insights into the development of his poetics. His criticism of Edouard Manet and his writings on Berthe Morisot, Edgar Degas, James Abbott McNeill Whistler,[4] and Richard Wagner clearly articulate his aesthetic tendencies and his theoretical views on art and the artist's relationship to nature, subjectivity, objectivity, and choice.

In the later nineteenth century, artists in both arts reconceptualized and reactivated the "faithful representation of nature" doctrine fundamental to the traditional painting-literature analogy. On the conceptual level, both arts strove toward a definition of mimesis as the enacting of the life force through representation,[5] rather than as an imitation of external nature divorced from the subject. Formally as well, there are many similarities between pictorial and literary aspirations and innovations of the period. It should be noted that in endeavoring to multiply the potential of poetic signs, Mallarmé most certainly explores and exploits the differences between verbal and visual signs, but, in fact, he does so only to activate and, ultimately, to transgress the traditional semiotic boundaries between the visual and verbal.[6]

The tendency to isolate Mallarmé from the tradition of *ut pictura poesis* and the relative critical neglect of the influence of the pictorial arts on Mallarmé's work probably stemmed both from critics' association of Mallarmé's work with music and from a lack of theoretical apparatuses to analyze and semiotically compare both the textual practices of the poetic and pictorial events and the passage from one sign system to another.[7] This scholarly neglect of Mallarmé's aesthetics in relation to the visual arts was further compounded by the fact that his art criticism was rarely studied, and, more important, by the absence of one of his most passionate and articulate articles on painting from the 1945 Gallimard/Pléiade edition of his complete works. While "Le jury de peinture pour 1874 et M. Manet," (*MOC* 2:410–15), an article condemning the jury's refusal to admit Manet to the official Salon, has elicited regular study, the article of the same period that most clearly demonstrates the breadth of Mallarmé's grasp of the visual premises of this "new painting" and the more global crisis in artistic values, has not, until recently, received comparable attention. This 1876 article, "The Impressionists and Edouard Manet" (*MOC* 2:444–70), demonstrates Mallarmé's sophisticated grasp of the mechanisms underlying Manet's and the impressionists' innovations. Moreover, the article's foregrounding of the relationship between the pictorial arts and literature provides many insights into Mallarmé's aesthetic thought and the techniques exploited in his poetic language.[8]

In what follows, I will trace the parallels between aesthetic theories and techniques in painting and poetry, as both arts moved toward a reconception of the principal tenets of *ut pictura poesis,* especially the faithful representation of nature. Although Penny Florence expresses reservations about the "very comfortable" description of impressionist art forms as an attempt to represent the effects of light and nature, she nonetheless accepts that what they aspire to objectively relay is based on "nature" as it is received or even distorted by the observing subject (*Mallarmé, Manet and Redon,* 3). Further, while Florence insists that the impressionists' and Mallarmé's art reexamined their own categorizations of cultural production, and that innovations occurred in relation to "something," that something is not specifically defined in terms of the ways in which epistemological thought about perception and nature's interaction with human consciousness may have affected artists of the period.

As James Kearns quite rightly points out, the poet himself describes his interest in the historical development and the fusion of the arts and industry as an endeavor that is "celle de l'âge moderne tout entier."[9] Though I am indebted to Florence's application of poststructuralist models to analyze the innovative semiotic operations of Manet and Redon and their relation to Mallarmé, conceptually and technically, the progression toward such innovation has much more to do with a "comfortable" process of naturalization (which she says both art forms resisted) and an infiltration of scientific and mechanistic thought than Florence suggests (38). Even if one chooses to focus on the unconscious in art as Florence does, one cannot discuss these innovations as completely unconscious, particularly when one insists that they are taking part in a "socio-political upheaval" (38). Julia Kristeva, Florence's source for the "upheaval" of avant-garde innovation, acknowledges this space where unconscious desire (semiotic eruption) and existential practice meet to "traduire le procès dans les institutions établies," as "le texte" (*La révolution du langage poétique,* 425).

As discussed in chapter 2, Taine's theory of image production (psychic and textual) and "the impression," as well as his naturalization of visual and verbal signs, provides the groundwork for a description of nineteenth-century epistemologies that might account for such a conscious attempt at crossovers between semiotic systems. Further, we should recall that Mallarmé's conception of image production and his exploitations of movement and multiplicity, as well as his aspirations toward immediacy and his preoccupation with the questions of subjectivity and objectivity are, as noted in chapter 3's discussion of "Igitur," grounded in a visual model of subjective functioning that is analogous to the optical afterimage. Such tendencies, and the aspiration to "invisible action rendered visible" ("The Impressionists and Edouard Manet," *MOC* 2:455), are in fact paralleled in preoccupations of the pictorial artists of the period.

Aesthetic alliances, and especially Mallarmé's alliance with Manet, provide valuable insights into the personally engaged side of Mallarmé's art criticism and the significance of his criticism for his own art theory. In particular, his texts on Manet reveal a Mallarmé with a vested interest in maintaining the cult value of art as well as its status and price structure. An examination of Mallarmé's critical pieces reveals not only his own artistic identifications and aesthetic principles but also his anxieties about the aesthetic and speculative commercial context to which he responds. While Mallarmé wrote on ballet, theater, mime, music, painting, the decorative arts, and even fashion, his art criticism and theoretical writings rarely deal—at least not explicitly—with one specific innovation affecting the pictorial arts of his era: photography.

The issues that Mallarmé addresses in his 1876 article on Manet often point to problems that began much earlier in the nineteenth century, deriving from scientific developments in optics and chemistry, and particularly from a transformation in theories of cognition and perception. As we have seen, the advent of photography brought to the fore many of the issues being discussed in the pictorial arts of the time. In the following analysis, I aim to demonstrate that both the emergence of photography and a conscious reworking of *ut pictura poesis* emerge as subtexts in Mallarmé's art criticism.

Photography profoundly affected the conditions of artistic production in the nineteenth century. Escalating and aggravating contradictions of both art theory and the art market, the photographic process had complex implications for the replication of visual phenomena and the mass reproduction of art. In Mallarmé's article on Manet, although photography seems to be a point of comparison, it is not an explicit one. Aside from the poet's persistent habit of erasing his frameworks,[10] one hypothesis for photography's absence is that despite the photographic image's acceptance by a public that called for verisimilitude and pictorial truth, there was in the artistic community a certain stigma attached to photography and "photographic style." Although the photographic image entered into the mainstream of nineteenth-century art, many artists either hid their use of photographs or kept silent on the subject in fear of the financial implications of a link between facile reproduction and market pricing. This silence was thus to a large degree a pose—much like that of the *poète maudit* or "ivory-tower poet" who at the same time consistently participated in industrial and commercial artistic production.

At this point, I should like to propose yet another hypothesis. While the subtext of photography is to be detected in many of the issues addressed in

Mallarmé's article, the impact of this technical innovation on the arts, and particularly the sciences, was by this time already absorbed by the artistic community, and certain effects integrated into aesthetic thought could be described by my own metaphoric use of the "photo" and the "graphic." This "photographic" provides a figure that can be used to emblematize and study the effects of modernization and an infiltration of scientific thought on artists' visions of cognition, image production, signification, and natural process. For the "photo" (light) and the "graphic" are in fact the pivot points of the reanimation of *ut pictura poesis* and the mimesis on which it is based. The aim of pursuing such a parallel is thus significant not only for analyzing Mallarmé's discussions of choice, focus, light, graphics, framing, and movement (and, later, his own textual use of such techniques), but also to illuminate the cultural norms affecting all the arts of his era. Certain aspects of these changing aesthetic norms are reflected in the full title of the journal in which "The Impressionists and Edouard Manet" appeared. Though the journal's title partially appears as *The Art Monthly Review* in the 1945 Gallimard/Pléiade edition (1623) and is also included as such on the opening page of the piece in Marchal's 2003 edition (444), the actual title conspicuously includes photography within the journal's purview. In full, it was *The Art Monthly Review and Photographic Portfolio, A Magazine Devoted to the Fine and Industrial Arts and Illustrated by Photography.*[11]

By the latter half of the century, and most certainly by the time Mallarmé wrote this article, few artists were unaware of the implications of the industrialization of art and the influence of the new medium and the technological and scientific advances that coincided with its development. What Kristeva describes as a pluralization of modern art forms that both renders and contests "truth," only to reveal a "seconde vérité" through the textual inscription of the trajectory of the first (*La révolution,* 61), is in fact a product of the polysemy of such art forms and their own explorations of interdisciplinary analogy: "La polysémie apparaît donc aussi comme le résultat d'une polyvalence sémiotique, d'une appartenance à divers systèmes sémiotiques" (60). Photography served in many cases to crystallize and heighten interest in trends that were already established in art, art criticism, and, of course, the sciences. I am specifically referring to the various aesthetic theories of the nineteenth century that reevaluate "nature," "truth," and representation's relationship to nature.

Questioning what it means to represent nature in art, Mallarmé's direct precursor, Charles Baudelaire, made the daguerreotype a cause célèbre in his 1859 *Salon,* and as early as 1840, Edgar Allen Poe, another significant figure for Mallarmé's intellectual development, had taken up the issue of the photographic process and nature. In his essay "The Daguerreotype," Poe writes:

> Perhaps, if we imagine the distinctness with which an object is reflected in a positively perfect mirror, we come as near the reality as by any other means. For, in truth, the Daguerreotype plate is *infinitely* (we use the term advisedly) . . . more accurate in its representation than any painting by human hands. . . .
>
> The variations of shade, and the gradations of both linear and aerial perspective are those of truth itself in the supremeness of its perfection. (38, emphasis in original)

Although Poe uses the word "mirror" and raises the issue of the faithful representation of nature, mimesis, he does not state that mimesis is the cornerstone of art. He does, however, assert that as a "positively perfect mirror" of reality, the photograph attains a status that exceeds human hands. If this is the case, then photography would have vast effects on pictorial representation and by extension, on the poetic tradition of *ut pictura poesis.* But what if photography revealed to its students more about nature and natural process than they had bargained for? Or more than they cared to admit?

Using the very expressions Poe had used some thirty years earlier, Mallarmé's 1876 article on impressionist painting explicitly takes up the troublesome relations between an *appearance* of facile reproduction of nature and art—relations of a commercial nature—while never specifically using the word "photography." Here, however, the transcripts from nature are in fact, those of human hands—impressionist hands. The "variations of shade" and light evoked in Poe's discussion of photography are discussed here in terms of impressionist "light productions"—not the daguerreotype (81). And finally, Mallarmé takes up the very delicate issue of the term "infinitely," which Poe explicitly says he uses "advisedly." Mallarmé, too, will use the term advisedly, only not to discuss a faithful representation of the laws of nature, but rather to allude to an appearance of rapid production and facile reproduction of nature in impressionist art. Mallarmé clearly recognized the infinite reproduction of art and the effects of the new medium on painting as a problem of a "commercial" order:

> Unfortunately the picture buyer, though intelligent enough to perceive in these transcripts from nature much more than a mere revel of execution . . . is the dupe of this real or apparent promptitude of labour, and though he pays for these paintings a price a thousand times inferior to their real value, yet is disturbed by the after-thought that such light productions might be multiplied *ad infinitum;* a merely commercial misunderstanding from which, doubtless, these artists will have still to suffer. (463)

In an article that treats issues such as "pictorial truth," "transcriptions from nature," and techniques such as "impressions" of "instantaneity," "spontaneity," the use of "light," "cropping," and the objective "eye," yet never mentions the influence of photography, Mallarmé himself suggests one possible reason: the effects of instantaneity achieved through these particular techniques, and the proliferation of landscape scenes and scenes from daily life, all suggested rapidity of production—and, ultimately, a facile reproduction of these images that would negatively affect their price structure.

Although they did not resemble the conventional realistic pictures associated with the pejorative term "photographic style," impressionist canvases produced scenes that could be termed "surphotographic"—that is, they based their transcriptions of nature on the effects of light and the impressions created as if one were experiencing the image at that very moment. The commercial menace of photography was thus not only significant because it was conceived of as reproducing nature to a degree that artists could not replicate, but even more so because by 1874 photography was no longer associated only with the realistic, but with the impressionistic, the "surimpressionistic," and the naturalistic, as artists and photographers sought to exploit and capture the action of light through either blurred or highly contrasted images. Paradoxically, this knowledge was then extended by analogy to study, exaggerate, and highlight the action of visual signification. As Kristeva points out, avant-garde art forms sought to mime the constitutive processes of the symbolic to account for the heterogeneity that escapes thetic and social constructions through a figurability and pluralization of the thetic itself (60). She states that impressionism "ramène le *procès* inconnu jusque dans la *toile*" (425, emphasis in original). Mallarmé's texts, too, foreground their own "mysterious" production.

Rather than analyze which works of art were copied from photographs or which poems inspired by them, it is more relevant to this study of Mallarmé's aesthetics to see how artistic works may have captured the novelties and innovations that the photographic image, process, and derivative metaphors crystallized and catalyzed: the ideas and techniques of representation extrapolated from the new art form and the developments in chemical and physical process that underlie its innovation. Such ideas may be traced to see how they may have affected both the visual arts and Mallarmé's vision of art. For, as Poe states in his essay on the daguerreotype:

> The results of the invention cannot, even remotely, be seen—but all experience, in matters of philosophical discovery, teaches us that, in such discovery, it is the unforeseen upon which we must calculate most largely. It is a theorem almost demonstrated, that the consequences of

> any new scientific invention will, at present day exceed, by very much,
> the wildest expectations of the most imaginative. (38)

LE CHEF-D'OEUVRE NOUVEAU ET FRANÇAIS[12]

In "The Impressionists and Edouard Manet," Mallarmé states that he will enter his subject matter without any "preamble" and that the conclusions of his article, "new from an art point of view," will come as the facts he relates "present themselves" (*MOC* 2:444). Nevertheless, Mallarmé begins with a brief lesson in art history and a rather lengthy lesson in contemporary art. I shall reproduce significant portions of this extraordinary and understudied piece to highlight certain strategies incorporated into Mallarmé's discourse. These strategies reveal the profound influences of the mechanical reproduction of art and the importance of such concepts as visual truth and nature. Simultaneously, Mallarmé's discourse neglects any mention of a photographic subtext while foregrounding a complex semiotic process of "light" and "graphics" that tends toward a diagrammatic reorientation of processes considered those of the visual arts. I will return to the "photo" and "graphic" in Mallarmé's poetic language in chapter 5; it is how Mallarmé describes and accounts for the modern movement in painting and its innovations that interest me at this juncture.

Although mostly devoted to impressionism and Manet, the article opens with Gustave Courbet, a central character in the drama of pictorial realism: "Rarely do our annual exhibitions abound with novelty . . . but about 1860 a sudden and a lasting light shone forth when Courbet began to exhibit his works" (444). "Novelty," then, seems to be first exemplified by Courbet and associated with "light." Mallarmé further explains that this "sudden" and "lasting light" coincided with a literary trend named "realism." Although he begins with a positive image of realism, he immediately qualifies his enthusiasm by defining realism as a movement that "sought to impress itself upon the mind by the lively depiction of things as they appeared to be and vigorously excluded all meddlesome imagination" (444). While Courbet's novelty is not in question, Mallarmé's description of Courbet is tempered—even undermined—by his comment on the exclusion of imagination. The poet-critic accentuates only the "new" and "sudden light" associated with the names of Courbet and realism and this is done only to situate his subject, the impressionists and Edouard Manet, in a historical context.

While Manet was closely associated with the impressionists in the mid-1870s, he was never considered an "impressionist"; he leaned toward a form of realistic (or even naturalistic) reportage in his chronicling of modern life. Yet, in this essay, Mallarmé explicitly positions Manet as *the* precursor to the impressionist movement and links them in his title. As he describes Manet, the suggestion of this artist's role is implicit in the poet's rhetorical choices: the words "preacher" and "doctrine," and the verb "preach."

> In the midst of this, there began to appear, sometimes perchance on the walls of the Salon, but far more frequently and certainly on those of the galleries of the rejected, curious and singular paintings . . . very disquieting to the true and reflective critic, who could not refrain from asking himself what manner of man is this? and what the strange doctrine he preaches? For it was evident that the preacher has a meaning; he was persistent in his reiteration, unique in his persistency. (445)

The terms signal and reinforce Mallarmé's identification with the image of the artist as both sacred and misunderstood. As is the poet, so is the painter?—*maudit?* Although the latter parallel is mine, Mallarmé's use of comparisons, the significance of a constant intermingling of literature and the pictorial arts, and repeated allusions to the contemporary movements in both arts are richly suggestive.

Mallarmé makes his writerly identification with the visual arts and their historical evolution quite obvious in the following presentation of Baudelaire as an "enlightened amateur":

> One who loved all arts and lived for one of them. These strange pictures at once won his sympathy; an instinctive and poetic foresight made him love them; and this before their prompt succession and the sufficient exposition of the principles they inculcated had revealed their meaning to the thoughtful few of the public many. (445)

The literary references continue with his presentation of Zola, who is also clearly one of the "thoughtful few":

> With that insight into the future which distinguishes his own works, he recognized the light that had risen, albeit that he was yet too young to then define that which we to-day call Naturalism, to follow the quest, not merely of that reality which impresses itself in its abstract form on all, but of that absolute and important sentiment which

> Nature herself impresses on those who have voluntarily abandoned
> conventionalism. (446)

As in the description of an "enlightened" Baudelaire, we see in the presentation of Zola yet another equation of the future and that which is "light" and "new." We also find the introduction of one of the key issues of representational theory that Mallarmé will subtly address in the article: nature. The "quest" for "reality" is described here as "not merely" a reality that nature itself imposes "in its abstract form," but as "that absolute and important sentiment which Nature impresses on those who have voluntarily abandoned conventionalism." Mallarmé dismisses the objective of this painting as "merely" the transcription of an impression and suggests that only the receptive artist who is not blinded by convention is capable of seizing and materializing the effects imprinted through his senses. Mallarmé is already evoking realist and naturalist arguments that subvert conventional realistic representation to transgressively support the representation of a *new* "reality"—a nature whose depiction, though unconventional, nonetheless maintains a claim to reality since its "impression" (in the fullest sense of the word) is based on "the natural." Although Penny Florence insists that Mallarmé's and Manet's "resistance to naturalisation" is related to "sociopolitical upheaval" (38), Mallarmé himself will historically situate, justify, and market this innovative reconceptualization of "nature" as a logical outgrowth of both artistic and literary tradition as well.

Significantly, this new painting obtains its justification and claims to authenticity through recognition by the "thoughtful few"—writers. Mallarmé, a member of that select coterie, contrasts reactions of the "enlightened" to those of other spectators at the 1867 special exhibition of Manet and his "followers." This last word emphasizes the immediate taking of sides in this new inquisition that focuses on a claim to reality. The references to religion and persecution in the terms "followers," "preacher," and "crusade" continue as the poet-critic addresses the jury's role in drawing sides in the debate (446).

Condemning the jury's use of the discourse of "morality," Mallarmé says the jury was hesitating between whether they should recognize Manet as "a self-created sovereign pontiff, charged by his own faith with the cure of souls, or . . . condemn him as a heretic and a public danger" (446). He remarks that their final decision was the latter. Mallarmé's earlier 1874 article had already denounced the jury's refusal of Manet. "Le jury de peinture pour 1874 et M. Manet" attests to Mallarmé's acute awareness of the need to reexamine the limitations placed on artistic choice (here, choice of subject matter) in the late nineteenth century:

> La question qu'il s'agissait de résoudre une fois de plus, et avec la
> même inutilité que toujours, tient tout entière dans ces mots: quel est,
> dans le double jugement rendu et par le jury et par le public sur la
> peinture de l'année, la tâche qui incombe au jury et celle qui relève de
> la foule? (*MOC* 2:413)

While Mallarmé does not, and would not, question the concept of choice as essential to any work of art, he already alludes to what he considers a shift in contemporary art, a cultural crisis that questions the past grounds of moral judgments regulating "selection" in art. His translation of Whistler's *Ten O'Clock* sums up the poet-critic's viewpoint as regards the role of the jury and morality:

> [L'Art] est une divinité d'essence délicate, toute en retrait, elle hait se
> mettre en avant et ne se propose en aucune manière pour améliorer
> autrui . . . n'ayant aucun désir d'enseigner, cherchant et trouvant le
> beau dans toutes conditions, et tous les temps. (*MOC* 2:838)

Moving on to address the public's encounter with the rejected work exhibited in Manet's atelier in 1874 and 1876, Mallarmé in "The Impressionists and M. Manet" begins his lesson in contemporary art with a rhetorical question that allows him to elude the details of the public's reaction in favor of an enlightening discussion of the pictures on view:

> And what found they there? A collection of pictures of strange aspect,
> at first view giving the ordinary impression of the motive which made
> them, but over beyond this, a peculiar quality outside mere Realism.
> And here occurs one of those unexpected crises which appear in art.
> Let us study it in its present condition and its future prospects, and
> with some attempt to develope [*sic*] its idea. (*MOC* 2:447)

This introduction enables him to explain the artistic philosophy and processes of his visionary friend Manet:

> Manet, when he casts away the cares of art and chats with a friend
> between the lights in his studio, expresses himself with brilliancy. Then
> it is that he tells him what he means by Painting; what new destinies
> are yet in store for it; what it is, and how that it is from an irrepressible
> instinct that he paints, and that he paints as he does. (447)

The implication of a new perception of painting is again rhetorically associated with the luminous ("lights," "brilliancy"). And it is in the following description of *how* Manet paints that Mallarmé shows the way in which the new art engages and positions itself in the debates concerning subjectivity and objectivity: "Each time he begins a picture, says he, he plunges headlong into it, and feels like a man who knows that his surest plan to learn to swim safely, is, dangerous as it may seem, to throw himself into the water" (447). Mallarmé thus describes the frame of consciousness to which Manet aspires for creation. The use of "plunge headlong" is rather ambiguous; Mallarmé appears to be saying that Manet throws himself into his work, oblivious of or at least momentarily disregarding convention and technique, in order to absorb a vision as it appears to the artistic mind. Yet this state of mind is not free association represented without form, nor is it a perfectly detailed photocopy of an external reality.

> One of his habitual aphorisms then is that no one should paint a landscape and a figure by the same process, with the same knowledge, or in the same fashion; nor what is more, even two landscapes or two figures. Each work should be a new creation of the mind. The hand, it is true, will conserve some of its acquired secrets of manipulation, but the eye should forget all else it has seen, and learn anew from the lesson before it. (447–48)

Although he insists on technique in the "acquired secrets of manipulation," he emphasizes here that what renders the work an art is "the eye"—the vision must be seen *for the very first time* within this particular artist's mind's eye, rather than in nature or in another artistic model. Mallarmé's 1887 sonnet "Surgi de la croupe" relates a similar idea: "Je crois bien que deux bouches n'ont / Bu, ni son amant ni ma mère / Jamais à la même Chimère" (*MOC* 1:42). What the hand remembers is a form of maintained convention, while the vision "should abstract itself from memory, seeing only that which it looks upon, and that as for the first time; and the hand should become an impersonal abstraction guided only by the will, oblivious of all previous cunning" ("The Impressionists and M. Manet," *MOC* 2:448).

We have a reversal here. While Mallarmé previously minimized the role of certain "secrets of manipulation," technique here becomes that which objectively materializes a mental negative and substantiates the reality of a transposed impression. Like the hand, the mind's vision becomes an "impersonal abstraction" rendered in a medium. Mallarmé is paradoxically moving toward a defense of the subjective, a valorization of an impressionistic, even idiosyncratic vision that is scientifically, industrially, and technologically charged, and thus justified by a dominant discourse grounded in "depersonalized" objectivity. This echoes his prior comment on Zola's quest for "that reality which nature impresses itself in its abstract form" (466). Very subtly, Mallarmé manipulates the rhetorical arguments of the opposing camp for his own purposes.

Well aware of the vogue for the photographic and verisimilitude, and of the arguments employed to describe and support them, Mallarmé promotes the use of objectivity in art to represent what is, or could be, a reality to the mind: "As for the artist himself, his personal feelings, his peculiar tastes, are for the time absorbed, ignored, or set aside for the enjoyment of his personal life" (448). Thus all "prejudices" about the artist and about what art is or should be, are to be put aside. "Such a result as this cannot be attained all at once. To reach it the master must pass through many phases ere this self-isolation can be acquired, and this new evolution of art be learnt" (448). Particularly slippery in this argument is the oscillation between the role of the subjective and the objective necessary for such "self-isolation." Mallarmé attests: "and I, who have occupied myself a good deal in its study, can count but two who have gained it" (448). His *textual* self-isolation—"and I"—emphasizes that attention is to be directed toward the poet-critic, he who, as exemplified in "Igitur," attempted such a radical depersonalization. By refusing to name the two artists "who have gained it," Mallarmé holds the reader's attention on himself.

The artistic depersonalization described here aspires to materialize the purely subjective through the objective. This challenge, the ultimate appropriation of realist and objective arguments for the exploration of the subjective in art, is justified by art historical references.

> Wearied by the technicalities of the school in which, under Couture, he studied, Manet, when he recognized the inanity of all he was taught, determined either not to paint at all or to paint entirely from without himself. Yet, in his self-sought insulation, two masters—masters of the past—appeared to him, and befriended him in his revolt. Velasquez, and the painters of the Flemish school, particularly impressed themselves upon him. (448)

After saying "the eye should forget all else it has seen" and asserting that Manet was "wearied" by the inanities of academic technicalities and training, Mallarmé invokes artistic models from the past. Not incidentally, both "masters" are now considered to be textbook precursors to impressionism because of their obsession with light. The works Mallarmé evokes, which captured the admiration of Manet, are in fact models that intermingled the imaginative pole, strong contrasts of light, and the use of blurred and residual images to evoke motion, emotion, and atmosphere.

> The wonderful atmosphere which enshrouds the compositions of the grand old Spaniard, and the brilliant tones which glow from the canvasses of his northern compeers, won the student's admiration, thus presenting to him two art aspects which he has since made himself the master of, and can mingle as he pleases. (448–49)

To exploit the popular opinion that valorized the objective and the realistic, Mallarmé implies that these images, though unconventional and perhaps even shocking to the public eye, are in fact rendered objectively and thus grounded in reality. The young student Manet masters aspects described as those "which reveal the truth, and give paintings based upon them living reality instead of rendering them the baseless fabric of abstracted and obscure dreams" (449). Mallarmé invokes past models and insists that these modes of representation communicated both "truth" and "living reality."

In these passages, Mallarmé develops a very clearly articulated argument for the representation of a newly materialized living reality that is not grounded in "the baseless fabric of abstracted and obscure dreams" but in artistic medium. The "strangeness" of this truth in art, renewed and modernized, implies a certain paradox in Manet's art as it does in Mallarmé's. Both arts seem to defy conventional notions of realism. And although many a study of both artists has sought to demonstrate their tendencies toward abstraction and idealism, it should be remarked that such criticism neglects to recognize that the transposition of the ideal (cf. Albert Sonnenfeld, "Elaboration secondaire du grimoire"), or the move toward abstraction through semantics (cf. Françoise Meltzer, "Color as Cognition in Symbolist Verse," 253) must be rendered in the artist's medium. The will to reality in its relation to the visual arts is invoked, and Mallarmé responds with a theory of representation that creates the impression that something truthful and animated emanates from the material reality of the works themselves.

Fully engaged in the debate, as were his literary ancestors, Mallarmé directly addresses the issue of imitation and the question of artistic models. The poet-critic asserts that while Manet could have imitated French masters, he sought more remote models: "An incomparable copyist, he could have found his game close to hand had he chosen his quarry there" (449). Although he signals the masters to whom Manet turned, Mallarmé subtly suggests that Manet is nonetheless against "imitation." If we recall that "the artist must forget all else he has seen" and examine the models proposed (artists recognized for their departure from what could be described as photographic-style realism), Manet's position becomes explicit. While imitation is not completely dismissed, the models he chooses suggest the need of "something more," a supplement.

> But he sought something more than this, and fresh things are not found all at once; freshness, indeed, frequently consists—and this is especially the case in these critical days—in a co-ordination of widely-scattered elements. (449)

Implying a crisis in conventional theories that provokes a reexamination of the balance between an imitation of nature and creation, Mallarmé suggests that the originality of Manet's work lies in the artist's refusal to copy or imitate any external reality; his genius lies in a creative synthesis of the heterogeneity, the "widely-scattered elements" perceived in "these critical days." It is this coordination of multiple elements, a synthesis that entails a "simplification apportée par un regard de voyant" ("Le jury de peinture pour 1874 et M. Manet," *MOC* 2:411) that Mallarmé sets out to trace. To discuss Manet's artistic development, Mallarmé turns his attention in the 1876 essay to the term "manner." "Now the old writers on art expressed by the word "manner," rather the lavish blossoming of genius during one of its intellectual seasons than the fact fathered, found, or sought out by the painter himself" (*MOC* 2: 449). Why does he take the time to correct the commonplace misunderstanding of "manner"? The actual "find," the objective "sought" by the artist, is left ambiguous and implied to be less significant than the process of finding one's artistic purpose and the modes of representing one's own vision; it is in this process of selection that one finds genius. Mallarmé asserts that the painter's truth—his "self"—will in fact come out objectively in what he chooses: "that in which the painter declares most of his views is the choice of his subjects" (449). He immediately evokes the literature–painting analogy to show the significance of choice in the sister arts, as parallel and as similarly subject to the crisis in aesthetics of the period. "Literature often departs from its current path to seek for the aspirations of an epoch of the past, and to modernize them for its own purpose" (450).

Literature, invoked earlier in the article in the description of self-isolation and vision, appears here to insist upon the parallel modernization of traditional aesthetic principles within the sister disciplines. Mallarmé gives currency to Manet's art by establishing historical precedents through past models in literature and in painting. He then relates Manet's work to a tendency toward renovation grounded in literary history, thus linking past artistic trends to a modern faith in objective truth; this innovative and piercing gaze seeking the essence of the vision it aspires to represent is described as an outgrowth of tradition. In painting, he says, "Manet followed a similarly divergent course, seeking the truth, and loving it when found, because being true it was so strange, especially when compared with the old and worn-out ideals of it" (450). Mallarmé asserts a firm parallel between the "sister arts," and his own portrayal of Manet parallels his description of the contemporary movement in literature: "Manet fell under the influence of the moment" (450).

To illustrate further the characteristic "elements" of the "new" art and its aesthetic moment, Mallarmé addresses Manet's famously scandalous *Olympia,* whose unconventionality he attempts to vindicate: "all the surrounding accessories, were truthful, but not immoral" (450). To accentuate the gap between conforming to reality, nature, and art, Mallarmé discusses the question of choice, and, once again, he invokes the literature parallel. He very clearly states that genius amounts to knowing what is new and effective; the artist sees what will be "captivating" yet relevant: "such types as he gave us were needed in our ambient life" (451).

Although Mallarmé begins the aesthetic lesson that follows by taking the position of a member of the public observing this controversy, he concludes as a member of the literary world:

> If our humble opinion can have any influence in this impartial history of the chief of the new school, I would say that the transition period in it is by no means to be regretted. . . . Its parallel is found in literature, when our sympathies are suddenly awakened by some new imagery presented to us; and this is what I like in Manet's work. It surprised us all as something long hidden, but suddenly revealed. (450–51)

Mallarmé identifies *choice* as the principal function of artistic genius in poetry and in painting. Choice of the object of representation and the manipulation of artistic medium is what renders the work new and original. The "surprise" he describes, akin to the literary "hangnail" or "ungrammaticality" evoked by Michael Riffaterre (*Semiotics of Poetry*) or the pictorial *punctum*—"piqure . . . et aussi coup de dés"—described by Roland Barthes (*La chambre claire,* 49) is what catches our attention. Mallarmé's description of the "something long hidden" seems to indicate that an aspect of the subject represented rings true and catches our attention as suddenly obvious.[13] Mallarmé clarifies that, in Manet's work, such normally unnoticed aspects are selectively perceived to sum up the subject of the representation:

> Often they attracted attention by something peculiar in the physiognomy of his subject, half hiding or sacrificing to those new laws of space and light he set himself to inculcate, some minor details which others would have seized upon. (451)

Here Mallarmé invokes another characteristic element of the new art: "new laws of space and light." He insists, however, that these laws are integrated in original ways. Manet's art may leave aside certain details that an undiscriminating eye might have chosen to copy, or he may choose to accentuate one aspect of them as the essence of the tableau itself. The artist, Mallarmé asserts, is aware of this special process of selection. And in the case of Manet and his works, despite their impressionistic appearance, "there was nothing vague, general, conventional, or hackneyed" (451). This artist's creations are a precise rendering of a carefully chosen vision—and, as such, they embellish reality. Well before Barthes's *punctum,* Mallarmé insists upon a similar "ce qui pique" in Manet's art and shows that the "new laws," brought to the fore by the realist school's art and further developed by later artistic movements, do not take precedence over artistic vision (as it is suggested may occur in the realist or "photographic" style's fetishes about detail, implying reproduction without discrimination). Choice clearly takes precedence over any law; this brings us back to the question of selection, or framing (*cadrage*), as essential to both the genius of the artwork and the artist's foresight of what to choose.

The "laws" to which Mallarmé refers had been put to work in the mid to later half of the nineteenth century and manipulated in various ways in artistic speculation, choice of subject matter, and technique. Though such innovations in the use of light, space, and tone may distort a painting from what was formerly seen as an exact copy, Mallarmé asserts that these paintings do show the truth of the nature they represent. However, these "laws of nature" are often seized in unconventional ways. The expression "sacrificing to" in the article suggests that "impressionist" forms of art sought to multiply and emphasize the effects of the light spectrum in its various manifestations or even its effects on the subject. The discovery of light and color as products and processes of the perception of light waves—these truths of nature coming to the fore with the dissemination of Hermann von Helmholtz's optical studies and the mishaps of photography[14]—created what I have referred to as a "sur-

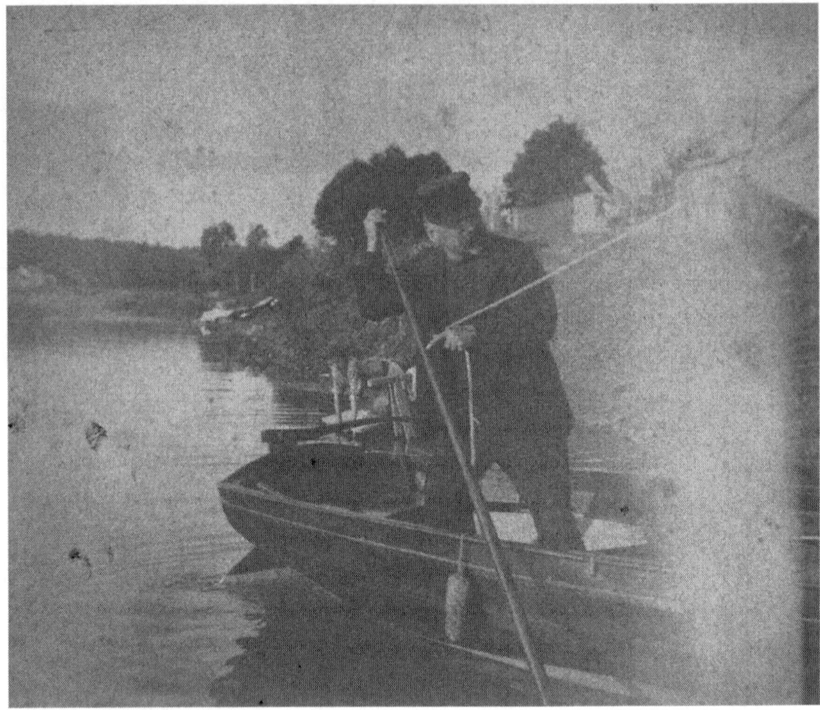

PLATE 11
Mallarmé in boat at Valvins, 1896.
Bibliothèque littéraire Jacques Doucet, Paris.

photographic" style. Again, I am using "surphotographic" here to insist upon the departure from conventional visual representation as evidenced in the photographic images. Though the descriptor "photographic style" was most often used pejoratively to characterize detailed pictorial works that exhibited little or no selection, the works Mallarmé refers to nonetheless manifest certain analogies with aspects of photography.

In *Image, Music Text,* Barthes suggests that the presentation of an immediate image that abolishes the distinction between past and present was initiated with photography (17).[15] Leaning on Barthes's analysis, Florence likens the autonomy of the texts afforded by "the obliteration of the poet in words and the painter in the action of eye and hand . . . to that of the photographic text" (39). The potential of such depersonalized texts that foreground "new laws" and immediacy, be it in impressionist painting, in the "disparition élocutoire du poète" ("Crise de vers," *MOC* 2:211), or syntactic fragmentation, is, in fact, analogous to that of the photographic text's.[16] Indeed, a key point in Mallarmé's article is his assertion that this potential is an essential contribution of a new art responding to modern times.

Both Mallarmé's and Manet's genius lies in appropriating the "new" and knowing which aspects to focus on to evoke the essential nature of one's subject. Mallarmé states that Manet attempted to cultivate, "to educate the public eye—as yet veiled by conventionality" (451). He insists that the present time is one of struggle, "a struggle to render those truths in nature which for her are eternal, but which are as yet for the multitude but new" (451). Mallarmé thus explicitly defines the goal of this art as "to render truths" of nature—the old painting like nature, poetry like painting, are nonetheless *both* regulated by a new conception of selection and nature.

Mallarmé explains that the public should accept this work as it accepts truth and truthful representation. Practically coming out with a sign theory of convention and signification, explaining that this art is truth and that meaning is conventional—as are representations of nature—Mallarmé shows the public that such innovations, permeating and diffusing into a new theory of tonality in painting, are an effect of what is called "the truth."

Addressing one of the common charges leveled against Manet—that he paints vulgarity and ugliness—Mallarmé states that this is due to "the fact that he paints the truth" (451). The realists, of course, used the same justification. Here again, Mallarmé strategically appropriates the realists' argument. Yet, there is something more here, and it corresponds to that other register that Kristeva refers to as a "seconde vérité" (*La révolution,* 61), which at once reveals and exceeds those "truths" achieved through convention.

Enumerating the difficulties Manet encountered with several of his paintings, Mallarmé highlights the Salon's rejection that year of *Le linge,* "a work which marks a date . . . in the history of art," setting out to elucidate "the painter's aim very exactly" (*MOC* 2:452). The aim, he insists, was not to create a momentary sensation, but was achieved by "steadily endeavoring to impress upon his work a natural and a general law, to seek out a type rather than a personality, and to flood it with light and air: and such air! air which despotically dominates over all else" (452).

Addressing "the theory of open air," which he describes as "that truism of to-morrow, that paradox of to-day" (452), as well as the effects of light on which it rests, Mallarmé insists that "the natural light of day penetrating into and influencing all things, although itself invisible, reigns also on this typical picture," which can be considered "a complete and final repertory of all current ideas and the means of their execution" (454).

The poet-critic shows how this "new" knowledge is being used to recuperate the reality claim for impressionist art, and how light is used to evoke movement and distortions in conventional mimetic reality and perception. This is the modern doctrine of art, a new art laying claim to a reality that, though unconventional, nonetheless proposes itself as a mimetic representation of nature. In *The Colors of Rhetoric,* Wendy Steiner suggests that in the realms of aesthetic theory and production the "moderns" exchanged the notion of a natural or pictorial quality in verbal discourse, *enargeia,* for the actualization of potency or dynamism, *energeia* (10). In fact, Mallarmé systematically reappropriates all arguments of both *enargeia* and *energeia,* nature and science, as proof for his argumentation.

In examining Manet's choices, Mallarmé is able to decipher what is modern in the exploitation and transformation of past models. Known for its shocking effects, Mallarmé's work, though not "repulsive" in the same sense, could be described the way he describes Manet's: "Captivating and repulsive at the same time, eccentric, and new, such types as he gave us were needed in our ambient life" (451). This genius entails knowing which modes to exploit as changes in technology affected human perception and created an era (and an art market) in rapid transition.

Note how in the following description of the use of air and atmosphere Mallarmé evokes the new discoveries of photo-graphic functioning:

> Everywhere the luminous and transparent atmosphere struggles with the figures, the dresses, and the foliage, and seems to take to itself some of their substance and solidity; whilst their contours, consumed by the hidden sun and wasted by space, tremble, melt, and evaporate into the surrounding atmosphere, which plunders reality from the figures, yet seems to do so in order to preserve their truthful aspect. (455)

Here Mallarmé recognizes the use of light to create and represent movement in art. The "new laws of space and light," seem to distort convention, yet they are exploited here to recuperate a claim to "reality" and "truth" for impressionist art. The new art is depicted as a faithful recreation of nature's mimetic capacity in the semiotic system. The significance of *energeia* is clearly delineated in the passage. Although *energeia* has for centuries been more associated with poetry than painting, Mallarmé praises Manet's aptitude for creating an atmosphere that exploits the use of light to evoke movement. This concept is appropriated analogically by poetry as well. The action of Mallarmé's poetry in particular, however, is not simply the temporal movement typically associated with narrative progression in the verbal arts, but one that incorporates instantaneity and visual and graphic dynamics. As the various retinas and lenses of the camera showed, the way in which perception occurs is not as conventional realistic representation in painting has practiced it: perception is shown to be a product of process. The perception of nature may appear "consumed by the hidden sun and wasted by space," it may "tremble, melt, and evaporate into the surrounding atmosphere, which plunders reality from the figures, yet seems to do so in order to preserve their truthful aspect" (455). These passages are markedly reminiscent of Baudelaire's "De la couleur":

> Supposons un bel espace de nature où tout verdoie, rougeoie, poudroie et chatoie en pleine liberté, où toutes choses, diversement colorées de seconde en seconde par le déplacement de l'ombre et de la lumière, et agitées par le travail intérieur du calorique, se trouvent en perpétuelle vibration, laquelle fait trembler les lignes et complète la loi du mouvement éternel et universel. (*BOC* 2:422)

The two poet-critics, Mallarmé and Baudelaire, propose models that defy conventionally static, "realistic" representation and that are based on the laws of nature and the movement of light waves as they might be perceived. The representation of this air is the representation of its variable perception—the multiplicity of actual vision and the attempt to visualize (and often accentuate) the actual movement of the physical world so characteristic of impressionist painting. Mallarmé can thus announce in his 1876 essay the scientific objectivity of such works:

> Air reigns supreme and real, as if it held an enchanted life conferred by the witchery of art; a life neither personal nor sentient, but itself subjected to the phenomena thus called up by science and shown to our astonished eyes, with its perpetual metamorphosis and its invisible action rendered visible. (*MOC* 2:455)

Mallarmé explains the way in which this movement, a movement he incorporates in his poetry, is created by art's "witchery": "And how? By this fusion or by this struggle ever continued between surface and space, between colour and air" (455). The conflicts between surface and depth, signifier, signified, and perception, are resolved here in a visual model based on invisible processes.

> The search after truth, peculiar to modern artists, which enables them
> to see nature and reproduce her, such as she appears to just and pure
> eyes, must lead them to adopt air almost exclusively as their medium,
> or at all events to habituate themselves to work in it freely and with-
> out restraint: there should at least be in the revival of such a medium, if
> nothing more, an incentive to a new manner of painting. This is the
> result of our reasoning, and the end I wish to establish. As no artist has
> on his palette a transparent and neutral colour answering to open air,
> the desired effect can only be obtained by lightness or heaviness of
> touch, or by the regulation of tone. (456)

He then describes Manet and his school's use of light, citing "natural" reasons
for the effects created. Though "their results appear to have been attained at the
first stroke," Mallarmé dismisses the idea that this impression of instantaneity
coincides with rapidity of production and insists that it is, on the contrary, a
technique appropriated from the modern world and "that the ever-present
light blends with and vivifies all things" (456).

Here the two poles of the paradoxical nature of the debate over photography come to light. For in its first stages, the photographic image was criticized for its excessive contrasts and for being too static and therefore an
unnatural representation. At the same time, however, developing methods (like
the calotype and glass plates) and phenomena such as halation produced
blurred images capturing the movement and "strange" effects of light.[17] This
provided a means for the study of how such movement may be perceived and
reconstituted by the retina. The impressionists integrated and exploited many
of the dramatic effects of contrast (e.g., in the works of Manet) and the grada-
tions of light, tone (e.g., in the works of Claude Monet), and blurring (e.g., in
the works of Edgar Degas) to be found in such images.

> As to the details of the picture, nothing should be absolutely fixed in
> order that we may feel that the bright gleam which lights the picture, or
> the diaphanous shadow which veils it, are only seen in passing, and just
> when the spectator beholds the represented subject, which being com-
> posed of a harmony of reflected and ever-changing lights, cannot be
> supposed always to look the same, but palpitates with movement, light,
> and life. (456)

The new, modern, and rapidly changing world, which Zola represented as
living and breathing, is evoked. While the impressionists generally leaned

toward an emphasis on shimmering games of light and tone, Manet more often tended to exploit games of light through contrast.

This passage is startlingly evocative of Mallarmé's own use of flashing images and graphic games, of particular interrelated choices of vocabulary, and his cross-referencing of images such as frames and various reflectors (mirrors, prisms, and jewels) that evoke movement and thematize the visual. The linking of apparently unrelated snapshot images in an unconventional fashion, the unexpected (but nonetheless related) juxtapositions, presented so that the reader or spectator does not have the time to assimilate the images in a coherent linear narrative, produces the simultaneous effect of instantaneity and a movement that is not one of narrative development. This is particularly obvious in the use of adjectives and colors that form matrices among themselves: brilliant, shiny, glistening, black, white, and, of course, "l'azur," which evokes the reflecting sky and open air. Yet despite this apparent fragmentation, the "harmony of reflected and ever-changing lights" suggests a strong insistence on the technical nature of the work and the importance of unity in works specifically created to center this effect. The reciprocal reflections of apparently unrelated and "ever-changing" fragments suggest a game of reflection based on an analogy with nature as an ever-changing life force. The coordination and the constant creation of analogies animate this movement of "light" and "life"—a metaphor for perception and thought. We recall Mallarmé's suggestion to François Coppée: "Ce à quoi nous devons viser surtout est que, dans le poème, les mots . . . se reflètent les uns sur les autres jusqu'à paraître ne plus avoir leur couleur propre, mais n'être que les transitions d'une gamme" (*MOC* 1:709).

In his article Mallarmé next addresses the issue of perspective, space, and "cutting-off" in relation to composition and convention. Denying that "composition" in the traditional sense plays an important role for the impressionists, Mallarmé explains that Manet, the transitional figure leading to impressionism, "is pleased to dispense with it, and at the same time to avoid both affectation and style" (*MOC* 2:457). Instead, the act of perception is posited as the sine qua non of artistic creation:

> He must find something on which to establish his picture, though it be
> but for a minute—for the one thing needful is the time required by
> the spectator to see and admire the representation with that promptitude which just suffices for the connection of its truth. (457)

It is thus the truth of the subject represented, the vision the artist selects to convey, that takes precedence over composition, or motif, or anecdotal meaning.

This "something" is the impression of instantaneity; a rapid and spontaneous perception of a truth is suggested. But this "new truth" that Mallarmé proposes goes against conventional realist representations of "truth" and perspective.

> If we turn to natural perspective (not that utterly and artificially classic science which makes our eyes the dupes of a civilized education, but rather that artistic perspective which we learn from the extreme East—Japan for example)—and look at the sea-pieces of Manet, where the water at the horizon rises to the height of the frame, which alone interrupts it, we feel a new delight at the recovery of a long obliterated truth. (457–58)

Mallarmé thus dismisses Renaissance perspective as a function of accepted convention. But where did this dismissal of perspective come from? The Orient? Perhaps, but the photograph is rather conspicuous by its absence. For photography demonstrated to artists that many conventions of perspective (as well as representations of movement) were in fact quite inaccurate. The introduction of framing as the key to this "long obliterated truth" is significant for Japanese focal point and the segmenting of canvases, as well as for Manet's paintings, where the horizon often goes all the way up to the frame and where scenes show figures whose arms and legs are in effect cropped off by the edge of the canvas. This type of "framing" was commonly seen in photographic snapshots. Centered or decentered, choice takes precedence over composition, and choice *of* subject matter in effect yields to choice *as* subject matter. This foregrounding of semiotic process is quite simply a matter of framing.

In the paragraph that follows, Mallarmé confirms his interest in focus, frames, and framing, and sheds light on his later exploitation of graphics. He states: "The secret of this is found in an absolutely new science" (458). This knowledge, although not new, is, in fact, newly in vogue and is to be found in the technique of cropping, which in turn raises the question of focal point:

> The manner of cutting down pictures . . . gives to the frame all the charm of a merely fanciful boundary, such as that which is embraced at one glance of a scene framed in by the hands, or at least all of it found worthy to preserve. (458)

One can almost see the photographer of today, hands framing the image and the selection of the scene to isolate. All the elements are there: the *coup d'oeil,* a flash of vision as if one was observing a scene embraced by what is only seen as an imaginary limit. One has the impression of a spontaneous slice of a reality whose fragmentation functions to overflow and surpass the limits of its frame.

> This is the picture, and the function of the frame is to isolate it . . . the one thing to be attained is that the spectator accustomed among a crowd or in nature to isolate one bit which pleases him, though at the same time incapable of entirely forgetting the abjured details which unite the part to the whole, shall not miss in the work of art one of his habitual enjoyments, and whilst recognizing that he is before a painting half believes he sees the mirage of some natural scene. (458)

Though Mallarmé admits the objection that these techniques and methods have all been used in the past, he insists that this technique of framing, or "cutting the canvas off," has never been pushed so far—so why now?

> Some will probably object that all of these means have been more or less employed in the past, that dexterity—though not pushed so far— of cutting the canvass off so as to produce an illusion—perspective almost conforming to the exotic usage of barbarians—the light touch and fresh tones uniform and equal, or variously trembling with shifting lights—all these ruses and expedients in art have been found more than once in the English school, and elsewhere. But the assemblage for the first time of all these relative processes for an end, visible and suitable to the artistic expression of the needs of our times, this is no inconsiderable achievement in the cause of art, especially since a mighty will has pushed these means to their uttermost limits. (458–59)

Mallarmé essentially affirms that there was a need at this place and time to represent movement and light in this fashion. Despite the obvious absence of the word "photography," he does mention that the need is pressing, since "a mighty will has pushed these means to their uttermost limits." A mighty will? Manet? Or Manet inspired by the encouragement, progress, and popularization of scientific thought, optics, psychophysiology, and the photographic image, which brought all these "expedients" to light? In *Art and Photography,* Aaron Scharf notes:

> Almost every definable characteristic of photographic form had been anticipated by some artist before the invention of the photographic camera. The cutting-off of figures by the frames frequently seen in

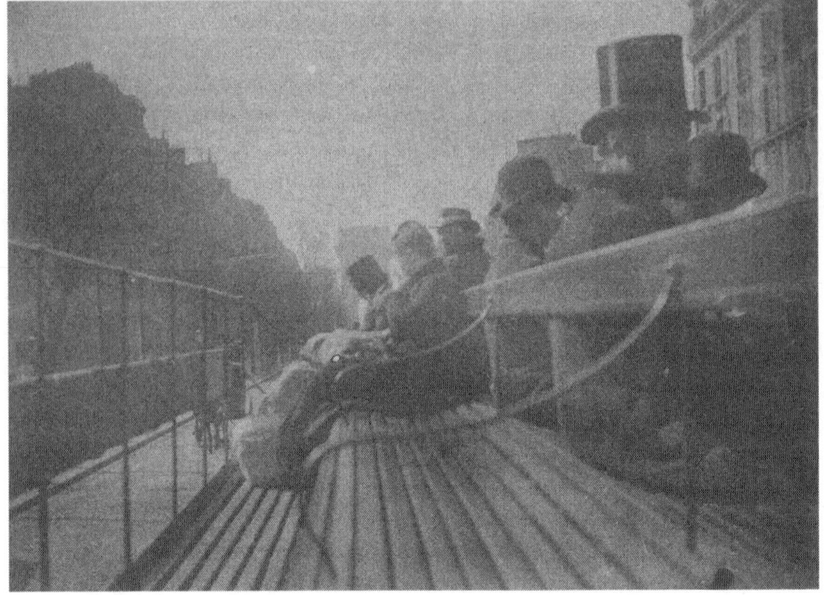

PLATE 12
Rivière, Scènes du rue de Paris: passagers sur l'impériale d'un omnibus, vers 1889.
Paris, Musée d'Orsay.
©Henri Rivière.
©Photo RMN/© Droits reserves.

snapshots, for example, can be found in Donatello's reliefs, in Mantegna, in Mannerist painting and in Japanese prints. . . . Other prefigurations might also be described in respect of tone, perspective scale and instantaneity of pose and gesture. Even the strange residual images encountered in photographs of moving objects were rendered by Velasquez. . . . What is important, however, is that none of these things, nor others of the kind, had any currency in nineteenth-century European art until they appeared in photographs . . . there can be little doubt that photography served to heighten the artist's perception of both nature and art. (11–12)

Rather than discussing even the slightest possibility of Manet's being inspired by technological developments, which were more or less taboo among serious artists, Mallarmé explains that Manet is well versed in techniques and conventions of the past and, at the same time, original:

> But the chief charm and true characteristic of one of the most singular
> men of the age is, that Manet . . . seems to ignore all that has been
> done in art by others, and draws from his own inner consciousness all
> his effects of simplification, the whole revealed by effects of light
> incontestably novel. This is the supreme originality of a painter by
> whom originality is doubly forsworn, who seeks to lose his personality
> in nature herself, or in the gaze of a multitude until then ignorant of
> her charms. (459)

Returning to the idea of an abdication of individuality for some sort of universal objective truth, Mallarmé asserts that although Manet's production was diverse, all of his works were born of a unique theory: "the absence of all personal obtrusion"—a technique of which Manet is in "full possession" (460). In fact, he states that "each work of genius, singular because he abjures singularity, is an artistic production, unique of its kind, recognisable at first sight among all the schools of all ages" (460). And it is here that he begins to discuss Manet's "followers," the impressionists.

Describing their unity as based on the theory of "open air" that "influences all modern artistic thought" (460), Mallarmé asserts that Monet, Sisley, and Pissaro exhibit one very similar trait: "they each endeavor to suppress individuality for the benefit of nature" (461). And while he highlights this similarity, he does add that each artist's vision manifests particularities and preferences affected by their milieu. For example: "Claude Monet loves water, and it is his especial gift to portray its mobility and transparency" (462). Sisley is to be noted because he "seizes the passing moments of the day; watches a fugitive cloud and seems to paint it in its flight" (462). Pissaro, meanwhile, "loves the thick shade of summer woods . . . and does not fear the solidity which sometimes serves to render the atmosphere visible as a luminous haze saturated with sunlight" (462). The descriptions of all three artists (and he does add that Manet "sums up" all of these qualities) are characterized by the selection of one aspect: movement, a natural movement expressed by light, color, and tone. Mallarmé explains that this movement, created through another approach to reality and the visible, gives an impression of instantaneity that, as we recall, is often misunderstood by the public.

Moving on to certain artists whose works may differ, but whose aesthetic theories actually have much in common with the aforementioned, he invokes Morisot, Whistler, Renoir, and Degas. Mallarmé describes how the "luminous, ever moving atmosphere" of Degas's ballet dancers is artistically rendered: "M. Degas . . . does not care to explore the trite and hackneyed view of his subject. A master of drawing, he has sought delicate lines and movements"

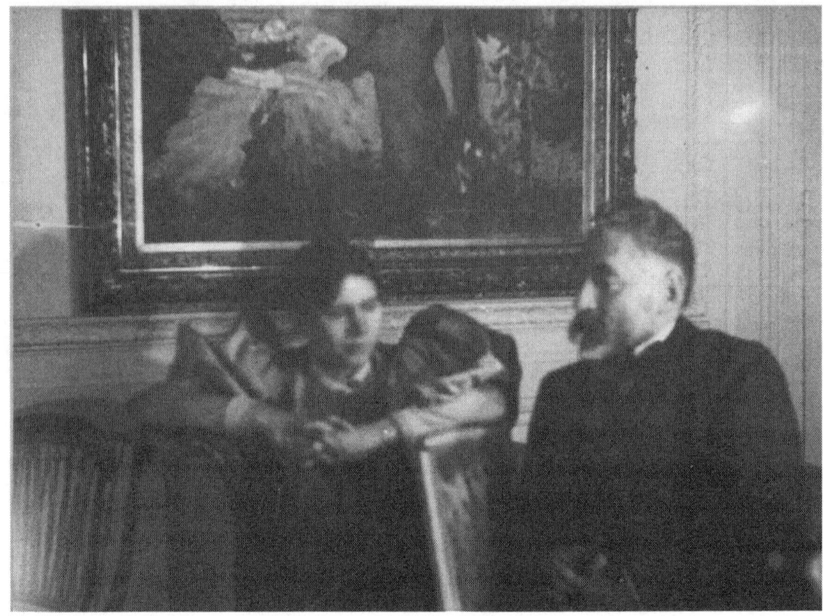

PLATE 13
Degas, Portrait de Stéphane Mallarmé et Paule Gobillard, cousine de Julie Manet.
Paris, Musée d'Orsay.
©Photo RMN/© Hervé Lewandowski.

(464). In describing Morisot's vision, Mallarmé concentrates on the atmosphere of purity, the use of light and shade, and air. "The airy foreground, even the furthermost outlines of the sea and sky, have the perfection of an actual vision" (465). Renoir's "aspect" focuses on reflection:

> The shifting shimmer of gleam and shadow which the changing reflected lights, themselves influenced by every neighbouring thing, cast upon each advancing or departing figure, and the fleeting combinations in which these dissimilar reflections form one harmony or many. (465)

Mallarmé insists on the role of these artists as visionaries in "a confused and hesitating age" (466). Their collective accomplishment is to have portrayed "an extraordinary and quasi-original newness of vision" (466). This new "aspect" that each artist frames and focuses upon creates an illusory impression that "make[s] us understand when looking on the most accustomed objects the delight we should experience could we but see them for the first time" (466).

Now, after many pages that are much more an art lesson than Mallarmé might admit, he recapitulates:

> Impressionism is the principal and real movement of contemporary painting. . . . At a time when the romantic tradition of the first half of the century only lingers among a few surviving masters of that time, the transition from the old imaginative artist and dreamer to the energetic modern worker is found in Impressionism. (466–67)

Emphasizing this idea of the present and its implications for the future, Mallarmé makes a very explicit social statement, one that would be a bit out of character for an artist often described as unconcerned with daily life.

> The participation of a hitherto ignored people in the political life of France is a social fact that will honour the whole of the close of the nineteenth century. A parallel is found in artistic matters, the way being prepared by an evolution which the public with rare prescience dubbed, from its first appearance, Intransigeant, which in political language means radical and democratic. (467)

He renders his point more strongly by relating these "visionaries" to social transformations of their time: "To day [*sic*] the multitude demands to see with its own eyes; and if our latter-day art is less glorious, intense, and rich, it is not without the compensation of truth" (467–68). Speaking as grand master of art and no longer as a part of the innocent public, Mallarmé defines the modern or contemporary period as a

> critical hour for the human race when nature desires to work for herself, she requires certain lovers of hers—new and impersonal men placed directly in communion with the sentiment of their time—to loose the restraint of education, to let hand and eye do what they will, and thus through them, reveal herself. (468)

Mallarmé insists, however, that artists undertake this revelation of nature not "for the mere pleasure of doing so" but to offer nature a way "to express herself, calm, naked, habitual, to those newcomers of to-morrow" and "to place in their power a newer and more succinct means of observing her" (468).

In these last comments we see a very astute and engaged commentary on the relationship between art and contemporary life. The new "means of observation" refers both to the changing nature of artistic production and nature as seen or transformed through the work of art. Mallarmé situates his vision of this aesthetic crisis, or turning point, in a context of industrial, social, political, and epistemological evolution. Clarifying his conception of the new art for the newcomers to the artistic market, "the mighty numbers of an universal suffrage" (468), he again insists upon the relationship between the crisis in aesthetics and the advent of impressionism: "We shall thoroughly have considered our subject when I have shown the relation of the present crisis—the appearance of the Impressionists—to the actual principles of painting—a point of great importance" (468–69). Mallarmé's conclusion sums up the crisis in nineteenth-century aesthetics and indicates a valorization of truth and reality that has shifted toward a new vision of nature, natural law, and perception:

> The scope and aim (not proclaimed by authority of dogmas, yet not the less clear), of Manet and his followers is that painting shall be steeped again in its cause, and its relation to nature. . . . what can be the aim of a painter before everyday nature? To imitate her? Then his best effort can never equal the original with the inestimable advantages of life and space. — "Ah no! this fair face, that green landscape, will grow old and wither, but I shall have them always, true as nature, fair as remembrance, and imperishably my own . . . that which I preserve through the power of Impressionism is not the material portion which already exists, superior to any mere representation of it, but the delight of having recreated nature touch by touch. I leave the massive and tangible solidity to its fitter exponent, sculpture. I content myself with reflecting on the clear and durable mirror of painting, that which perpetually lives yet dies every moment, which only exists by the will of Idea, yet constitutes in my domain the only authentic and certain merit of nature—the Aspect. It is through her that when rudely thrown at the close of an epoch of dreams in the front of reality, I have taken from it only that which properly belongs to my art, an original and exact perception which distinguishes for itself the things it perceives with the steadfast gaze of a vision restored to its simplest perfection." (469–70)

Here, the poet-critic deals with every aspect of the function of art and the artist at issue, and, taking on the voice of the painter (and a very subjective "I"), he clearly expresses his own aesthetic vision, which, in its review and revision of its own artistic sources and methods, modernizes them: "art and thought are obliged to retrace their own footsteps, and to return to their ideal source, which never coincides with their real beginnings" (469). The slippage (around the shifter "I") between painting and the poet's own art, in a conclusion that states that "painting shall be steeped again in its cause, and its relation to nature" (469), is obvious. For Mallarmé, too, joins a re-creation of nature touch by touch in his own mirror of art; an art of the "aspect," one that selects and frames the vision, foregrounding its process and stripping it of any accessory, in order to endow it with purified and pluralizing force.

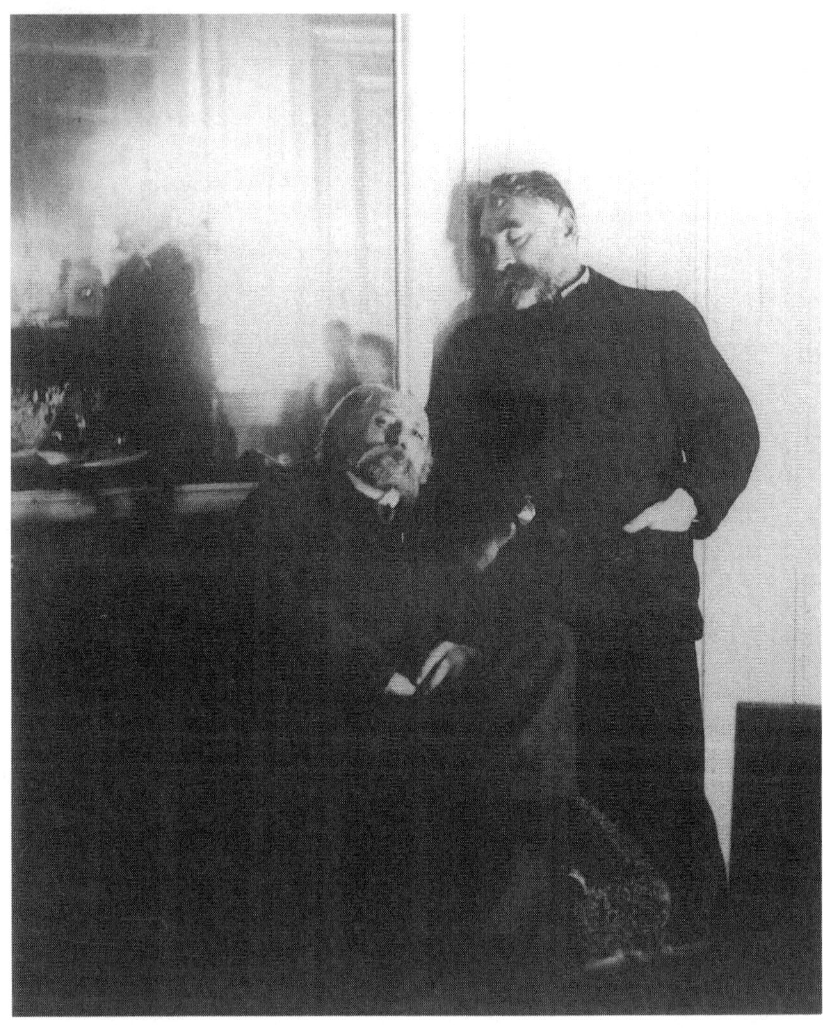

PLATE 14
Degas, Photograph of Mallarmé, Renoir and Degas, 1895.
Bibliothèque littéraire Jacques Doucet, Paris.

FRAME *WORKS* FOR MALLARMÉ

Dans l'oubli fermé par le cadre se fixe
De scintillations

NEW LAWS, NEW PAINTING, AND MALLARMÉ'S "POÉTIQUE TRÈS NOUVELLE"

THE PRESENT CHAPTER examines how Mallarmé's delineation of the multiple levels of representation helped him to fabricate a "poétique très nouvelle" ("A Cazalis," *MOC* 1:663) that dramatizes the process of signification as a new "reality"—one that has many affinities with the "new" painting of the impressionists he so admired. In Mallarmé's analyses of the "new" painting, I remarked that: (1) the "subject matter" is in fact shown to be the "nature" of the sign; and (2) he deals with the nature of these new signs and the advent of the "impression" from perspectives as diverse as conception, production, and reception. In this chapter, I show how his insistence on the framing of the signifying event and the "nature" of the impression to which he alludes elucidate the "new laws" governing his own "poétique très nouvelle."

WINDOWS, MIRRORS, AND FRAMES: *J'AI TROUÉ DANS LE MUR DE TOILE UNE FENÊTRE*[1]

To return to our principles of mimesis, *ut pictura poesis,* and imitation, we recall that the mirror has played a central role in the theorizations of both painting and poetry, as have windows and frames. Mallarmé often exploits transformations in the representations of these images to discuss closure, opening, and reflection. Evocations of mirrors, windows, frames, and even light may be seen as emblematizing and articulating a new perspective on mimesis and mimetic capacity in his poetic language. Rather than indicators or reflectors of the real, such images in Mallarmé's texts become ciphers of a conceptual map that sights, activates, and comments on how the poet-critic envisions the nature of signs. They present a commentary on and questioning of the place of reality in representation that destabilizes the illusion of transparency, exposing the acts of mirroring, framing, and viewing. This self-reflexivity obviously fascinated Mallarmé. Given his study of linguistics as a "science," his view of cognition as virtual, inherently linguistic, and analogous to optical perception, as well as his familiarity with Plato, Descartes, and Taine, such a perspective on Mallarmé's conception of verbal signs cannot be considered anachronistic.

Yves Bonnefoy contends in "La poétique de Mallarmé" that the poet is quite aware of the absence-presence dichotomy as regards referentiality in representation. He suggests that this consciousness manifests itself in Mallarmé's work as an oscillation between a lucid acceptance and a poignant nostalgia for a presence that has most aptly been described by Richard Stamelman as "lost beyond telling."[2] Nevertheless, as I have demonstrated, Mallarmé is less nostalgic than he is exploratory in his displaying of the dialectic operations of the word as sign and its aspirations to presence. His texts underscore the action of their own production and thereby insist on their own distinct nature and mimetic capacity. Rather than being transparent representations or imitations of some external nature, his works, he states, are modeled on and inscribe natural process: "j'imite la loi naturelle" ("A Aubanel," *MOC* 1:703). As noted in chapter 4, Mallarmé himself makes it all quite clear: by staging the nature of representation, he insists on nature as painting itself through the "aspect."

Mallarmé's mimesis is not located in the external world; it is modeled on the internal world in its relation to both signification *and* the outside world. Although Mallarmé rarely discussed mimesis as such, he explored in depth its principle association with the mirroring function.[3] His works insistently pose and expose the problem of representation. To address the "grimoire" of signification that his texts present, and their position in relation to mimesis, it must be understood that his conception of the "aspect," his use of fragmentation, light, and graphics, all develop outward from his ontic model of perception and signification. This model, we recall, invokes a mechanistic conception of the mind as camera, a machine whose product—a graphic re-presentation of photic phenomena—and process were regularly and publicly described in the popular press as examples of either nature reproducing itself, light drawings, or light tracing itself. Such descriptions are strikingly analogous to the way in which, in "Igitur," Mallarmé metaphorizes thought: as light illuminating itself.

Mallarmé consciously attempted to exhibit and control the process of verbal signs textually. The text in "noir sur blanc" can thus be viewed as the materialized positive of a mental and inherently fictive negative. To actualize such an aspiration in verbal art, the poet mobilized a keen awareness of how the verbal and the verbal-poetic sign functions. Many critics have documented this "pre-Saussurian" exploration of the sign and the signifying event in Mallarmé's work and thought. For example, Guy Michaud writes:

> On peut affirmer sans nulle exagération que Mallarmé . . . avant Saussure, jetait à sa manière les fondements d'une linguistique structurale . . . et qu'un siècle . . . avant Barthes, il définissait à peu près le langage poétique comme un language pluriel, d'une nature autre que celle du langage ordinaire. (*Mallarmé: L'homme et l'oeuvre*, 6)

Mallarmé's insistence on signs as systems of synchronically functioning layers of "anchors" and "relays" metaphorizes and foregrounds the space of analogy itself.[4] The dialectical fluctuation between internal and external reference of Mallarmé's texts, the effort to motivate signs in a signifying chain by paradoxically insisting on their arbitrariness, can be seen as an attempt to multiply the potential of verbal signs and to insist upon the poetic and signifying process as inherently mobile. We recall his evocation of the signifying event in "Le mystère dans les lettres":

> —Les mots, d'eux-mêmes, s'exaltent à mainte facette reconnue la plus rare ou valant pour l'esprit, centre de suspens vibratoire; qui les perçoit indépendamment de la suite ordinaire, projetés, en parois de grotte, tant que dure leur mobilité ou principe . . . prompts tous, avant extinction, à une réciprocité de feux distante ou présentée de biais comme contingence. (*MOC* 2:233)

Elsewhere in his later work, Mallarmé most often exploited analogies with music, the theater, and dance to suggest a type of representational dynamism, an aesthetic *movement* that was also gaining impetus in impressionist art. In his texts, music's "mystery" and "obscurity" served as an allusion to an integral psychic process of representation and perception he sought to inscribe and index in the text. However, as noted in our earlier discussion of

"Le mystère," comparisons with music and the performative arts, exploited to invoke the movement occurring in the animated *kamera* of the mind, are most often initiated through a subtle use of visual allusion, graphic analogies, and games of light.

Certain effects integrated into aesthetic thought and practice, which I describe by my own metaphors of the "photo" and the "graphic," can be used to emblematize and examine the effects of modernization and an infiltration of scientific thought and metaphors on artists' conceptions of psychic and textual image figuration in relation to nature. The "photo" and the "graphic" as the pivotal points of a reconceptualization of the *ut pictura poesis* and mimesis frameworks allowed me to contextualize Mallarmé's critical discussions of choice, light, graphics, framing, and movement. The analysis of light and graphics that closes this chapter's "photo-graphic" reading of Mallarmé's writings on dance will reveal how his own texts institute a complex semiotic chain that aspires to varying degrees of diagrammatic iconicity,[5] grafting one set of representational relations onto another to initiate a new genre of movement in poetry.

*L'ARMATURE INTELLECTUELLE . . . SE DISSIMULENT ET TIENT—A LIEU—
DANS L'ESPACE QUI ISOLE LES STROPHES ET PARMI LE BLANC DU PAPIER*[6]

Perhaps more than any other technological innovation, photography captured the minds of the public and aestheticians of the mid to later nineteenth century; while to some it represented a perfect mimesis, for others, the innovation presented a stimulus for *tekhné*. The varied impact of this technology on visual artists such as the impressionists is well documented *and visible* in such techniques as framing, cropping, highly contrasted fields, and blurred representations of bodies in motion. However, photography's effect on the aesthetic field was not limited to provoking transformation or retrenchment in painting, nor was it limited to heightening already existent trends in art and art criticism. Of particular relevance here are the ways in which photography informed the various aesthetic theories and practices of the nineteenth century that reevaluate "truth" and representation's relationship to nature in the less conventionally visual arts. I am referring specifically to how the currency of photographic effects and the diffusion of metaphors—epistemological models based on the camera and the photograph—generated innovation in the verbal arts as a new, reanimated, and rejustified genre of *ut pictura poesis* developed.

What I call Mallarmé's "photo-graphics"—the complex use of light, frames, and framing that distinguishes his texts and gives viability to their aspirations to spatial presence *and movement*—can be understood as a strategic response to the history of the painting–poetry analogy and in particular, to its biases about what poetry may lack. While, as noted, in *Pictorialist Poetics* David Scott acknowledges the importance of the interrelationships between poetry and painting in the nineteenth century, he does not view the Horatian tradition or the concept of imitation as fundamental catalysts in the innovations that occurred between the visual and the verbal arts. Similar critical dismissals of the tradition are to be found in works such as that of Mary Lewis Shaw, whose otherwise insightful *Performance in the Texts of Mallarmé* reads as follows:

> Mallarmé's aesthetic attitudes toward the visual arts seem considerably less complex [than his attitudes toward the performing arts]. He was a staunch supporter of the Impressionists and a close friend of Edouard Manet and Odilon Redon, who illustrated some of his work. And the few essays that he wrote on visual artists point to interesting parallels between his own writing and their work. *Un coup de dés,* his last complete text published in his lifetime and the first modern concrete poem, has an extremely important visual aspect. But the relative lack of both ekphrastic poetry and visual art criticism in Mallarmé's work and the complete absence of reference to painting and sculpture in his plans for the book suggest that the relationship between literature and these arts does not figure prominently in his aesthetic theory. Indeed, this relationship is barely touched on at all. (3–4)

In contrast to such arguments, the discussion and readings that follow demonstrate not only the degree to which *ut pictura poesis* can be seen as a significant frame of reference for Mallarmé, but also, precisely how painting and the visual arts *figure,* not only prominently, but also practically, in his diagrammatic aesthetics. Indeed, the readings illuminate how Mallarmé's work responds to the tradition—textually—through paradoxical analogies with the framed work. I say "paradoxical" because while it would seem that his work aspires to escape some of the biases and precepts of the tradition—and this is in fact the case—he does so through analogies with the visual arts, precisely the comparison from which he has been distanced, and which critics have contended he dismissed. Exploiting insights gleaned from the framed work (particularly framing, cropping, and effects of light), he creates a new and reanimated species of *ut pictura poesis* that responds to the tradition and elucidates the developing movements in both poetics and the visual arts of his time.

DEVELOPING MOVEMENTS

As we recall from the previous chapter, Steiner cites the shift in emphasis from *enargeia,* a pictorial quality in verbal discourse, to *energeia,* the actualization of potency or movement, as a key element in the evolution of the aesthetics of the moderns (10). As early as the 1870s, Mallarmé praised just such a tendency in his art and literary criticism. In fact, he deemed the aspiration to kinesis a major characteristic of the developing movements in the visual and the verbal arts alike. Nowhere, perhaps, does Mallarmé more explicitly expose this shift in aesthetic values and its significance for both literature and painting than in his writings on Manet and the impressionists, as discussed in chapter 4. Could the advent of photography, often regarded as the epitome of stasis, have something to do with the dynamism this poet-critic consistently praised in the art of his time? Might the invention somehow illuminate his vision of art and his own artistic production?

Mallarmé's defense and justification of Manet and the impressionists consistently related the developing movements in the pictorial arts to contemporary trends in the verbal arts. Not incidentally, he also insisted that the developing movement in the pictorial arts was a result of the "true artist's" ability to seize what is "captivating" in modern, "ambient" life. He associates this kinesis in painting with the assimilation and appropriation of "widely scattered elements" ("The Impressionists and Edouard Manet," *MOC* 2:449) and insists that the modern understanding of "new laws of space and light" (451) is never a matter of slavish imitation. He emphasizes that artistic vision and choice take precedence over any law. In effect, Mallarmé presents the new movement in painting as a new and improved referentiality, grounded in natural law and distinguished by at least two major characteristics: the desire to render movement, and a new conception of framing. Both aspire to capture effects and action of the light spectrum and its perception, which more often than not did not conform to conventions recognized by the Academy or the various juries of the official French Salons.

In his written commentaries on the official Salons of the 1840s and 1850s, Baudelaire, too, had insisted that movement was essential to modern (romantic) art, that it was animation and the life force that the photograph could not render, but that painters and writers could. For similar reasons, color, which at the time Baudelaire was writing could not be reproduced photographically, was highly valorized in his writing. One could propose that the importance he placed on such qualities was related to a desire to protect the place of painting and the role of the artist against the machine and its capacity to produce an exact mechanical reproduction of nature with which artists could not compete. As early as 1839, François Arago, a scientist and Republican member of the Chamber Deputies, announced at a meeting of the Academy of Sciences that in the daguerreotype, "light reproduces the forms and proportions of external objects with almost mathematical precision" (Aaron Scharf, *Art and Photography,* 25). Like Poe,[7] Mallarmé would, of course, also concede that competition in view of exactitude was futile: "La Nature a lieu, on n'y ajoutera pas" ("La musique et les lettres," *MOC* 2:67). Still, if Baudelaire, with great savvy, seemed to competently and confidently dismiss the faithful representation of external nature as an end for, and of, art, there may have been still other reasons for his uneasiness with regard to this machine. Indeed, the technology represented much more than a menace to artistic imagination. The invention, as critic Jules Janin enthusiastically noted, was useful to the artist "who does not have the time to draw." This calls up an unnerving issue, articulated by Mallarmé in his 1876 article as a "commercial misunderstanding" (*MOC* 2:463) that could negatively affect the reception and pricing of artistic production. Furthermore, the machine, according to Janin, was capable of accurately reproducing artworks themselves. He notes: "It is destined to popularize among us, and cheaply, the most beautiful works of art of which we have now only costly and inaccurate reproduction" (quoted in Scharf, 26). While Baudelaire appeared overtly less concerned than Mallarmé with the commercial menace than with what such a strict interpretation of mimesis might mean to demands on artistic production, he did emphasize the dangers of "industry" impinging on art and, somewhat paradoxically, announced photography's real task as being a servant of the sciences and of the arts, but a very humble servant. It is precisely this role as servant that will interest us as we examine how photography and its metaphors—as objects of and for study—reinforce developing notions of visual perception, unsettling the aesthetic landscape.

Photography was initially criticized for being too static, for its inability to fix moving objects without blurring, and because tones of certain colors were grossly distorted. To Baudelaire such defects presented a window of opportunity for painting and the artistic imagination, which could supply the movement and color he so cherished. But can the valorization of movement really be divorced from this technology? While Baudelaire insists that it is the movement of the artist's nature and vision that should be framed, suggesting that the industry of photography can never attain such an art, Mallarmé actually paints a very different picture.

Indeed, since photography did act as a servant to the arts and sciences and provided the means to make visible aspects of the light spectrum not usually perceived by the eye, the move toward presenting process as product and the valorization of the impression of instantaneity were quite often informed by this very technology artists aspired to exceed. Simply put, the impact of photography on the pictorial arts provoked an interest in rendering movement in painting. Although it was criticized early on for its "unnatural" stasis, photographic representation explored its own particular capacity to render animation as seized in individual images and in attempts to trace movement over time through sequential snapshots and fragments that simulate kinesis. While Eadweard Muybridge's famous 1887 studies are the culmination of this focus on the possibilities of representing movement in time, this type of investigation was well underway and in fact becoming commonplace, as accounts of innovations in biophysics (such as Étienne-Jules Marey's highly publicized experiments) and technical gimmicks for mass amusement were advertised and popularized in the specialized and daily presses.[8] This fascination with capturing movement, I contend, elucidates the operations of Mallarmé's aesthetic frames of reference and how his frames work.

TEMPORALITY:

LE BLANC SOUCI DE NOTRE TOILE[9]

As we have seen, in his 1876 article on the impressionists and Manet, Mallarmé systematically addressed all the main precepts of the *ut pictura poesis* tradition with respect to painting and then related them to literature. These issues, to my mind, framed out the underlying "armature" of the article. The expression "frame out" is not gratuitous. Although the article introduced the principles and criteria by which painting had been judged and then applied these to modern pictorial and literary art forms, the piece explicitly presents itself as an inductive process of spatiotemporal discovery: Mallarmé states that the written "facts" of the text "present themselves . . . as they may" (*MOC* 2:444). The movement, which he says, "seems to emanate" from the article as the development of its meaning, presents an animation that is meant to be analogous to what he described as characteristic "aspects" of the new art: the impression of "novel" perception and most significant, the making visible of "invisible action" (455).

In this 1876 piece, rather than merely describing the work of Manet and the impressionists to paint (so to speak) a verbal picture, Mallarmé's article seeks first and foremost to situate the new art forms—historically, aesthetically, and ideologically—to illustrate their principles. While it bestows high praise on the new art, his article nonetheless marginalizes the actual works in order to center, valorize, and appropriate what he sees as their formal processes. To this end, he firmly situates their reconceptualization of representation within a very traditional discourse of verisimilitude. Explaining that the public have been fooled by "an artificially classic science," that they are the "dupes of a civilized education" and therefore "ignorant" of nature's charms, Mallarmé explains that the new art, its framing of process, and its framing process offer "a new delight at the recovery of a long obliterated truth" (457–58). The poet-critic exploits all the arguments for a faithful representation of nature and applies them to a dynamic reenactment of the life force in Manet's art. Clearly, he recognized analogies with the new art's mimetic capacity in his own art.

In describing the innovations of the impressionists, Mallarmé sheds light on his own quest for novelty and his practical means for achieving it in writing. His "descriptions," which often include explicit comparisons with literature, can be seen as commenting on the articulatory strategies of the text itself. This applies in particular to the illusion of a temporal present created as the "graphic" development the text "presents" and to the tactical use of lexical items that refer to the "light," "air," and "animation" so characteristic of impressionist signs, while simultaneously indexing these very "aspects" as somehow present in the text.

As with the "new" painters, Mallarmé's innovation occurs as an assimilation and appropriation of "widely scattered elements" (449). As in the new painting, such "elements" may be grounded simultaneously in past aesthetic "models" (451), "new" elemental "laws" (451), or in "the influence of the moment" (450). The intermingling of past "models," always implicit in traces, does not impinge upon the autonomy of the new works; he considers them neither "imitations"[10] nor pure creations completely divorced from nature or natural process. Mallarmé identifies with the impressionists' use of analogies with atomistic photo functioning to create impressions of movement; he appreciates their innovative use of fragmentation and framing, and he insists that these aspects are grounded in natural process and therefore "truthful." Indeed, while he notes how the "luminous and transparent atmosphere struggles with the figures" in these paintings, he signals that "the surrounding atmosphere, which plunders reality from the figures . . . seems to do so in order to preserve their truthful aspect" (455).

Historically, a deeply entrenched valorization of verisimilitude and truth, visual imagery, and description dominated conceptions of mimesis in both poetry and painting.[11] In this sense, Mallarmé's poetics represents a dramatic rupture with tradition. Similarly, the "shared subject matter" or the "necessary anecdote" of narrative and allegorical art and poetry that conventionally joined the sister arts as "content" seem to disappear in Mallarmé's later verse. However, as Mallarmé explains in his art criticism, this content dimension also fell to the wayside in the "new" painting. According to Mallarmé, the neoclassical insistence on choice or selection of subject matter as that which is lofty in nature or human nature no longer seems to apply in either art. As we recall, choice *of* subject matter yields to choice *as* subject matter; the focus is on the presentation of the artistic process in each medium. This insistence on the role of selection and choice itself in the material functioning of a formal medium, a collapse of the form–content split, articulates another trait of Mallarmé's "modern" reconceptualization of mimesis. Indeed, rather than articulating the death of *ut pictura poesis,* the "old parallels" of the comparison that seem to have become obsolete are actually recuperated and modernized in Mallarmé's texts through "aspects" that often exploit techniques traditionally considered to be those of the visual arts. In a dazzling reversal, this canny speculator observes conventions via their modernization; the traditional distinctions of the two arts actually become points of intersection that form a new species of *ut pictura poesis.* This new species is achieved through a complex use of light and graphics that rethinks art's relationship to nature, and the verbal arts' relationship to movement via temporality. Let us review these "distinctions."

While poetry was considered similar to painting as an imitative art, in terms of subject matter (selection of the worthy) and often in terms of their so-called shared visual appeal,[12] it was because of the distinction of the formal media, one spatial and visual, the other temporal and verbal, that the two arts were considered incomparable and comparisons between the two were dismissed as superficial. So what happens when artists explore and display the reversibility of these attributes? Or as W. J. T. Mitchell's work in *Picture Theory* more appropriately asks: *When did they ever not?*

The long disputed time–space dichotomy is of particular interest here with respect to the different arts' capacities for expressing movement. Poetry and, more generally, the verbal arts, were said to possess a movement that entailed the unfolding of the story or the anecdote over time. While, on the one hand, time was said to be the *bien* of poetry, space, on the other hand, was the property of painting. Any movement to which painting might aspire was toward the outside of the picture's frame—that is, how the image might call up in the sociolect a story, anecdote, or fable, or refer to a historical event about to happen. Such moments, and most often those when it appears that a character is about to do, hear, or say something, were referred to as "pregnant moments" (Steiner, 40). Surprisingly, perhaps, in Mallarmé's discussion of impressionist painting, this is not at all the type of movement to which he alludes. His descriptions explicitly present impressionist art as unconventional, and he insists that this new movement in painting is grounded in new laws of space and light that are faithful to the nature of the impression they seek to capture, inscribe, and, by extension, to reinvoke. Rather than the anecdote, allegory, or historical allusion being central, according to Mallarmé, these works insist on the mise-en-scène of the visual sign in its reconstitution and reenactment of perception. The framing of the nature of the visual sign itself distinguishes the works as he describes them. Painting, then, as it is explicated by Mallarmé, clearly aspires to another genre of movement. Moreover, as I will demonstrate, his identification with this genre of movement sheds light on his own aesthetic and his verbal analogues of impressionist movement. Rather than simply suggest at this point that poetry's "canvas" might aspire to the spatial, which is in Mallarmé's work most visibly the case, my investigation will zoom in on how Mallarmé reenvisions temporality and movement within the framework of the verbal arts.

CENTERING THE PERIPHERY:
J'AI TOUT FAIT POUR QUE LE TEMPS QU'ELLE SONNA RESTÂT PRÉSENT[13]

Frames and the framing process, traditionally seen as peripheral elements in the verbal arts, became central to Mallarmé's poetic creation, to his poetics, and particularly, to the incorporation of what I call "ekphrastic effects"—that is, the verbal representation of aspects often considered to be those of visual representation. The ekphrastic effects that I will address at this juncture do not envision ekphrasis as a "minor genre" of descriptive verbal representation—a poem creating a verbal picture, as it were—nor will I limit my study to what Murray Kreiger refers to as the "ekphrastic principle": "when the verbal object would emulate the spatial character of the painting" (*Ekphrasis: The Illusion of the Natural Sign,* 9).[14] Rather than extending (or reducing) the definition of ekphrasis (the verbal representation of visual representation), I will limit this discussion to ekphrastic effects that envision and enact an innovative, graphically conceived genre of "movement" in Mallarmé's writing. I will suggest how such aspects may frame Mallarmé's interventions—theoretical and practical—in the *ut pictura poesis* tradition. What might seem, then, to be a cursory dismissal of the double mimesis associated with ekphrasis, is, as I will show, supported by Mallarmé's writings on the impressionists. It will also be seen that the descriptive possibilities conventionally associated with verbal representations of the visual arts become secondary in his art criticism. The framed object he seemingly seeks to present is not only marginalized, however; somewhat paradoxically, its frame is recuperated. The *cadre* (frame, framework), the *encadrement* (framing), and the *cadrage* (centering, cropping, placement) traditionally associated with the visual arts are analogically centered as Mallarmé reenvisions movement in the verbal arts.

Most noteworthy in Mallarmé's rethinking of the movement that can be incorporated in verbal art is that the only mobility associated with the verbal was a temporal one that occurred via narrative progression. Ekphrasis would then entail the stilling of the narrative's temporal development by a description of a work of visual art as it is presented in verbal art. Anyone familiar with Mallarmé's poetry will certainly remark that lengthy and detailed descriptions that stop any kind of a story are few and far between—as are stories per se, for that matter. Mallarmé's ekphrastic effects, rather than merely stopping temporal movement of a narration to describe an object or to evoke yet another narrative in the sociolect (as per the conventional pregnant moment in painting), simultaneously aspire to institute another kind of movement. These ekphrastic effects, and particularly his analogical appropriation and reorientation of the triggering principle of the pregnant moment, occur via what might collectively be called "framing processes": the framing of the processes of the text; the discourses about visual and verbal operations that frame his aesthetic; and *cadrage,* the placement of all "aspects" within the matrices of his writing.

Mallarmé's reinterrogation of art's mimetic capacity and his use of analogy—interdisciplinary and intermedia— reactivate the "reality claim" of the *ut pictura poesis* comparison from within the poetic framework. While such a declaration supports the direction of many recent discussions of ekphrasis as a verbal product of age-old interartistic power struggles, what interests me here is how a rewriting of the faithful representation of nature *as the faithful representation of the nature of the sign*—a rewriting that entails a shift from *enargeia* to *energeia*—informs Mallarmé's response to the aesthetic hierarchies of his era and simultaneously elucidates his semiotic production.

Defined and occasionally limited to a spatial aspiration, Mallarmé's rethinking of temporality exceeds the typographic "stillness" or "spatial form" of *Un coup de dés* for which he has become so well known. While ekphrastic effects in Mallarmé's writing may seem to "still" temporal movement, most often they simultaneously provoke another kind of temporal movement (a "suspens vibratoire") that is analogous to that of the pregnant moment, but one that does not *only* rely on the movement of narration or the "suite ordinaire" of any narrative description. At the semantic, phonic, or even purely visual level (word shape, blanks, or the graphics of punctuation marks), the stilling of the temporal progression of the text by each isolated word paradoxically coincides with its triggering of a movement among select semiotic and semantic elements (rather than only to a tangential narrative). It is hardly surprising, then, that in his art criticism, Mallarmé offered high praise for the instantaneity of the "new" pictorial arts. Such immediacy, he said, was an effect of movement, light, and life. Recall that "nothing should be absolutely fixed," that the "represented subject . . . composed of a harmony of reflected and ever-changing lights . . . palpitates with movement, light and life" (456). Indeed, via the artist's framing, the viewer should have the experience of seeing it for the very first time. By expanding the classical definition of "choice" (of lofty subject matter) to include the material substrate of his own art, Mallarmé simultaneously displays that choice of the aspect[15]—framing—may in fact be something that "properly belongs" to his art.

In Mallarmé's distinct effort to incorporate certain effects that distinguish the "new" poetics from previous models of poetic potentiality, he stressed poetic form and accentuated the direct sensorial impact of poetic signs—a move toward iconicity, which, like visuality, was considered a property characteristic of the pictorial arts. In addition to this superficial insistence on the visible signifier, he layers the primary visual aspect of the text with semantic allusions to pictorial categories that destabilize the narrative progression to diagram a form of kinesis that is both grounded in a visual model of epistemology and akin to the new movement in painting. "Invisible action rendered visible" (455) redefines mimesis, the underlying premise of the *ut pictura poesis* tradition. Mallarmé, however, conspicuously avoids discussing the tradition of the painting–poetry analogy.

Mallarmé's analogies with the other arts often serve as thematic supports (or metaphoric indexes) to emphasize effects that respond to and surpass the attributes traditionally ascribed to poetry. Furthermore, his intentional indexing of poetic potential via analogies other than painting serves, paradoxically, to veil fundamental developments in poetics that parallel those occurring coincidentally in the visual arts. However, and more important for the purposes of this discussion, such analogies are, nonetheless, grounded in a specular model of poetic signification, and, as we shall see in the reading of dance that closes this chapter, they are most often articulated with "visual" effects. In short, allusions to and comparisons with other arts exploit visual effects and seem to point anywhere but to painting; they insist on the sensory and post-sensory impact and action of the verbal signification and seek to distinguish Mallarmé's art from its historical rival and from the realist biases associated with *ut pictura poesis*.

Despite this strategic obfuscation, the fundamental significance of the painting analogy for Mallarmé's theoretical framework sheds light on how his innovative poetic practice is initiated. The following excerpt from Mallarmé's preface for Berthe Morisot's exhibition catalogue is revelatory of his philosophy of poetic language and his practice, in that he illustrates his philosophy by focusing on a reconception of mimesis that aspires to graphic *energeia,* or animation.[16]

> Poétiser, par art plastique, moyen de prestiges directs, semble, sans intervention, le fait de l'ambiance éveillant aux surfaces leur lumineux secret: ou la riche analyse, chastement pour la restaurer, de la vie, selon une alchimie,—mobilité et illusion. (*MOC* 2:151)

The condensation and fragmentation of Mallarmé's syntax cannily institute an aesthetic *prise de position* and a destabilizing, spatial, and figurative appropriation of the pregnant moment that is *both* an ekphrastic effect and an ekphrasis. Mallarmé clearly envisions the aspirations of the poet in a similar fashion: "Quel génie pour être un poète! Quelle foudre d'instinct renfermer, simplement la vie, vierge, en sa synthèse et loin illuminant tout" ("Sur la philosophie dans la poésie," *MOC* 2:659). In the previous passage on Morisot, Mallarmé's text does not merely attempt to describe Morisot's work, but to initiate analogically, via a play of light and graphics, his own "mobilité" and "illusion." In other words, his text on Morisot *enacts* the very same phenomenon he finds in the painter's work. The process-oriented conception and production of mobility and illusion he details do not insist on the anecdote or action that one is to attribute to the framed object, but rather on the potential for animation of the work's surface. In "Whistler et Mallarmé 1888–1898," Jacques Roujon states: "Mallarmé observe avec un oeil de peintre les vibrations de la lumière non seulement sur les eaux mais sur la chair, sur les étoffes, sur les arbres et il prétend les traduire par des vibrations de mots dont le son lui importe autant que le sens" (641). Heuristically accepting that Mallarmé's "descriptions" often reflect not only back on their own language, but on his poetic practice in general, this insistence on the conflict of ambiance and surface, light, movement, and the coordination of the elements of a formal medium, suggests not only the acoustic dimensions of his poetic language or even any primary denotations of words; rather, it implies the movement between the surface of the verbal symbol (auditory and visual), the meanings of words (denotations), and the possible meanings of words in multiple contexts (connotations). As in Morisot's canvas, Mallarmé enacts movement in this passage through a series of nonanecdotal pregnant moments. It is the application through praxis of this technical analogy with an art whose capacity for movement was considered limited that destabilizes this Mallarméan text, bolstering its potential for movement and multiple meanings, and taking his own version of *ut pictura poesis* to yet another level—a diagrammatic one. This textual "description," and, more generally, his own impressionist aesthetic, sets up a tension—a "suspens vibratoire"—between the surface of words, their arrangement, and their variable vibrations in the text and in the mind. In all of Mallarmé's writings, the fragmentation of the syntax, the desire to "poetiser par art plastique," to achieve immediacy—"moyens de prestiges directs"—would restore an illusion of kinesis through framing, another genre of movement activated among selected aspects of a matrix.

CE VITRAIL. LA CHAMBRE SINGULIÈRE EN UN CADRE[17]

In his piece on Manet and the impressionists, Mallarmé implies that along with the absolute abdication of individuality, the new laws of light, space, and movement, and the staging of choice as subject matter, another "find" of the new art was to be found in "an absolutely new science" that involves "cutting down the pictures" (*MOC* 2:458). This new science, which Mallarmé globally refers to as "the function of the frame" incorporates two distinct yet reversible elements. The first, the frame, is never temporally distinguishable from the second, the framing operation. The latter, depending on the degree to which one cuts the picture down, implies one of those "aspects" we consider characteristic of modern art: selective cropping or fragmentation. For Mallarmé, the frame in the pictorial arts may become "a fanciful boundary, such as that which is embraced at one glance of a scene framed in by the hands," or a means of isolating and enclosing those "aspects" "found worthy to preserve" (458). The spectrum of the frame thus encompasses decomposition—the cutting down into fragments and what could be considered "choice" of the aspect on an elemental level. Particularly germane here is that Mallarmé's description of the graphic "science" of the frame has, once again, parallels with his descriptions and deconstructions of thought and language as both made up of active particles analogous to the elemental functioning of light rays and their perception as afterimages.

As a consequence, Mallarmé displays and delineates conventions of temporal movement in the written text via games with light and graphics.

Even his "aboli bibelot d'inanité sonore" ("Ses purs ongles," *MOC* 1:98), the verse most often evoked to insist upon his ludic use of sonority, comes from a highly "visual" poem demonstrating rigorous attention to choice of subject, focus, and image, as well as the selective and reflective arrangement of the "scattered elements" of his medium.[18] Described by Mallarmé as being "as white and black as possible," this poem, originally entitled "Sonnet allégorique de lui-même," emblematizes its own production through densely layered framing techniques.

> Ses purs ongles très haut dédiant leur onyx,
>
> L'Angoisse, ce minuit, soutient lampadophore,
>
> Maint rêve vespéral brûlé par le Phénix
>
> Que ne recueille pas de cinéraire amphore
>
> Sur les crédences, au salon vide: nul ptyx,
>
> Aboli bibelot d'inanité sonore,
>
> (Car le Maître est allé puiser des pleurs au Styx
>
> Avec ce seul objet dont le Néant s'honore.)
>
> Mais proche la croisée au nord vacante, un or
>
> Agonise selon peut-être le décor
>
> Des licornes ruant du feu contre une nixe,
>
> Elle, défunte nue en le miroir, encor
>
> Que, dans l'oubli fermé par le cadre se fixe
>
> De scintillations sitôt le septuor.

A tightly structured sonnet in *"-yx,"* "Ses purs ongles" thematizes the creative act through a meticulously structured, graphic cross-referencing of lexical items alluding to visual phenomena (light, reflection, frames that evoke both mirrors and the pictorial arts, and windows) as well as items that, by their shape or typography, form visual (or aural) patterns among themselves. "Onyx" and "minuit," for example, both conjure up blackness. A luminous color and a precious stone, "onyx" etymologically recalls *onux* or claws (the French "ongle," [claw, nail], is derived from the Latin *onyx,* Gr. *onux*) and metonymically connects with the poem's opening "ses purs ongles." These "ongles," in turn, are a synecdoche for the artist's hand and the verb Mallarmé used most often to connote writing—"griffer"—itself derived etymologically from the graphic.

Graphically offset by the references to darkness are the evocations of photic phenomena via flames ("brûlé," "Phénix," "feu") and the light ("or," "scintillations") entering from the northern window frame ("la croisée"). This window is itself a framing structure that encloses a matrix of smaller framed squares ("cadre"). The "or" of the light framed by the window sparks a harmony with another light in the "lampadophore." These internally reflective snapshots evoking flashes of white and light, the disposition of sounds ("or") and word shapes ("or") that call up light or reflection in the sonnet, are fixed and *mises en abyme* in the frame of the mirror. Rather than an experiment in sound without meaning or a window onto nature, we find a window onto the nature of signification and a reflection of and on a reanimated *ut pictura poesis.* In this poem, the coordination of the "widely scattered elements" that Mallarmé praised in Manet's art (*MOC* 2:449) is embodied as the poem's captivated, scintillating action is framed: "dans l'oubli fermé par le cadre se fixe / De scintillations."

The graphic frame and the act of framing physically and metaphorically frame the idea or impression and its components, as well as the operations of its semiotic production and performance. "Framing" refers to varying degrees of a reversible phenomenon modeled on natural law, yet created in a completely artificial medium: a semiotic system that is both visual and verbal. The frame thus conceived is manifold, reversible, and potentially both infinite and infinitesimal in scope: it is the artistic frame, the process of framing, and framing as *cadrage*—an operation characteristic of a modern perspective on choice. As in the impressionist paintings he described, in Mallarmé's poetry the "function of the [textual] frame" and the act of framing physically and metaphorically encompass selection, choice of theme, subject matter, formal structure or genre (the choice of the sonnet, for example), choice of technique and its disposition in the artistic medium, and finally closure, the framing of the artistic space, or "choice" at the macroscopic level. The "scintillations" enclosed by the frame in "Ses purs ongles" might thus refer to the constellation in the evening sky, to each of the terms in the matrix alluding—visually or aurally—to light in the poem, or to the sonnet itself.

JE TE PARLERAI PENDANT DES HEURES[19]

Mallarmé's mimesis, no longer a copy but a discrete creation with mimetic capacity, does not exclude allusions to visual "aspects," nor does it marginalize the use of "painterly techniques"—quite the contrary. In "Ses purs ongles" and elsewhere, his texts provocatively displace realist biases of poems (or paintings) as windows onto nature, to display their performative capacities as signifying events. Images of windows, mirrors, and frames thus insist first and foremost on their distinction from, and only then on their relation to, the outside world. The graphic frame analogically appropriated as aesthetic choice, rather than remaining marginal in the verbal arts, becomes central, and functions at every level of the semiotic production of the text. At stake in the Mallarméan frame-work is a rethinking of the question of temporality via movement *in and of* space and time.

This kinetic mimesis, no longer grounded solely in narrative develop-ment, analogically centers attributes conventionally ascribed to the pictorial arts. Mallarmé's "photo-graphic" technique involves a diagrammatic iconicity initiated through ekphrastic effects. Delineated through indexing features that stop the reader at an aspect of the text, his photo-graphic *cadrage* synchronically creates an afterimage-like "suspens vibratoire" that overlays the text's diachronic progression. As we reconsider the dissimulated "échafaudage(s)" of a theorist who announced that "l'armature intellectuelle du poème se dissimule et tient—a lieu—dans l'espace qui isole les strophes et parmi le blanc du papier" ("Sur la philosophie," *MOC* 2:659); of a poet who placed such stock in the material trace and vibratory dimensions of the word and the text; and of a critic who stated that one must always "crop the beginning and the end of one's work" ("A Cazalis," *MOC* 1:657), there can be no doubt that for Mal-larmé's aesthetic frameworks the significance of this "photo-graphic" *cadrage* is anything but marginal.

OFFENSIVE MOVES IN MALLARMÉ: DANCING WITH *DES ASTRES*

We have seen how the history of the painting–poetry analogy and epistemo-logical thought about visual and psychic perception are resolved in Mallarmé's vision of mimesis and what I have described as his "framing processes." The same perspective can be used to elucidate the poet's analogies with arts other than painting. Indeed, Mallarmé's recourse to music, theater, and dance in his later works suggests a representational dynamism that was also animating the impressionist movement in art. I next address what I consider some very "offensive" moves on the part of a painstakingly self-conscious artist. In partic-ular, my focus will be on how Mallarmé's interartistic frameworks respond to a long history of comparison between the pictorial and the verbal arts. "Offen-sive moves" refers simultaneously to the poet's aesthetic moves—his speculative strategy—and to the practical implications of such speculation: an innovative and destabilizing institution of kinesis. "Dancing with *des astres*" suggests how this movement, often associated with dance in his writing, is imprinted in the verbal text through ekphrastic effects, envisioned and enacted via games of light and graphics. In particular, stars, constellations, and the reflection of light, which all figure prominently throughout Mallarmé's corpus, take on a specific role when associated with dance. Recourse to dance is exploited textually to index the theatrical signifying operations of the dance itself *and* to affiliate this visual body-writing with movement. Simultaneously, such allusions are meant to point to (or index) the kinesis—what Mallarmé might call *the music*— embodied in the photo-graphics of the text that discusses it.

Although Mallarmé's recourse to music and dance is typically explained as a dismissal of the painting analogy that valorizes movement and nonimitative art, his texts beg to differ—and to defer. The suspension effect that Mallarmé describes when he discusses dance *as* poetry is effected by dance in space, and by poetry via a series of pregnant moments situated spatially in the *cadrage* —the cropping, arrangement, and spacing out of the text. While there may be no mirror of, or window onto, nature (a big maybe, given the sheer number of lexical items that call up mirrors and windows in his work), there is a faithful representation of the nature of the sign—*a faithful representation of a diagrammatic kind.* Rather than an escape from the visual, recourse to these arts is exploited to expose and foreground the effects of another vision of mimesis; a new and reanimated *ut pictura poesis.* This is, however, a "primary mimesis," an enactment modeled on a principle, a performance of process that defies reproduction of the same, and thus generates a spectacular poetics that envisions, embodies, and stages its own performativity.[20]

LA FORME THÉÂTRALE DE POÉSIE PAR EXCELLENCE[21]

Considered by many critics (primarily outside Mallarmé studies) as a founding father of dance theory and later anointed "métaphysicien du ballet," Mallarmé was fascinated by a variety of dance forms, by the dancer Loïe Fuller, and, more precisely, by the specular and spectacular action of her veils.[22] Of the *Crayonné au théâtre* (*MOC* 2: 160–203), pieces Mallarmé penciled at the theater between 1886 and 1897, two focus specifically on dance. They are ostensibly dance reviews. The first, entitled "Ballets" (*MOC* 2:170–74) was published in 1886, and the second, "Autre étude de danse: Les fonds dans le ballet" (*MOC* 2: 174–78) first appeared in the *National Observer* in 1893 as "Considérations sur l'art du ballet et la Loïe Fuller." The latter was subsequently reprinted in

1895 in *La revue franco-américaine,* under the broadened heading of "Etude de danse." This generalizing evolution in the second title, veiling but not effacing the temporal and the circumstantial, is noteworthy. Although perhaps indicative of the move away from traditional ballet and the rising popularity of new forms of modern dance, the generic nature of the later title is also characteristic of the ambiguity of the poet-critic's objectives in such dance reviews. While Mallarmé's writings on dance take up a specific performer or performance as a pretext (as do his less-studied writings on painting), they most typically present universalizing meditations on this art and highlight its relationship to his own. It is thus no surprise that the poet's use of dance is not limited to these two reviews. Indeed, dance appears to animate a number of his performative "studies," such as the *billet* to Whistler, "La musique et les lettres," and the pieces collected in *Crayonné au théâtre.*

Mallarmé designated ballet the "forme théâtrale de poésie par excellence" (*MOC* 2:175). Insisting that all in dance is, as theatrical art would demand, "fictif ou momentané" (163), he praised this "écriture merveilleuse et immédiatement significative de la danse" (*Corr* 3:83) as the "incorporation visuelle de l'idée" (*MOC* 2:173)—a sign, both visible and visual. While this montage of quotations was cropped from four different Mallarmé texts, the overall effect is one of coherence. Indeed, there are constants in all Mallarmé's writing on dance. As I have suggested, the most general of these entail how dance is used metaphorically to speak of its own processes and analogically to speak about those of poetry. Another constant is that dance is insistently allied with both fabrication and performative immediacy. Finally, Mallarmé's writings systematically exploit dance to entwine a mobility and a visuality that are expressed in his texts via a constellation of lexical items referring to light, reflection, and stars. Even when focusing on movement, it is most often the visual facet of the dance's movement that Mallarmé chooses or selects to frame.

L'INCORPORATION VISUELLE DE L'IDÉE[23]

As with dance, so with the dancer. She too explicitly functions as a metaphor. In his review entitled "Ballets," Mallarmé proposes the following axiom: "la danseuse *n'est pas une femme qui danse,* . . . elle *n'est pas une femme,* mais une métaphore" (*MOC* 2:171, emphasis in original). This dancer, he insists "te livre à travers le voile dernier . . . la nudité de tes concepts et silencieusement écrira ta vision à la façon d'un Signe, qu'elle est" (174). The dancer, then, according to Mallarmé, is metaphor, sign, and writer. As sign, she would be both signifier and signified, using her body—the signifier—as a visual vehicle or embodiment of a signified. While this self-reflexivity might appear to diminish the significance of any external reference, he insists that she is also a metaphor; she still stands—or dances—for something else: the operations of dance. Finally, as the verb "écrira" suggests, she is a writer: "elle te *livre* . . . la nudité de tes concepts et silencieusement *écrira* ta vision" (174, emphasis added). Anyone familiar with this self-conscious author's work would freeze at the graphic presentation of the third-person conjugation of the verb "livrer." Certainly, the syntax offers no other possibility than "she delivers unto you." And yet, when Mallarmé writes the letters *l-i-v-r-e* (book) in a sentence whose principal verb is "écrire," his verbal precision and his attention to the visual aspect of his texts guarantee

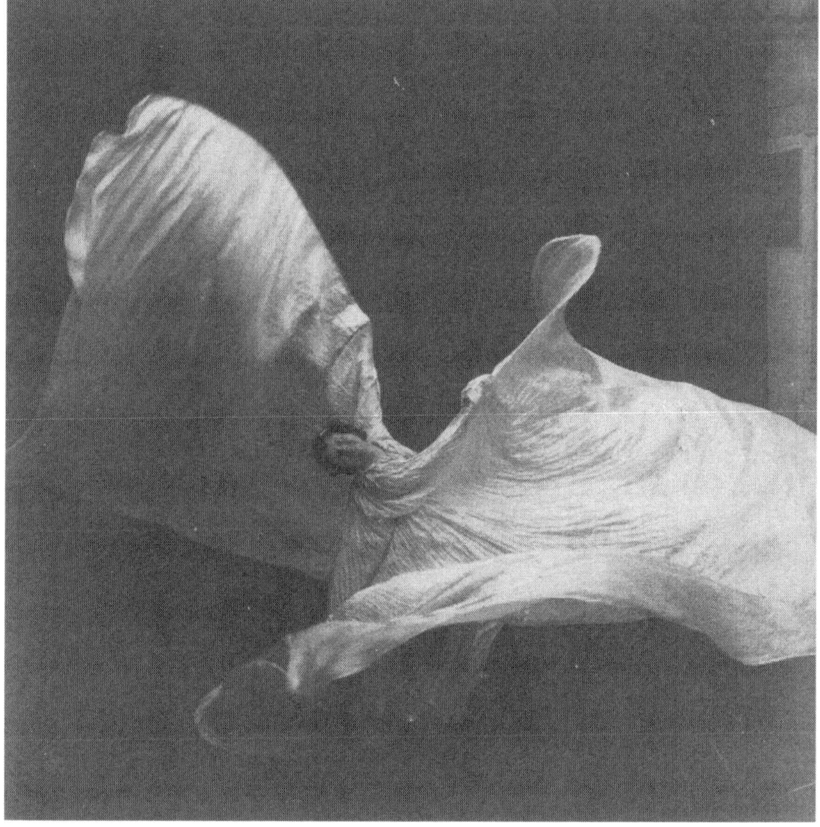

PLATE 15
Taber, Loïe Fuller dansant avec son voile, 1897.
Paris, Musée d'Orsay.
Photo RMN/© Michèle Bellot.

that the word is not gratuitous: the reading is suspended while a choice of shifting possibilities and impossibilities overlays the temporal unfolding of the text. This lexical and (syn-)tactical suspension is not merely a matter of chance.

THE DANCING FRAMEWORK

Similarly held in suspense, the dancer or visual sign "par une présence volante et assoupie de gazes . . . paraît, appelée dans l'air, s'y soutenir" (170). And in that suspense, she does not even dance. She suggests, she writes, becomes, and performs a poem, a poem that upstages she who performs it: "*elle ne danse pas*, suggérant . . . avec une écriture corporelle ce qu'il faudrait des paragraphes en prose dialoguée autant que descriptive, pour exprimer, dans la rédaction: poème dégagé de tout appareil du scribe" (171, emphasis in original). The suspense of this depersonalized body writing is transposed into the verbal text at a variety of levels. In terms of sonority "par une présence volante et assoupie de gazes" seems to lift off with the patter of alliterating *p*'s of "par une présence," gaining further momentum with its series of vibrating fricatives and sibilants in "volante," "presence," and "assoupie de gazes." The clause, however, is then suspended, visually and syntactically, by the fragmentation of the commas that follow: "elle paraît, appelée dans l'air, s'y soutenir." Playing on the mobility inscribed in what Derrida refers to as "incalculable choreographies," Evlyn Gould notes that the suspense created by Mallarmé's "choreographic syntax" multiplies the semantic potential of the text.[24] The reader is forced to hesitate, to choose from among a variety of levitating meanings. Somewhat paradoxically, however, it is the visual halting of the narrative "suite" by visible commas and spaces—graphic effects—that stimulates and simulates the semantic *jeté* of the "dance."[25]

Musing on the "incalculable choreographies" in the passages from these reviews—the constant oscillations Mallarmé proposes as inherent to dance, as well as the insistent shifting between dance and verbal text—leads me to the necessary question: To what end might he aspire in equating poem and dance? As an element in my contention that much of Mallarmé's poetics and his recourse to analogies with arts other than painting can be understood as a dialogue with the tradition of *ut pictura poesis* and, in particular, its biases about poetry's inadequacies, I will here explore how, like music, dance is used in this poet's texts as a power play—a metaphor of metaphor that indexes and bolsters poetry's potential in the interartistic power struggle subtending the painting-poetry analogy. According to Richard Klein, "metaphors of metaphor are figures that allude to their own allusiveness, signify their power of signifying, intend their own intentionality" ("Straight Lines and Arabesques," 64). What might dance as a metaphor of metaphor have to say, or perhaps even *show,* about the figurative potential of writing in Mallarmé's texts?

In his discussions of visual and corporeal signification in the two reviews on dance, Mallarmé uses allusions to visual phenomena to illustrate how he envisions the functioning of words and the mystery of his own art. Grounded in an analogy with visual perception, he insists that words trigger a cascading spectacle of dancing light in the theater of the mind. "Dancing with *des astres*" refers precisely to how such allusions to visual phenomena aspire to co-*mneme*-orate effects of the verbal signifying event that parallel those in dance. Textually staging how his poetic performance may be placed in relation to the visual arts, he thematizes and enacts a movement that is not conventionally associated with verbal representation. He exhibits how the instituting of a synchronic movement systematically overlays the diachronic "suite ordinaire" of the text, enacting the movement he discusses through a series of syntactically and lexically charged pregnant moments. Ironically, it is the putting into practice of this technical analogy with an art whose capacity for movement was considered limited that maximizes yet again the Mallarméan text's potential for movement and multiple meanings—even, perhaps especially, in his writings on dance.

THE "PHOTO" AND THE "GRAPHIC":
THE DANCING FRAME WORKS

Up to this point, I have analyzed Mallarmé's dance reviews as "pretextual" texts. However, it is worthwhile to resituate these pretexts in context. "Ballets," the first review to which I have alluded, is highly critical of the work that it addresses. Although he praises Elena Cornalba, who was in fact the ballerina held in suspense, Mallarmé castigates the spectacle at the Eden theater. He condemns the staging of the ballet as well as the lack of art and animation of the setting. With typically Mallarméan irony, he then mocks the use of stars in the mise-en-scène as borderline sacrilegious: "Les astres, eux-mêmes, lesquels j'ai pour croyance que, rarement, il faut déranger pas sans raisons considérables de méditative gravité . . . je feuillette et j'apprends qu'ils sont de la partie" (*MOC* 2:170). For a poet who associated his ideal poetic with a "complexité stellaire" in which one could read "le hasard infinis [*sic*] des conjonctions" ("Igitur," *MOC* 1:483), it is not surprising that the reduction of the infinite and mysterious potential of pure brilliance to the lowly task of spelling out the name of the star of the show sparks a searing touch of sarcasm: "et l'incohérent manque hautain de signification qui scintille en l'alphabet de la Nuit va consentir à tracer le mot VIVIANE" (*MOC* 2:170). The final denouncements in fact all relate to the failed spatial arrangement, the failed placement of stars with respect to *the* Star. The perfect *cadrage* in the ballet-poem would frame the reflective constellation of the visibly moving corps de ballet and its *étoile.*

In the text on Loïe Fuller, the poet's own light-writing and "choreographic syntax" parallel those of the first essay, but lead us through to a completely different story. Admitting that with respect to this dancer "tout a été dit" (174), Mallarmé is nonetheless poised for the exercise: "L'exercice, comme invention, sans l'emploi, comporte une ivresse d'art et, simultané un accomplissement industriel" (174). *Theoretically speaking* of Loïe Fuller's dance, Mallarmé bestows high praise for the technical, industrial nature of this art and its electricity. His sentences—like the movements of the dancer—appear, in the most literal sense, to enact what he says the dancer performs: a "transition de sonorités aux tissus . . . instituant un lieu" (175–76). The parallel here with the "rien n'aura eu lieu que le lieu," a commandment of Mallarmé's ultimate gamble with the spatial *Un coup de dés* is all the more striking when allied to a materialization of sonorities referenced in the texture of the fabric (*MOC* 1: 384–85). Loïe Fuller, known for her innovative use of electricity to light the moving veils that *were* her scenery, embodies, for Mallarmé, rhythm itself and the site of signification. Allusions to the texture of the text as fabric, typical Mallarméan metaphors for the poetic text, are even more germane here since the dancer, illuminated with these swirling gauzes and described as "radieuse," is presented here as a "figurante qui illustre maint thème giratoire," embodying and enacting a vertiginous anima akin to light: "il faut pour les mouvoir, prismatique . . . le vertige d'une âme comme mise à l'air par un artifice" (*MOC* 2:174–75).

Concluding a verbal exercise that transposes the spatial pirouettes, *tours jetés,* and reflections of his subject, Mallarmé praises a "mobilité chorégraphique" and a stage free of accessory: a "scène libre, au gré de fictions" (176). He further suggests that "la mode," the fashion of the moment, disseminate this miraculous modern art of light; that fashion should "extraire le sens sommaire et l'explication qui en émane et agit sur l'ensemble d'un art" (176). However, in that sentence, he does not designate the art to which he refers. The text, which preaches a study and dissemination of Loïe Fuller's "fusion," and reflection in art,[26] highlights the transposition of such effects in the art that enacts them. In this essay, Mallarmé also textually enacts "maint thème giratoire" (174). Exposing the spatial, his games with commas, spacing, and allusions to light halt the text and reflect among themselves, subverting verbal art's conventional capacity for movement to create an impression of suspension: a dance between multiple meanings and levels of reference.

Clearly, this synchronic movement is meant to analogize the sensorial impact of another art through verbal discourse. However, a close examination of the text raises the issue of whether that art is, in fact, dance. Whereas there are, according to certain critics, no real examples of ekphrasis in Mallarmé's texts—that is, moments where a verbal work of art represents a pictorial one— ekphrastic effects are in reality all-pervasive. Rather than stopping the movement to present a verbal picture, ekphrastic effects seek to simulate aspects of the visual arts and to stimulate a "suspense vibratoire." This movement among a variety of cropped and arranged images is actually an innovative *ut pictura poesis:* pregnant moments in the frames of these texts function as a series of freeze-frames that simultaneously fix and multiply meaning.

As we are moved via graphic and visual effects to Mallarmé's genre of textually initiated movement, another genre of reanimated *ut pictura poesis* shifts the conception of mimesis subtending it: we find a mimesis of the signifying operation, an enactment meant to commemorate an event or a figure of figuration. By tactically playing with synchronic movement in his texts, Mallarmé offensively eschews the standard version of *ut pictura poesis.* "Dancing with stars" not only makes sport with how this movement is embodied in Mallarmé's texts. It signals the significance of stars, constellations, and light in the subject matter of the two illuminating dance reviews cited and the importance of these reviews for Mallarmé's conception of signification and his aesthetic. It will be remembered that *Un coup de dés* not only announces that "rien n'aura eu lieu que le lieu," it also mandates that "rien / n'aura eu lieu / que le lieu / *excepté / peut-être / une constellation*" (*MOC* 1:384–87, emphasis added). Finally, "Dancing with *des astres*" most obviously alludes to the risks involved in Mallarmé's "offensive" poetic games; to how analogies with pictorial representation destabilize the reading process, audaciously revisiting poetic convention, and gambling with public reception. Of course, Mallarmé was conscious of this effect. His response to Marcel Proust's accusations of unintelligibility and obscurity are limpid in his essay "Le mystère dans les lettres": "Si, tout de même, n'inquiétait je ne sais quel miroitement, en dessous, peu séparable de la surface concédée à la rétine,—il attire le soupçon" (*MOC* 2:229).

The destabilizing nature of Mallarmé's texts is explicitly linked in the ekphrastic effects of the previous quotation to a shimmering akin to the scintillation on the surface of the retina. This vibratory suspension—often thematized as proper to dance or even music—is actually imprinted and blueprinted in the visual.[27] It is this offensive movement that animates Mallarmé's work, from early texts such as "Hérodiade" though the dance reviews written near the end of his life. It is also these offensive moves that caused his texts to be caricatured, denied publication, and dismissed as "unintelligible." As Mallarmé ironically laments: "les malins, entre le public, réclamant de couper court, opinent, avec sérieux, que, juste, la teneur est inintelligible" (229).

Dancing with the stars in Mallarmé's light-writing chances more than a mere aesthetic speculation on the capacity for visuality and performativity in verbal art: it pushes the odds to the point of dancing with receptive disaster. But, as I suggest, the best defense might be a good offense. In this case, it is not only that Mallarmé will be remembered as an early theorist of dance, it is that he is able to highlight how supposed properties of various arts are integral to the experience of poetic writing. In this sense, his "Employer des comparaisons prises à tous les arts mais la poésie les résume" ("A Henri de Regnier," *Corr* 2:306) is indicative of more than a fusion of the arts. Indeed, it is doubtless much more literal than heretofore assumed.

CHAPTER 6

Interartistic Frameworks

*Employer des comparaisons prises à tous les arts,
mais la poésie les résume*

DE LA MUSIQUE AVANT TOUTE CHOSE?[1]

MANY CRITICS LOOK UPON the music-literature analogy as the supreme metaphor for symbolist poetry. Texts such as Paul Verlaine's "Art poétique," which places "la musique avant toute chose," and certainly Paul Valéry's portrayal of the symbolists' intention as taking back from music what properly belonged to poetry ("Existence du symbolisme," 700) seem to provide ample support for a host of definitions that characterize symbolism by a preoccupation with musicality. Since critics are quite aware that Valéry was actually paraphrasing Mallarmé in his essay,[2] there exists a conflationary tendency to equate Mallarmé with the symbolist movement and to suggest that in his work the music analogy reigned supreme.[3] While studies of analogies with music are both accurate and useful in the examination of certain aspects of Mallarmé's poetry, approaches that support the omnipotence of music in his work often bypass the contextual aesthetic history of *ut pictura poesis* and the place of the visual in Mallarmé's texts.

> [L]e trésor profond des correspondances, l'accord intime des couleurs,
> le souvenir du rythme antérieur, et la science mystérieuse du Verbe,—
> est requis, et tout entier s'émeut, sous l'action de la rare poésie que

149

> j'invoque, avec un ensemble d'une si merveilleuse justesse que de ses
> jeux combinés résulte la seule lucidité. ("Symphonie littéraire," *MOC*
> 2:282)

Mallarmé's work has in many ways been categorized, explained, and in a sense rewritten in the critical process. Like art criticism, which often determines the value of the art object through verbal commentary on "meaning" or exegesis exterior to the works themselves, Mallarmé criticism has by and large been a process of explaining meaning, rather than a study of process. Consequently, the place and relative importance of music, which became a most obvious point of comparison in Mallarmé's later texts, has been intensely studied. Such a critical phenomenon, however, might actually be attributed to a trap set by a poet who not only practiced the veiling and overlaying of his "armature intellectuelle," but explicitly ascribed the place of such "échafaudages" to the "blancs" ("Sur la philosophie dans la poésie," *MOC* 2:659).

Both Mallarmé's classification with music and his uniqueness have contributed to a sort of critical isolation, a status that until recently tended to decontextualize him from the poets who influenced him most and from the movement in which he began his career, the Parnassians. Although he was later named "chef" of the symbolist school, as we have seen, Mallarmé was an early admirer of highly "visual" writers such as Charles Leconte de Lisle and Théophile Gautier, who, like Baudelaire, was also an art critic. Describing his aspirations for a work in progress in an 1873 letter to Catulle Mendès, Mallarmé stated: "Je chanterai le *Voyant* qui, placé dans ce monde, l'a regardé" (*MOC* 1:766, emphasis in original). This "Voyant," none other than Gautier, Mallarmé portrayed in the same letter as endowed with a "don mystérieux de voir avec les yeux" (37). The resulting poem, "Toast funèbre," refers to Gautier as "Maître" and attributes the greatness of this master's art not to his ear but to his "oeil profond" (*MOC* 1:27, 93).

As noted in chapters 1 and 2, Mallarmé's work developed out of both the romantic and Parnassian trends. The latter, highly visual and characterized by a self-proclaimed association with both the pictorial and the plastic arts, manifests a marked aspiration to iconicity and object status that Mallarmé's work seems to incorporate. Despite Mallarmé's later categorization with the symbolists and a critically oversimplified and idealized conception of "the symbol," Mallarmé's art consistently exhibits a very Parnassian preoccupation with the visual. However, in its intricate examination of the symbolic nature of poetic language, Mallarmé's work loses the strictly descriptive quality characteristic of the Parnassians and instead tends to stage the anatomy of its own signifying process; progressively, his texts explore the role of the visual in written verbal signification.

The fundamental place of the visual, which Mallarmé's poetry seeks both to exploit and to surpass, is grounded in several aesthetic aspirations and techniques shared by and shaping the different artistic movements. By replacing his work within the tradition of the painting–poetry comparison, I have shown that critical endeavors that continue to ascribe Mallarmé's entire aesthetic framework to the music analogy regrettably neglect the importance of the visual arts in his model of verbal signification, as well as the frames of reference to which his "steadfast gaze" and what I call his "photo-graphic" impressions respond. I say "regrettably" because a study of the place of the visual arts in Mallarmé's thought and practice simultaneously clarifies many "aspects" of Mallarmé's allusions and explicit recourse to analogies with music to discuss the place of auditory signification in his work. Ironically perhaps, in Mallarmé's exploration of the functioning of the word as symbol, the painting–poetry analogy takes precedence, not only chronologically, conceptually, and structurally, but in the particular way the painting analogy addresses, informs, and structures Mallarmé's exploitations of interartistic analogy and particularly, "le souvenir du rythme antérieur"and "l'action de la rare poésie" ("Symphonie littéraire," *MOC* 2:282) that he invoked.

THE "ME," THE "I," AND THE "EYE"

Modernity in art is often characterized by a renewed interest in the painting–literature analogy and mimetic capacity and a shift away from the nineteenth-century preoccupation with the music analogy.[4] This preoccupation with music, often equated with aspirations to the affective, and especially the effusions of the romantic *moi,* does not, however, characterize Mallarmé's work or his allusions to music. Even obvious invocations of the music analogy to allude to movement in Mallarmé's texts, and the theoretical and practical insistence on music's basic affinity with verbal art—its phonic dimension and "mysterious" capacity to trigger impressions—cannot be divorced from the historical traditions of *ut pictura poesis* and mimesis. Furthermore, although French criticism and literature of the nineteenth century certainly invoked the music analogy, the painting–literature analogy was fundamental, not marginal.

In criticism by writers throughout the century such as Stendhal, Gautier, Baudelaire, and Zola, not to mention works on the philosophy of art such as the widely read texts of Charles Blanc and Hippolyte Taine, the painting–literature analogy remained a constant. Moreover, in French literature of the period, even allusions to music in the representation of the poetic persona, or poetic subjectivity, respond to the aesthetic theorization of the painting–literature analogy and the questions of specularity, subjectivity, and objectivity that the comparison poses. Mallarmé's poetics is much more an affair of the "eye" and the "I" and a rethinking of mimetic capacity than it is of "expressivity" or the self.

In chapter 3 I proposed that Mallarmé's conception of psychic and textual image production can be glimpsed in his description of Igitur's encounter with his self as afterimage in the mirror. Although Mallarmé's mirrors aspire to seize subjective process and its breakdown in order to stage the textual reinstitution of that action, such an endeavor can hardly be described as an effort to express subjectivity; on the contrary, it attempts to objectify the latter. The reflection Mallarmé explores in that photo-graphic mirror, and more precisely, in the mirror of the text, can once again be seen as similar to that of a photographic image, only this time in the sense that both fix a reflection and *an effect* of what Carol Armstrong describes as "an authorless image made by the action of light and the responding activity of the eye rather than the hand or human generation" ("Reflections on the Mirror," 121).

Mallarmé considered the absolute distinction between the inner consciousness of the artist, the representation in the work, and the presentation of the work to be one of the major "trouvailles" of his time. He states this explicitly in a congratulatory letter to Emile Verhaeren in 1888: "Là je vous félicite d'un sens spécial. Ou plutôt l'ouvrier disparaît (ce qui est absolument la trouvaille contemporaine) et le vers agite un sentiment avec ses sursauts" (*MOC* 1:798). Similarly, Mallarmé's description of the frame of consciousness to which Manet aspired when creating could not be characterized as an "expression of the self" or "expressivity." While Mallarmé and the impressionists attempted to explore, integrate, and initiate subjective and optical process in representation, the distinction between the text, the agent of its production, and its reception remains absolute.

As I proposed in chapters 1 and 2, much of the crisis of literature that Mallarmé announced revolves around a rethinking of manner, medium, and convention. Mallarmé specifically stated that at such moments of crisis art returns to its "sources" to modernize them. Indeed, his texts reveal themselves as taking part in a reconception and rethinking of referentiality and the mirroring function as the source of art. The overwhelming evidence of Mallarmé's obsession with mirrors, windows, and a variety of frames and reflectors indicates more than the writer's persistent preoccupation with this major aesthetic frame of reference for Western art; his constant staging of the representation problem serves to make the reader conscious of the traditional aesthetic assumptions to which such images are bound. This exhibitionism in Mallarmé's work can be seen as one of the main traits of the late nineteenth-century reconceptualization of mimesis, a move toward an objectification of the subjective and of the signifying process. To this end, art forms of the latter half of the nineteenth century, and Mallarmé's in particular, often relied on interartistic crossover and the application of different epistemological systems to the production of art.

Chapter 3 demonstrated that the self projected in Igitur's mirror is explored as both the subject and object of a gaze that is visual (the mirror), auditory (the rhythmic heartbeat), and verbal (the mirror of the text). It was also noted that Mallarmé's texts often compared the "nature of the impression" that precedes synthetic thought to light's action on the retina, to its action on darkness, and to the movement of the symphony. Both the phonic aspect of music and the visual function of painting are clearly points of comparison for Mallarmé's verbal art and his conception of its symbolic functioning. The effort to study the effects of sensations on the mind and then to reproduce the effect in the text can, in both cases, be seen as attempts to index varying levels of diagrammatic, imagistic, and metaphoric iconicity in the verbal text. Such aspirations, and the use of interartistic analogy to amplify symbolic process, can be seen as responses to the history of painting–poetry comparison.

STAGING THE "PHOTO" AND THE "GRAPHIC":
UN SPECTACLE D'ENCHANTEMENT MODERNE[5]

Mallarmé's use of analogy explored, experimented, and exploited the poetic possibilities of all the disciplines. His attempts to purify his poetic language and his aspirations toward a perfection of form manifest a hypercognizance of aesthetic strategy, a poetic technology of effect. And although his early appropriations of the nomenclature and images of musical instruments are often used to promote the commonplace equation of Mallarmé's symbolism with the musical, one would be hard-pressed to compare their number to his use of visual-arts terminology and the deployment of allusions to light, color, mirrors, reflection, and shadows. In fact, not only are his early interdisciplinary mobilizations of musical nomenclature paralleled before 1885 by semantic items referring to the *toiles,* paintings, tableaus, mirrors, windows, and frames that the text thematizes, but on careful scrutiny, one often finds that even the instruments Mallarmé does exploit in his earlier works published in *Le Parnasse contemporain* (1866) are often rare and archaic instruments suggestive of something mythical that is no longer there, obsolete and only a metaphor for some other kind of music that this poetry is not.

The complete title of the original version of the following occasional piece addressed to Cécile Brunet was "Sainte Cécile jouant sur l'aile d'un chérubin"; it was written in 1865 for her name day. The 1883 poem "Sainte" (*MOC* 1:26, 83, 114), a rewrite of "Sainte Cécile," at once gives a good indication of Mallarmé's evolution as regards his use of the musical analogy and a clear indication of the painting analogy's significance in his work.

SAINTE

A la fenêtre recélant

Le santal vieux qui se dédore

De sa viole étincelant

Jadis avec flûte ou mandore,

Est la Sainte pâle, étalant

Le livre vieux qui se déplie

Du Magnificat ruisselant

Jadis selon vêpre et complie:

A ce vitrage d'ostensoir

Que frôle une harpe par l'Ange

Formée avec son vol du soir

Pour la délicate phalange

Du doigt, que, sans le vieux santal

Ni le vieux livre, elle balance

Sur le plumage instrumental,

Musicienne du silence.

As Charles Mauron has shown, M. Brunet, "poète provençal, était artisan en vitraux," and Cécile Brunet's patronymic saint implies music and the lyrical

(*Mallarmé par lui-même,* 180). One immediately sees the coincidence of both interartistic analogies in the circumstantial situation—which is, however, erased from the poem. The insistence on the window at which the "Sainte" is situated evokes the metaphor with the *vitrail,* or the stained-glass window, which will become the reigning metaphor of the poem itself. As the musical instruments and the musical analogy progressively disappear, the window and its relation to the *vitrail* are placed in the foreground, the two forming a metaphor of the poem as a process that frames and reflects the creative space.

If one regards the poem itself as a "vitrage," one sees how the entire work becomes "ce vitrage d'ostensoir," a pictorial ornament containing a sacred host: the "musique de la parole." But what is this "music of the word," if not a metaphor of metaphor that serves to index the activity of the language in which it is expressed? Indeed, this music referred to itself undergoes a transubstantiation (note the present participles) in becoming poetic signification—a music of silence that reflects on the movement of signification. The word "vitrage," on the other hand, suggests not only an ensemble of windowpanes but a translucent curtain that elliptically implies the window frame that encloses the space. In this sense both the poem's thematization of poetry and the painting–literature analogy are accentuated—as is the role of the poet-saint, "à la fenêtre, à ce vitrage."

The development of the poem, commencing with a sort of material negation of the instruments and of the *Magnificat,* corresponds to a metamorphosis into the new music by the finger of the Saint—"musicienne du silence"—and, by extension, the hand of the poet. One is left with a silent "vitrage," a pictorial poem dramatizing the representation and framing it in a multiartistic work that indexes images of disappearing musical instruments.

A similar coincidence of archaic instruments, protective glass "vitre," and the hand of the poet is found in "Le démon de l'analogie" (*MOC* 1:416–18). This prose poem ends when the narrator notices his hand's reflection in a "vitrine," behind which he sees outmoded instruments and antiques. His hand is the only object reflected in the "vitre," as the mirror of his fantasy becomes reality. L. J. Austin notes that in his "Préface" for Berthe Morisot, Mallarmé suggests an analogy between the "vitre protectrice" of the canvas and that of the painter's art ("Mallarmé Critique d'Art," 157–58). When Mallarmé's constant association of hands ("griffes," "onyx," "doigts," "ongles"), wings ("ailes," "plumage"), outdated instruments, windows,[6] mirrors, frames, and "vitres" allude to the other arts, they serve to index a particular facet of the literary text. Such allusions are invoked to reinforce the potential and effect of the poem's commentary on its own genre. Given this self-reflexivity, the analogy between the protective "vitre" and the "vitre" of the painter's art can be seen as applying to the "vitre" of poetic language where, as in music, "à travers des voiles feints . . . un sujet se dégage" ("Le mystère dans les lettres," *MOC* 2:231). The "vitrage" of "Sainte" could thus be seen as both "vitre" and "voile": "Toute maîtrise jette le froid: ou la poudre fragile du coloris se défend par une vitre, divination pour certains" ("Berthe Morisot," *MOC* 2:149). The "voile" is, in this sense, an allusion to the material signifier.

STAGING WORDS, SOUNDING LIGHT

Mallarmé performs his own transformation of the effect of visual imagery verbally—with the material medium of the written word. The reaction sought is a performative one that receives, hesitates, retraces, and provokes an actual process; the creation of this meaning is a newly created "spectacle d'enchantement moderne" (*MOC* 2:151). The use of the word "spectacle" here to evoke the theatrical metaphor, etymologically and conventionally suggests both specular processes and action. "Enchantement" evokes enchantment with the work as it engages the participant, and it insists upon the repetitive dimensions of the *chant* as the idea of an incantation.

Another example of Mallarmé's dense use of interartistic analogy is to be found in "Hérodiade" (*MOC* 1:17–22, 85–89). Accurately stressing the frequency of allusions to both painting and music in Mallarmé's correspondences, Austin states:

> The "musical overture" to *Hérodiade* is also described in pictorial terms. Mallarmé claims that the dialogue between Hérodiade and the Nurse is to the overture what an *image d'Epinal* is to a canvas by Leonardo da Vinci. Elsewhere he evokes all the complex conditions that must be fulfilled if his ideal is to be realized, and once again music and poetry are invoked on equal terms. ("Mallarmé on Music and Letters," 25)

The fact of the matter is that while terms such as "Prélude" and "Ouverture" appear in the conception of the original work, the only segment of the dramatic poem that was published during the author's life was the section envisioned as "Scène." Furthermore, even the "Ouverture ancienne," a highly pictorial section that was drafted as part of the unfinished work, is not marked by allusions to music or musical terms, but by the use of unexpected juxtapositions and devisualized games with triggers of light ("ors nus," "caprice / Solitaire d'aurore au vain plumage noir"); reflectants and mirrors ("Du bassin, aboli, qui mire les alarmes," "le cygne / Inoubliable: l'eau reflète l'abandon"; "désolée / Par le diamant pur de quelque étoile"); and frames ("La chambre singulière en un cadre") ("Ouverture," *MOC* 1:137–39). These games of light and reflection are further developed in "Scène," a section that dramatically thematizes Hérodiade's self-specularization as her pictorial image is seized and framed in the mirror. The performative action of the text in this segment lies less in the fact of the dialogue than in the semantic arrangement. The following passage, for example, paradoxically insists upon stasis through a system of internally repetitive semantic reflectors. The images insist on solidity, sterility, absence, and illusion while highlighting the process of perception itself.

H.

Assez! Tiens devant moi ce *miroir.*

O miroir!

Eau froide par l'ennui dans ton *cadre* gelée

Que de fois et pendant des heures, désolée

Des *songes* et cherchant mes *souvenirs* qui sont

Comme des feuilles sous ta *glace* au trou profond,

Je m'apparus en toi comme une ombre lointaine,

Mais, horreur! des soirs, dans ta sévère *fontaine,*

J'ai de mon *rêve* épars connu la nudité!

(*MOC* 1:19, emphasis added)

The aspiration to semantic flashing of visual effect functions to structure a response in the same way as the incantatory games of sonority and repetition. In Mallarmé's terms, these techniques, which multiply poetic dimension and effect, serve to "abolish" a good deal of the inevitable "hasard" of reception.

Mallarmé often uses the nomenclature and techniques of the visual arts in a seemingly nonvisual medium to subvert the contingent drawbacks of visual imagery as a copy of reality and to reject the narrative verisimilitude of temporality usually associated with descriptive poetry. Verbal art thus acquires and exploits visuality by triggering processes conventionally associated with visual *enargeia.* Such interartistic analogies serve to supplement and reinforce verbal art's own possibilities of reenacting a "new" reality and thereby attaining object status.

Expressed through a thematization of self-specularity and a poetic language exploiting games of reflection, light, and semantic mirrors, the "spectacle" is evoked in "Hérodiade." The theatrical analogy, suggesting both internal spectacle and external action, finds its place in Mallarmé's interdisciplinary aesthetics as it does in the Faune's "need" for theatricality and Igitur's crisis of narcissism. These works, first conceived in the 1860s, are all intellectually and practically preoccupied with specularity, cognition, and image theory; they are marked by an effort to objectify the subjective in a highly static representational frame, yet they aspire to an internally performative art that displays the action of signification and explores its possibilities—sonority being one of them.

EMPLOYER DES COMPARAISONS PRISES À TOUS LES ARTS,
MAIS LA POÉSIE LES RÉSUME[7]

Mallarmé's interdisciplinary analogies with painting, music, dance, and the theater are, in fact, all innovative exploitations appropriated to achieve literature's pretensions not only to theatricality and musicality, but the state of a "supreme art," a poetic language not merely capable of assimilating the attributes and dimensions of all the other disciplines through poetic technique, but one endowed with them.

As we have seen, early on Mallarmé praised music's mystery and promoted a comparable use of the hieroglyphic status of musical and poetic signs. As Austin notes:

> In strong reaction against the democratic, not to say demagogic, poetry of Victor Hugo, he was already seeking to lay the foundations of an aristocratic poetry, intelligible to the initiate alone. If he appeals to Music it is merely because music possesses its own language, its own form of notation, there is no suggestion here that poetry is music's debtor or creditor. ("Music and Letters," 24)

Mallarmé envied music's form of notation and invoked the analogy in his early prose comparisons as a way of distinguishing both music and writing from the spoken word. As demonstrated in chapter 2, the musical analogy provided a figure to facilitate poetry's discussions, evaluations, and examinations of itself. It served to reinforce certain poetic effects to which his work aspired; through analogical correspondence he reminded the reader of what to experience.

In Mallarmé's earlier works and letters, the theme of music was exploited as an example of what poetry is and exceeds. And while in his early essay "Hérésies artistiques" (*MOC* 2:360–64) Mallarmé envied music's mysterious signs and proposed the exploitation of certain compositional techniques, especially those of rhythm, surprise, and emotive movement, in "Le mystère dans les lettres" (1896), we saw how these techniques were intended to be actualized:

> On peut, du reste, commencer d'un éclat triomphal trop brusque pour durer; invitant que se groupe, en retards, libérés par l'écho, la surprise.
>
> L'inverse: sont, en un reploiement noir soucieux d'attester l'état d'esprit sur un point, foulés et épaissis des doutes pour que sorte une splendeur définitive simple. (*MOC* 2:232)

The compositional techniques to suggest movement obviously invoke music. But the stylistic suggestions concentrate on sentence structure and propose that the effect to be achieved should parallel the pictorial technique of chiaroscuro. The musical analogy, mobilized to reassert the importance of an animated evocation in writing, is nevertheless articulated through an analogy with visual technique.

Mallarmé's later comparisons with music, like those with dance, facilitated his discussions of representation; they furnished a rhetorical tool to evoke the movement that goes on in the "blancs" in which perception and signification occur. By demonstrating literature's potential for representing and reenacting process, Mallarmé brings literature closer to being an art that creates a reality rather than an imitation of one. Such comparisons with music are deployed, as was pictorial technique, to reinforce poetic language's capacity to exceed transparent mimetic representation.

In his later essays, although music was invoked in the name of mystery, the analogy with music was not exploited in the name of pure obscurity—or pure poetry. Addressing Valéry's paraphrase of Mallarmé's "reprendre notre bien," Austin refutes the literary commonplace that states that: "the stolen property in question is the sound of words, and that Mallarmé's intention was to group together words devoid of any logical or grammatical coherence, hoping that they would thereby produce similar effects to those of music" ("Music and Letters," 24). Severely critiquing Gustave Lanson's popularization of this definition of "poésie pure," Austin asserts that this was

> a complete travesty of Mallarmé's real intentions. For while he began by envying Music its mystery, he ended by asserting repeatedly that Poetry is superior to Music precisely because it is intelligible, because it has a discursive meaning; and while his use of language was

> undoubtedly highly original, he always insisted that syntax is the guar-
> antee of poetic intelligibility. (22)

Furthermore, due to the relatively sparse study of Mallarmé's art criticism, it has not been noted that a variant of the famous "reprendre notre bien," so often used to insist upon the importance of music for Mallarmé's aesthetic thought, was also applied to nature in his 1876 article on Manet: "I have taken from it only that which properly belongs to my art" (*MOC* 2:470).

Austin's reading of Mallarmé's intention is borne out in "Le mystère dans les lettres," where Mallarmé attempts to claim music's "mystery" for poetry, yet never reduces his aesthetic intentions to a lack of meaning. This is true as well in "La musique et les lettres," Mallarmé's 1894 Oxford and Cambridge lecture (published in 1895). In this essay we see a gradual movement toward clarity of meaning through contrast. As in "Le mystère dans les lettres," where Mallarmé declared that music has learned from nature and from the heavens her alternatives of light and shade, the effects of movement, associated with music and to be exploited in poetry, are actually achieved through *visual,* impressionistic effects of chiaroscuro. The musical effects discussed are verbally achieved through pictorial allusion:

> une *réminiscence* de l'orchestre; où succède à des rentrées en *l'ombre,*
> après *un remous soucieux,* tout à coup l'éruptif multiple sursautement de
> la *clarté,* comme les proches *irradiations d'un lever de jour.* (*MOC*
> 2:68–69, emphasis added)

Another well-inked path linking Mallarmé and music is found in critical commentary of the poet's text on Wagner. However, the apparent primacy of music in "Richard Wagner: Rêverie d'un poète français," only serves to veil and reflect a deeper aesthetic issue (*MOC* 2:153–59). In this text on Wagner, as in "Le mystère dans les lettres" and "La musique et les lettres," Mallarmé is involved in an aesthetic debate that decenters conventional mimesis and centers on movement.

Mallarmé's essay on Wagner, published in August 1885, is a text admittedly inspired by music, and apparently by Wagner's music. The title does not, however, mention music, musicality, or composition. Wagner becomes little more than a pretext for this "rêverie," described by Mallarmé as "moitié article, moitié poëme en prose" (*MOC* 2:1622). Mallarmé never cites Wagner's work in particular, and though he takes up certain Wagnerian themes, Wagner is curiously absent except as a challenge to poets and a commentary on contemporary art. It is, in fact, writing and its theater which prevail. The same phenomenon is apparent in the poem "Hommage" (*MOC* 1:39, 99). In this poem, dedicated to Wagner, the theme of poetry is accentuated much more than that of music and, significantly, it begins with "Le silence."

Unlike Baudelaire, who described himself in a letter to Wagner as "vaincu" (*BOC* 2:1452), Mallarmé was never willing to concede poetry's position to music. Mallarmé's essay on Wagner opens by addressing the issue of verisimilitude. While he clearly identifies with Wagner's fusion of the arts and praises his transformation of the conventional mimetic theater, in the essay, as in his art criticism, Mallarmé is exploiting the opportunity to expound the aesthetic principles of a "new" art.

Given Mallarmé's aesthetic identifications with Manet, Degas, Whistler, and other impressionists, as well as his participation in several public aesthetic debates, one could regard his engagement in the Wagner debate as being less based on an admiration of music's possibilities than on the exploitation of some very general aesthetic premises that parallel those of the impressionists. Mallarmé's praise of the impressionists' depersonalization parallels his own earlier preoccupations and his aspiration to objectify the subjective and the creative process. Furthermore, Mallarmé's praise of Wagner's theater, like his defense of the impressionists, crystallizes around both arts' rejection of conventional verisimilitude and their ability to create a new reality at the moment of their reception. As in "The Impressionists and Edouard Manet," where he praised the "new" art for creating the impression of an animated vision taking place "just when the spectator beholds the represented subject" (*MOC* 2:456), Mallarmé is establishing and dictating the framework of his own aesthetic, an aesthetic that seeks to represent, accentuate, and reenact the very same raw processes of perception that preoccupied him in his "conte dramatique," "Igitur."

As Mallarmé's use of condensation and ellipsis became more developed, both his analogies with visual technique and his allusions to music became more refined. Indexing effects of both arts to generate psychic movement through visual and auditory stimulation, Mallarmé leaned toward highly static texts that internally stimulated unconscious movement through matrices of flashing and fragmented images, semantic cross-referencing, and games of sonority. Mallarmé's music, then, functioned much as his pictorial cross-referencing and reflectors did: to insist upon the material presence of related signifiers within the signifying chain. As in "Ses purs ongles," where the light of the "lampadophore" and the stars flash back and forth among the black of onyx and midnight, the sounds of words are used to reflect among themselves within the textual frame. The text activates and then silences and erases both Echo and Narcissus. In the poem, his multilayered approach to *cadrage* is apparent not only in the selection and reflection of specific interrelated images to focus upon, but in the thematization of reflection, as the window and the room are mirrored and fixed by the "cadre" (*MOC* 1: 37, 98). The epitome of this technology and multiplication of sensory effect is, of course, found later in his final text, *Un coup de dés* (*MOC* 1:365–407).

In Mallarmé's aesthetic, neither the music analogy nor the painting analogy can justifiably be considered the mimetic mirror of the poet's inner substance. His exploitation of these interdisciplinary analogies is, on the contrary, the result of a well of new ideas redefining the mimetic. What began as a subjective response to the menace of photographic realism and its implications for mimesis became an objectification of the very concepts artists were exploiting to subvert conventional mimesis. The rejections of conventional pictorial mimesis in painting, and in poetics, are at once a reaction against the effects of the photograph and an incorporation of the knowledge acquired by the new medium and technological developments in the visual. This reinterrogation of mimesis eventually provided the impetus to impressionistic landscapes and the scientific justification for what can be called "subjectivity objectified."

In the final analysis, Mallarmé's invocations of music can be seen as an analogy for the movement inherent in perception itself, as an effort to represent objectively an observed psychic and specular state.

> Avec véracité, qu'est-ce, les Lettres, que cette mentale poursuite, menée, en tant que le discours, afin de définir ou de faire, à l'égard de soi-même, preuve que le spectacle répond à une imaginative compréhension, il est vrai, dans l'espoir de s'y mirer. ("La musique et les lettres," *MOC* 2:68)

Mallarmé's reinterrogation of art's mimetic capacity, his keen awareness of semiotic and specular functioning, and the interdisciplinary parallels and analogies he exploits to achieve his "depersonalized" and "objective" poetic language reactivate and recenter the painting analogy's reality claim from within the poetic "frame." "The secret . . . is found in an absolutely new science . . . the manner of cutting down" ("The Impressionists and Edouard Manet," *MOC* 2:458). No longer grounded solely in narrative development, Mallarmé's kinetic mimesis involves a diagrammatic iconicity initiated through ekphrastic effects. His photo-graphic *cadrage* synchronically creates an afterimage-like "suspens vibratoire" that overlays the text's diachronic progression. As we reconsider the dissimulated frameworks of a theorist who announced that "l'armature intellectuelle du poème se dissimule et tient—a lieu—dans l'espace qui isole les strophes et parmi les blancs du papier," it not at all surprising that while Mallarmé openly compared poetry to music and dance, he rarely explicitly compared poetry and the pictorial arts—"significatif silence" ("Sur la philosophie," *MOC* 2:659). Indeed. For a poet who placed such stock in the material trace and vibratory dimensions of the word and the text; for a critic, who stated that "il faut toujours couper le commencement et la fin de ce qu'on écrit ("A Cazalis," *MOC* 1:657), that there can be no doubt that for Mallarmé's aesthetic frameworks the significance of this photo-graphic *cadrage* is anything but marginal. "Employer des comparaisons prises à tous les arts, mais la poésie les résume"?

Without doubt. The precept elucidates an allusive poetics whose most distinguishing feature is the way in which it aspires to commemorate its own process and performativity. It might, additionally, and very quietly, celebrate a lucid gaze that reconceived time and movement in verbal art; the work of a poet who lived and textually died "selon un pacte avec la Beauté," a beauty whose "transformations" the visionary charged himself to *see,* in all its brilliance ("Etalages," *MOC* 2:223).

Exposing Change

Quotidian frameworks and developing movements

STÉPHANE MALLARMÉ'S lucid analyses of the transformations of his age are now earning the scholarly recognition that they deserve. The rupture he announced— "une exquise crise, fondamentale"—is *monnaie courante*. In theory and in deed, the scintillating textual displays and appraisals of this once-marginalized poet-critic continue to incite speculation and to accrue literary and market value on a global scale. The practices of this avant-garde journalist whose writings revolutionized "la guerre des petites revues" and subsequently, theoretical engagements of thinkers from Valéry and Lacan to Kristeva, Derrida, and Deleuze are now maturing as a brilliant speculative investment in contemporary commerce and the ambient quotidian of his era.[1]

Throughout this study, I have focused on the "displays" of this paradoxical chronicler of verse, fashion, journalism, and modernity, herald of the "new" art and the "new laws" of light and air, tracing the poet's masterful assimilations of the daily and the modern as well as his innovative reenvisioning of conventions of time, space, and mimesis. This coda recapitulates the ways in which Mallarmé's engagements with the history of art, consumer culture, and technology exhibit a cunning take on the newly emerging markets he wished to play, a take that appears to underwrite what I have termed the "photo-graphic" logic of his practice and a pragmatic aesthetic that thematizes and exposes *actualité* as the product of carefully calculated cultural production.

Mallarmé's ruminations on the ups and downs of the world of commerce, transformative markets, and the play of publicity might seem at odds with the slow-to-dissipate ivory-tower image that he so productively cultivated. Still, recent criticism and the preceding chapters irrevocably alter any stable vision of the disengaged poet, oblivious of the modernization of contemporary life and literature. Moreover, for readers worldwide, Bertrand Marchal's meticulously prepared 2003 second volume of Mallarmé's *Oeuvres complètes* has radically reframed the poet's production in relation to the press. It is no longer possible to dismiss Mallarmé's engagement with the world around him, nor can we overlook his take on the writer's market as evinced by his canny poetic articulations of the daily.

One case in point is the group of articles that Mallarmé wrote to document the London Annual International Exhibitions (1871–1872). Framed as letters to the editor, these brief circumstantial pieces herald the pageant of luxury wares he would later display in the 1874 *La dernière mode* and much of his production *à venir*, including many of the *Divagations* and most certainly the ingenious 1894 "Etalages."[2] The articles indicate the effects of the latest fashions and modes in industrial literature. In fact, these journalistic texts of the 1870s crystallize Mallarmé's post-"Igitur" engagement with the photo-graphic model of image production and his reorientation of figurative language as a fusion of modern artistic practice and context.

Until recently dismissed as part of Mallarmé's "besogne," a term the poet applied to jobs sought for financial purposes, many of Mallarmé's journalistic and occasional texts attest to his obvious cognizance of what is at stake aesthetically in his age. As early as 1871 he is clearly conscious of the politics at play when an event like the London Exhibition summons up issues such as the hierarchical status of the fine versus the industrial arts, the aesthetic versus the commercial, and international competition for cultural and industrial superiority. When viewed as what they are—lucid and often explicit expositions on the realities of demographic and economic change that might produce such "besogne"— these texts of the 1870s provide a window onto much of the innovative direction that Mallarmé's writing would later take. The poet-chronicler-cultural correspondent quite literally writes himself into the history of representation and consumer culture.

Engaging with political history and the history of the press, developments in transport, and internationalization, these texts allude to the rise of mass commerce and situate the vogue for international exhibitions. Their interest for me is less in their context than in how they expose the very act of representing history as epoch-relevant and epoch-making. Brief and playful journalistic explorations of contemporary aesthetics, they emblematize how a poetics of modern journalism displays the commerce of narrative and narratives of the modern as both product and inventory of their times.

The 1871 and 1872 pieces self-consciously exhibit a complex historical, theoretical, and poetic endeavor that reappraises and reinvests the luxury item with renewed and justified force. They also sound and reendow the figure of the writer with valorized currency in the new market. In effect, Mallarmé's discerning appropriation and appreciation of the dominant discourses of modernity—the influence of the moment—articulates how the power of verbal figurations of history may transform histories of representation. The poet-critic situates the work of the exhibiters, the products on display, and the exhibition itself as historically relevant because "modern," that is, as responding to changing commercial and increasingly industrializing cultures: "Nos exposants ne s'étonneront pas de notre solicitude pour leur tentative—vraiment celle de l'âge moderne tout entier—d'une fusion de l'art et de l'industrie" ("Première lettre," *MOC* 2:366).

As chronicles, historical documents, or *fait divers* that engage with the formation of social values, these documents acknowledge that they are indebted to the rise of consumer culture and, more significantly, to the commodification of events. Taking issue with what is worthy of modern critical appreciation in the production of culture, Mallarmé carefully elucidates why certain pieces should accrue value: "Les trouvailles sont rares par ce temps et valent qu'on les remarque" (367). It is precisely the novelty associated with the vital turnover of merchandise intrinsic to journalistic and avant-garde display that is deemed worthy. The use of the term "trouvaille" will be echoed in his 1876 article on the impressionists and Manet, where he cites the "trouvaille" of cropping or "cutting off," referring to the function of the frame and more generally to a new perspective on choice. It also evokes his comments on the "trouvaille" of the disappearance of the modern worker-poet ("A Verhaeren," *MOC* 1:798) and immediacy ("A Vielé-Griffin," *MOC* 1:799). Together, these "finds" articulate a reframing of mimesis. They promote the exhibition of a new *ut pictura poesis* enacted and informed by a visually encoded epistemology that underwrites the performative properties and the specular aspect of representation itself.

Portraying his "investigation" of the 1871 Exhibition as knowingly and justifiably "réduite à un regard usuel promené sur les objets de nécessité journalière" ("Deuxième lettre," *MOC* 2:369), Mallarmé intimates that his own "regard" is just as indispensable as the quotidian objects to which he refers. While this "regard" may indeed be tailored to the daily medium in which the piece was published, "usuel" takes on more meaning: rather that referring to the banal, Mallarmé invokes and actualizes "utility." In a stunning "appropriation de la structure, limpide, aux primitives foudres da la logique" ("Le mystère dans les lettres," *MOC* 2:232–33), Mallarmé intricately links an aesthetic interrogation of the "regard usuel" and the necessities of the times to the light so often associated with the modern illumination of impressionist art, to the spectacular displays of daily life, as well as to cognitive processing, knowledge, and the "heures retentissantes" ("Deuxième lettre," 369), the narrative time that marked his explorations of verbal image production and perception in the experimental text "Igitur."

As he would in his later essays on the impressionists and Manet, in *La dernière mode* and in the writings published in the later collection *Divagations,* Mallarmé positions himself in the texts from 1871 and 1872 as a chronicler of change. He corresponds as he would later say the poet lives, "selon un pacte avec la Beauté qu'il se chargea d'apercevoir de son nécessaire et compréhensif regard, et dont il connaît les transformations" ("Etalages," *MOC* 2:223). The degree to which the poet-critic is conscious of his endeavor as aesthetic opportunist and chronicler of his times, of the transformations of beauty, and of the market is evinced in the closing of the second letter from the 1871 exhibition. Even for regular readers of Mallarmé, the tone, lexical items, themes, and particularly the pseudonymic play of the following passage could easily have come from *La dernière mode,* were the letters not written three years before the inception of that ephemeral fashion magazine.

> Je suis heureux, Monsieur le rédacteur en chef, que vous m'ayez donné, à l'intention de vos lectrices, l'occasion de répandre, sur ce luxe de soieries et de dentelles déployées, l'écrin de nos bijoux exposés. C'est réunir, sous l'admiration d'un même regard, deux séductions spéciales que le monde, dans nos rues comme dans les allées de l'Exposition, envie traditionnellement au commerce parisien. L.-S. Price (*MOC* 2:372)

Mallarmé's text displays its own active appreciation of the periodical press. In a fashion that goes beyond mere amusement, Mallarmé consciously speculates on the verbal production of the text itself as a "piece." His clever signature, an anglicized pseudonym, is no doubt a measure of the degree to which Mallarmé commodifies the transformations in consumer culture and what they may mean to his modern art. The 1871 exposition was among the first to exhibit objects with prices on them. This is akin to the marketing innovations of the *grand magasins,* which also began to display fixed prices.[3] Further, his comments on the display of the new French culture of luxury and its "fusion de l'art et de l'industrie" ("Première lettre," 366) extend to his own journalistic pieces. He frames his writing about luxury commodities at the exhibition not just as cultural news, but as precious literary merchandise that is itself a show-cased jewel ("l'écrin de nos bijoux exposés"). Finally, by signing not as Mallarmé or Stéphane or Stéphane Mallarmé, but as "Price," he literally puts a price tag on his piece.

In the third and final letter on the 1871 exposition Mallarmé extends a double invitation to the display of modern life and, more specifically, to contemporary Parisian exhibition:

> Cette monographie exacte de la faïence moderne . . . finie dans la galerie d'une maison parisienne, j'invite le lecteur, à qui j'ai donné, d'une façon sommaire, les indications désirables, à regarder un instant nos étoffes et nos tapisseries. ("Troisième lettre," 376)

Beckoning the reader-consumer to examine fabric and the fabrication of daily, modern life, the passages on "étoffes" and "tapisseries" call up *La dernière mode* and a host of texts that have been referred to as the poet's *Propos sur la poésie*. They also strike resonances with "L'action restreinte," where the poet links the fabrication of the luxury text to display and inventory: "Ce pli de sombre dentelle, qui retient l'infini . . . assemble des entrelacs distants où dort un luxe à inventorier . . . et présenter" (*MOC* 2:215).

Mallarmé closes the final 1871 letter with "Nous songeâmes simplement, il vous en souvient, à noter . . . les transformations heureuses ou les hésitations de cet insaisissable esprit qui préside à la fabrication du décor familier de notre existence quotidienne" (379). He "notes" the verbal fabrication of the "décor familier" of the expositions discussed in these writings as refiguring something he calls "notre existence quotidienne." While he diplomatically evokes complicity via the "notre" of "notre existence quotidienne," there is no indication that he is not delicately calling up a royal "we" and thus, the role of the writer: the inscription of his own quotidian existence and his role in the daily.

In fact, Mallarmé's 1871 and 1872 articles on the London Exhibition articulate a new genre of writing and a new species of writer. He self-consciously exposes—in the press—changes in merchandising, modern readerships, consumption, poetry, and journalism. Extrapolating and rarely straying from the principles of image production and conception explored in the dossier for "Igitur" and later articulated in "Crise de vers," the 1871–1872 pieces also foresee his speculative processes of the 1880s and the 1890s. In his "Bibliographie" for the *Divagations,* published more than twenty years after the 1871–1872 articles, Mallarmé explained how the arrangement he adopted for the volume's disposition—its graphic choices—found synergy with those of the periodical press:

> Raison des intervalles, ou blancs—que le long article ordinaire de
> revue, ou remplissage, indique, forcement, à l'oeil . . . pourquoi ne pas
> le restreindre à ces fragments obligatoires où miroita le sujet, puis sim-
> plement remplacer, par l'ingénuité du papier, les transitions quelcon-
> ques? (*MOC* 2:226)

Explicitly commenting on the epoch-transforming ingenuity and impact of
the newspaper, the 1896 "Bibliographie" recalls the poet's discussion of the
integral mystery of French letters and reading: "Si, tout de même, n'inquiétait
je ne sais quel miroitement, en dessous, peu séparable de la surface concédée à
la rétine" ("Le mystère dans les lettres," *MOC* 2:229). It also corresponds to
how he relates verbal arrangements—in both the press and the book—to the
ekphrastic displays of his photo-graphic "poème critique":

> Les cassures du texte, on se tranquilisera, observent de concorder, avec
> sens et n'inscrivent d'espace nu que jusqu'à leurs points d'illumination:
> une forme, peut-être, en sort, actuelle, permettant, à qui fut longtemps
> le poème en prose et notre recherche, d'aboutir, en tant, si l'on joint
> mieux les mots, que poème critique. ("Bibliographie," *MOC*
> 2:276–77)

These comments on the production of the late 1890s *Divagations* articulate
how Mallarmé's "traitement de l'écrit" and the use of space—"les blancs"—
visibly reenact his explorations of image production and conception in
"Igitur," for the "poème critique" would "Mobiliser, autour d'une idée, les
lueurs divers de l'esprit" (277).

As Mallarmé was to state in the opening remarks to the *Divagations*,
"Nul n'échappe décidément, au journalisme" (*MOC* 2:82) The "poème-
critique," then, would indeed present a window onto itself as literary display, a
veritable exhibition and diagram of an aspect of modern thought. With an eye
to the rapidly transforming modern markets for literature, art, and fashion,
acutely aware of his own *prises de position* in the literary markets and movements, Mallarmé's speculative photo-graphic displays refigure his frameworks
as a recuperative poetics of dynamism and change, one that exposes the developing movements and the epistemological moment of an avant-garde poet.

NOTES

<hr>

INTRODUCTION

1. "Graphic" implies "vivid," "visual," and "of or pertaining to written or pictorial representation." Despite its origins in the Greek term for "writing," the term "graphic art" is, by definition, applied to the visual rather than the verbal arts. When I depict Mallarmé's art as "graphic" or his framing processes as "graphic aspects," I am specifically evoking the degree to which his work may be analogically modeled on a visually conceived diagram.

2. *MOC* 1:43, 102. Throughout *Frameworks for Mallarmé*, fragments of Mallarmé's voice punctuating chapters and sections of the book appear in italics and bear notes indicating the titles (or incipits) of the works from which they have been cropped.

3. Since I intentionally use fragments of Mallarmé's texts to punctuate and to resonate with my discussions, these disparate sound bites are at once isolated from their contexts and simultaneously recontextualized, most often to foreground a particular facet of the selected text and to incite the reader to re-view the text in light of my discussion. In this particular example, Mallarmé's phrase "M'introduire dans ton histoire" is appropriated to introduce my own text and to evoke what will later be discussed as Mallarmé's implicit positing of a theory of reception.

4. In the U.S. market, where the rapid publication of manuscripts and the spinning off of articles determines not only the maintenance of jobs for academic critics, but many of the trends affecting production in literary criticism, increasingly one sees not only studies that isolate an aspect of the writer's work, but also those that present a theoretical structure or theme and then explore that model in a number of writers' works. Although studies of Mallarmé outside the United States, particularly those published over the last two decades, do exhibit more contextualized approaches to the author's production, thought, and impact, one still finds, as evidenced in the recent centennial explosion of publications on Mallarmé, particularly in France, that the single-author manuscript remains the norm. Some

examples are: Eric Benoit's *Mallarmé et le mystère du livre* (1998), Peter Brown's *Mallarmé et l'écriture en mode mineur* (1998), Yves Delèque's *Mallarmé: Le suspens* (1997), Pascal Durand's *Crises: Mallarmé via Manet* (1998), Michel Gauthier's *Mallarmé en clair* (1998), Jean-Paul Hameury's *L'échec de Mallarmé* (1998), Serge Meitinger's *Stéphane Mallarmé* (1995), Jacques Rancière's *Mallarmé: La politique de la sirène* (1996), Jean-Luc Steinmetz's *Stéphane Mallarmé: L'absolu au jour le jour* (1998).

5. Some examples of this genre at its richest include: Dominique Fisher's *Staging of Language and Languages of the Stage* (1994), Rae Beth Gordon's *Ornament, Fantasy, and Desire in Nineteenth-Century French Literature* (1992), Evlyn Gould's *Virtual Theater from Diderot to Mallarmé* (1989), Françoise Meltzer's *Salomé and the Dance of Writing* (1987), Richard Stamelman's *Lost Beyond Telling* (1990), Richard Terdiman's *Discourse/Counter-Discourse* (1985), Nathaniel Wing's *The Limits of Narrative* (1986).

6. Graham Robb, *Unlocking Mallarmé* (1996); Roger Pearson, *Unfolding Mallarmé: The Development of a Poetic Art* (1996).

7. This claim requires some attenuation. Until 1998 notable exceptions to this critical neglect of the circumstantial included: Brown, *Mallarmé et l'écriture en mode mineur* (1998), Ross Chambers, "An Address in the Country" (1986), Roger Dragonnetti, *Un fantôme dans le kiosque* (1992), Lucienne Frappier-Mazur, "Narcisse travesti" (1986), Marian Zwerling Sugano, *The Poetics of the Occasion* (1992), and Gayle Zachmann, "Developing Movements" (1997). After 1998, the trickle of articles has become a torrent of scholarly monographs, including Damian Catani, *The Poet in Society* (2003), Roger Pearson, *Mallarmé and Circumstance* (2004), Hélène Stafford, *Mallarmé and the Poetics of Everyday Life* (2000).

8. See Zachmann, "*La Décoration!*" (1997).

CHAPTER 1

Chapter title fragment is from "Crise de vers," *MOC* 2:204.

1. "Crise de vers," *MOC* 2:211.

2. See the discussion in chapter 3 of frames of consciousness in "Igitur."

3. For a discussion of prephotographic optical devices that destabilize the model of the camera obscura, see Jonathan Crary, *Techniques of the Observer* (1990).

4. "Etalages," *MOC* 2:218.

5. See Claude Bellanger, Jacques Godechot, Pierre Guiral, and Fernand Terrou, eds., *Histoire générale de la presse française,* Vol. 2 (1815–1871) (1969).

6. Writers often published texts three or four times in different periodicals (e.g., the *roman feuilleton*) and sometimes in keepsakes and the like. This was widespread from at least the 1830s. For a study of the mechanisms of the literary market under Louis-Philippe, see: Lucienne Frappier-Mazur, "1843, 9 June, Publishing Novels" (1989) and Richard Terdiman, *Discourse/Counter-Discourse* (1985).

7. From 1850 to 1914, illiteracy in France fell from 39 percent to 4 percent. See Madeleine Ambrière, ed., *Précis de la littérature française du XIXe siècle* (1990), 326.

8. For documentation of Mallarmé's resistance to books "à bon marché" and difficulties with his editors (in particular, Vanier), see *Corr* 3.

9. See Christophe Charle, "L'expansion et la crise de la production littéraire" (1975).

10. Most artists were themselves from the bourgeoisie. As suggested earlier, there is a conscious effort among artists to promote their personas as "other."

11. It could be argued that the rise of the poet-critic preceded the nineteenth century, and this would be accurate; however, I am referring to the highly commercialized figure of the poet-critic as it emerged and whose numbers increased dramatically and proportionally with the expansion of the press and the rise of art criticism in the nineteenth century.

12. "Symphonie littéraire," *MOC* 2:283.

13. "Heroes" refers here to Baudelaire and the Parnassian poets. Poe à la Baudelaire is excepted, as are Lamartine and Béranger, who precede, and Hugo, who, while of the generation, spans most of the century. Mallarmé documents his admiration for Gautier, Baudelaire, and Banville in his 1865 triptych "Symphonie littéraire," *MOC* 2:281–84.

14. For an extended reading of the paradoxical status of the mid-nineteenth-century writer in France with respect to social representation and contestation, see Terdiman, *Discourse/Counter-Discourse.* See also T. J. Clark, *The Absolute Bourgeois* (1982).

15. I am both alluding to and willingly falling into the dialectic trap of Louis Althusser's "Contradiction et surdétermination" (1965) and his "Idéologie et appareils idéologiques d'état" (1976).

16. "Un spectacle interrompu," *MOC* 1:420, emphasis in original.

17. See Nathaniel Wing, *The Limits of Narrative* (1986).

18. See Erich Auerbach, *Mimesis* (1991); Gunter Gebauer and Christoph Wulf, *Mimesis: Culture—Art—Society* (1995); Christopher Prendergast, *The Order of Mimesis* (1986); Mihai Spariosu, *Mimesis in Contemporary Theory* (1984); Wendy Steiner, *The Colors of Rhetoric* (1982).

19. Art as a means to attain a reality that surpasses the physical appearance of the object world; cf. Baudelaire's "surnaturalisme."

20. "Le Phenomène futur," *MOC* 1:413.

21. For related readings see: Walter Benjamin, *Charles Baudelaire* (1973); Clark, *The Absolute Bourgeois* and *The Painting of Modern Life* (1985); Ulrich Finke, ed., *French Nineteenth Century Painting and Literature* (1972); David Kelly, "'Modernité' in Baudelaire's Art Criticism" (1974); and F. W. Leaky, *Baudelaire and Nature* (1969). For a study of Baudelaire's literary criticism, see Rosemary Lloyd, *Baudelaire's Literary Criticism* (1980).

22. Aristotle's *Poetics* protects the poets by insisting on them as "makers." He also includes the faithful representation of men's actions as an acceptable aspect of mimesis.

23. For a discussion of photography's influence on artists of the era and the use of photographs by painters, see Aaron Scharf, *Art and Photography* (1986) and Elizabeth Anne McCauley, *Industrial Madness* (1994). See also chapters 4 and 5.

24. "Toast funèbre," *MOC* 1:27.

25. Terdiman's "generation of 1848" and Chamber's "deterritorialized" poets.

CHAPTER 2

Chapter title fragment is from "Eventail de Madame Mallarmé," *MOC* 1:30.

1. It should be noted that *L'artiste* was one of the first truly interdisciplinary artistic reviews of its kind.

2. Baudelaire's article on Théophile Gautier foreshadows much of "Hérésies artistiques: L'Art pour tous." See *BOC* 2:103–28, especially pages 106–7 on the "foule"; pages 108, 114, and 128 on utility and progress; page 111 on the separation of "métiers" and the heresy of teaching, and pages 117–18 on mystery, "le sacré," "le jeu de hasard," and science.

3. "Hérésies artistiques," *MOC* 2:362.

4. "Etalages," *MOC* 2:223.

5. See, in particular, *Les gossips de Mallarmé,* a collection of most of his notices sent to the *Athenaeum* between 1875 and 1876. See also *La dernière mode, MOC* 2:485–654. As well as publishing in England several pieces that were not included in the 1945 edition of the *Oeuvres complètes,* Mallarmé published in the United States and tried for several years to negotiate various positions as a cultural correspondent with the United States and England. See *Corr* 2, particularly his letters to Mrs. Whitman and Mr. O'Shaughnessy.

6. See Vincent Kaufmann, *Le Livre et ses adresses* (1986): "Le Livre, semble-t-il, reste nécessairement et irréductiblement virtuel; il ne peut avoir lieu que sous forme de fragments, qui en font miroiter l'existence et la place" (23).

7. See *Corr* 3, particularly the letters to Edouard Dujardin, which document his support of the review and his exclusive engagement to publish all new work in *La revue indépendante.*

8. I am referring in particular to Mallarmé's positioning of himself as chronicler of the modern and the modern exposition for the 1871 and 1872 London International Exhibitions. This endeavor presents a speculative shot at the new markets, a space in which to form public tastes, and it forshadows *La dernière mode.*

9. "Sur la philosophie," *MOC* 2:659.

10. "L'action restreinte," *MOC* 2:215.

11.   See, for example, "Le jury de peinture pour 1874 et M. Manet," *MOC* 2:410–15; "The Impressionists and Edouard Manet," *MOC* 2:444–70; and "Crise de vers," *MOC* 2:204–13.

12. Works such as Michel-Eugène Chevreul's 1839 *De la loi du contraste simultané des couleurs* and Hermann von Helmholtz's *Handbuch der physiologischen Optik,* the first volume of which appeared in 1856, described and popularized theories of visual perception, as did the widely read texts of Charles Blanc, Hippolyte Taine, and Edmond Duranty. For a particularly pertinent analysis of the links between visual arts and the sciences in the 1870s and 1880s see Marianne Marcussen and Hilde Olrik, "Le réel chez Zola et les impressionnistes" (1980).

13.   "Magie," *MOC* 2:251.

14. Definitive title: "Renouveau." *MOC* 1:11, 105, 119.

15. See *Corr* 1. Mallarmé's early letters document that he and his correspondents were discussing and exchanging a wide variety of texts in philosophy and the sciences (Leibniz, Taine, Hegel, etc.). In 1866 he wrote to Aubanel: "J'en prends tristement mon parti, sur un divan, parmi des monceaux de livres. . . . Il est vrai que ce sont des livres de science et de philosophie" (232).

16. "Sur la graphologie," *MOC* 2:669, emphasis in original.

17. For a discussion of this naturalization in Taine, Zola, and the impressionists, see Marcussen and Olrik.

18. See *Corr* 1:154. In his second critique of Taine, Mallarmé writes: "En outre, il sent merveilleusement l'âme de la poésie, mais ne comprend pas *la beauté du vers,* ce qui est au moins la moitié de cet art" (*Corr* 1:170, emphasis in original).

19.   "Le mystère dans les lettres," *MOC* 2:229.

20. See, among others, Taine, *Philosophie de l'art,* 20.

CHAPTER 3

1. "A Lefébure," *MOC* 1:669.

2. The word "specular," etymologically rooted in the Latin *specularis,* from *speculum,* mirror, is also meant to suggest the Latin *speculari,* to observe and the Latin *spectrum,* defined in physics as the distribution of a physical system. The Latin *speculari,* to observe, evolves in English as the verb "speculate," while the Latin *spectrum* evolves in French as "spectre," meaning both specter and spectrum. The interfacing of these related definitions calls up the multiple levels of inquiry invoked by Mallarmé's poetic product and processes, especially as these are exteriorized and examined as in a mirror.

3. "Prose," *MOC* 1:29–30, 94–96, 129–30.

4. My choice of the expression "common currency" is by no means gratuitous. While scientific discourses were certainly commonplaces exploited as reality effects within texts, the use of such discourses in fictional texts and prefaces, to both explain *and justify* literary methods and production (as in Balzac's *Avant Propos à la Comédie Humaine,* for example), can be seen as more than a guarantee of authenticity; the incorporation of scientific discourses can be considered a way of ensuring marketability in a cultural environment that valorized such discourses. Bertrand Marchal, in his notes to the 1998 Gallimard/Pléiade edition of Mallarmé's works, also acknowledges the significance of an infiltration of scientific thought on Mallarmé's conception of language (*MOC* 1:1359–60).

5. The term "spectrum" denotes a range of related quantities, or a sequence of qualities, ideas, or activities. I also wish, however, to evoke its more precise meanings as pertinent here:

> *Spectrum.* 1. Physics. The distribution of a characteristic of a physical system or phenomenon, esp.: a. The distribution of energy emitted by a radiant source, as by an incandescent body, arranged in order of wavelengths. b. The distribution of atomic or sub-atomic particles in a system, as in a magnetically resolved molecular beam, arranged in order or masses. c. A graphic or photographic representation of such a system. 2. a. A range of values of a quantity or set of related quantities. b. A broad sequence or range of related qualities, ideas, or activities. Lat., appearance, *specere,* to look at. (*The American Heritage Dictionary,* 2nd ed.)

6. "Notes sur le langage," *MOC* 1:505, 504.

7. Michel Pierssens, in his early epistemocritical study, *The Power of Babel* (1980, translated from the 1976 *La Tour de Babil*), was one of the few critics to identify the importance of an infiltration of scientific discourse in Mallarmé's notes of 1869 and 1895. While in this book Pierssens focuses primarily on how such discourses are used in the poet's own anecdotal discussions of his "madness," in *Savoirs à l'oeuvre: Essais d'épistémocritique* (1990) he provides a reading of a number of Mallarmé texts, suggesting how such writings may have been informed by well-known linguistic studies from his era.

8. Descartes's *Discours* proposes itself both "comme une histoire" and "comme une fable."

9. The ordering, format, and emphasis of Marchal's presentation of the "Notes" differ from the 1945 edition here. In text, I have retained Marchal's choices. See *MOC* 1:507. These "Notes" in the 1945 edition are found on page 852.

10. In *Semiotics of Poetry* (1978), Michael Riffaterre defines poetic language's distinction from common linguistic usage as "indirection": "poetry expresses concepts and things by indirection. To put it simply, a poem says one thing and means another" (1).

11. The word "commemoration" (or here, "co-*mneme*-orates") suggests the integral role memory plays in the signifying event as conceived by Mallarmé. The term summons up the process of cognition, theories of psychic image resuscitation, and the psychic "impression"; the optical and technological epistemologies that inform these theories via devices and derivative metaphors; and the textual operations enacting and instituting a recalling and re-presentation of afterimage-like phenomena as a diagrammatically analogical a-visual afterlight.

12. In *The Colors of Rhetoric* (1982), Wendy Steiner explains that "the temporal limits of painting could be overcome by isolating a moment in the action that revealed all that had led up to it and all that would follow. This is the so-called pregnant moment" (40). We will later return to how Mallarmé analogically appropriates the conventional pregnant moment to institute a movement that exceeds that of narrative time.

13. In *Savoirs à l'oeuvre*, Pierssens defines the epistemological figure as "un savoir qui prend figure singulière . . . car par elle s'opère la greffe d'un savoir sur le discours ou la fiction" (11).

14. In *La révolution du langage poétique* (1974), Julia Kristeva describes this reconception of mimesis as it is articulated in modern poetic language: "Imitant la constitution du symbolique . . . le langage poétique moderne va plus loin que toute *mimesis* classique (théâtrale ou romanesque). . . . La *mimesis* nous paraît se placer en ce lieu de la transgression du thétique, *lorsque la vérité n'est plus un renvoi à un objet identifiable en dehors du langage, mais à un objet constructible à travers le réseau sémiotique,* posé cependant dans le symbolique et dès lors toujours vraisemblable" (58, emphasis added).

15. The nature of the "reanimated" *ut pictura poesis* to which I refer goes beyond the tradition that distinguishes the visual from the verbal in order to perpetuate the "things versus words" opposition; it is, on the contrary, highly conscious of the semiotic character of both arts. While I allude to Mallarmé's incorporation of textual and cognitive movement through "painterly" techniques, I am not referring to a verbal reproduction of visual effects that would entail an uncomplicated matter of imitation (the poet describing effects that the painter can reproduce visually), but rather, to analogies between aesthetic aspirations, techniques, and semiotic operations.

16. My use of "virtually" here is meant to suggest, as the adjective "virtual" does, at once a *potentially* visible phenomenon and, at the same time, concretely visual virtual images from which rays of reflected or refracted light appear to diverge.

17. Action, kinesis and *energeia* (the actualization of potency or dynamism), are used here in opposition to *enargeia* (a natural or pictorial quality in verbal art). The history of the painting–poetry comparison has typically associated temporality (narrative movement) with poetry. The action that I am referring to here entails a different type of movement, effected through a diagrammatic analogy with a visual technique: the pregnant moment. Highly germane are (1) that the experiential

    kinesis to which Mallarmé's writings allude is akin to retinal experience and optical reconstitution, and (2) that Mallarmé's insistence on kinesis or animation is directly related to a reconception of mimesis as performative. See chapter 5.

18. Dr. Bonniot, who in 1900 was engaged to Mallarmé's daughter Geneviève, found the notes for "Igitur" among Mallarmé's draft papers. Suspecting that it was different from the other unfinished drafts, he put the dossier aside.

19. *Un coup de dés,* Mallarmé's last work, is generally seen as taking up the principle themes, images, décor, and problems established in "Igitur."

20. In a letter to Henri Cazalis, November 1869, discussing his "conte," Mallarmé writes: "S'il est fait (le conte) je suis guéri; *similia similibus*" (*MOC* 1:748).

21. The critical interpretation of "Igitur" as a "failure" is rooted first in the commonplace view of Mallarmé as "impotent" and, second, in the more philosophically popular question of "le hasard," a question that critics generally attempt to answer with the text of *Un coup de dés.*

22. Paul Claudel, "La catastrophe d'Igitur," 111–17. Nuancing this somewhat, Maurice Blanchot remarks in *L'espace littéraire* (1955): "C'est plutôt par son abandon qu'*Igitur,* oeuvre non pas inachevée, mais délaissée, annonce cet échec, par là retrouve son sens, échappe à la naïveté d'une entreprise réussie pour devenir la force, et la hantise de l'interminable" (148). Blanchot underlines the fact that "Igitur" is abandoned, seeing in this abandonment a manifestation of artistic maturity, an attempt to maintain desire by maintaining the absence of the work.

23. While in chapter 5 we will return to Mallarmé's "framing processes," at present, this "metonymic metaphor" stands for the framing of the processes of the text, for the discourses about visual and verbal operations that frame his aesthetic, and for the *cadrage,* or placement, of all aspects of the matrices in his writing.

24. The word *igitur* is also found in a song that Mallarmé would certainly have known, *Gateamos Igitur,* a tune that is traditionally sung at the threshold of adulthood, when one takes one's place in society.

25. See Haskell M. Block, *Mallarmé and the Symbolist Drama* (1963) and Robert Greer Cohn, *Mallarmé's Igitur* (1981).

26. "Trappings of the romantic hero" alludes at once to the effusive hero whose lengthy monologues, typically articulated in isolated natural settings, present a character whose subjective experience of his own emotions dominates. Igitur's journey is explicitly "pas sentiment, ni esprit" (*MOC* 1:474). Emotion is nullified as this final hero of the romantic tradition, the last of his "race," takes his place among his ancestors. By the same token, the "traps of the verbal artist" here calls up the lengthy descriptions of emotive states, movement, and atmosphere conventionally associated with the representation of the romantic hero. The aesthetic principle deduced from such descriptions, namely, that movement in verbal art will always be limited to the progression of events during the time of the narration, will be one of the major conventional boundaries with which Mallarmé's aesthetic takes issue.

27. The verb "lire" in the third person singular ("lit") has as one of its homonyms the verb "lier" in the third person singular ("lie"). We will return to this *lien,* the relationship of Igitur's story to his ancestors, later in the chapter. The word "race" calls up the themes of the "Vie D'Igitur," as well as the following exhortation: "Ecoutez, ma race, avant de souffler ma bougie—le compte que j'ai à vous rendre de ma vie" (479). Interestingly enough, it is unclear whether this exclamation belongs to the voice of Igitur, another narrator, or the writer himself.

28. This segment is presented in the 1945 edition as "[ARGUMENT]." It is in brackets and capitals because it was Dr. Bonniot who gave it this title. It is preceded in the manuscript by a numbered outline that lists the four "morceaux": 1. Le Minuit, 2. L'escalier, 3. Le coup de dés, 4. Le sommeil sur les cendres, après la bougie soufflée. "Vie d'Igitur," which was found as a separate bundle of documents among the manuscript's drafts, was not included in the original outline. See *MOC* 1945:434; *MOC* 1:474.

29. The acceptance of a self, the possibility of an "I," is seen as a universal folly (or madness): "Un des actes de l'univers vient d'être commis là" (*MOC* 1:474). The separation and subsequent acceptance of the "folie" that occur in "Vie d'Igitur" at the moment when "Il se sépare du temps indéfini et il est!" (499) is thus recognized in the story as a fiction, a "glorieux mensonge."

30. "Le mystère dans les lettres," *MOC* 2:233.

31. Fragmentation is often produced through grammatical techniques. Here, the syntax and the use of commas bring the flow to a virtual standstill while semantic triggers insist upon movement, reflection, and perception.

32. While there is little doubt that Mallarmé would be aware of the etymology of the term "chambre" that he chose as his metaphor of the mind, as Joel Snyder and Neil Walsh Allen have argued in "Photography, Vision, and Representation" (1982), there are serious limitations to any analogy between the camera and the eye (or optical perception). This said, it is at once clear that both analogies are called up in the text and, more important, that the dominant analogy for the psychic processes presented in this specific camera of the mind remains in line with nineteenth-century conceptions of optical perception and, more generally, the dominant conventions of discourse that link seeing and knowing through metaphors of visual perception.

33. Leo Bersani's *The Death of Stéphane Mallarmé* (1982) provides a detailed reading of the emergence of the writing subject through an exploration of death.

34. Still, it is worthwhile to keep in mind that in typically Mallarméan style, this particular "joyau nul de rêverie" in "Crise" leaves to chance whether the "reciprocal reflections" replace the perceptible lyric breath *found in* the "ancien souffle lyrique" or whether the reflections replace the perceptible lyric breath *from within* the "ancien souffle lyrique."

35. One can suppose that Mallarmé was aware of the multivalence and usage of the adjective "virtuel":

> 1. Qui est seulement en puissance et sans effet actuel. 2. Terme de mécanique. Qui est possible. . . . On nomme déplacement virtuel d'un point, tout déplacement idéal et infiniment petit qu'il pourrait recevoir . . . le travail virtuel d'une force est le travail infiniment petit qui correspond à un semblable déplacement. // Vitesse virtuelle, espace infiniment petit parcouru dans la direction d'une force par le point d'application de cette force. // Moment virtuel, le produit de la force multipliée par la vitesse virtuelle. // 3. Terme de physique. Le foyer virtuel d'un miroir, d'une lentille, est celui qui est déterminé par la rencontre des prolongements géométriques des rayons lumineux. Le téléscope de Galilée augmente le diamètre apparent de l'objet autant de fois que le foyer réel de l'objectif contient de fois le foyer virtuel de l'oculaire." (Littré, *Dictionnaire de la langue française*)

36. Cf. "la Nuit resta avec une douteuse perception de pendule" ("Igitur," *MOC* 1:484).

37. See chapter 2. The conflation of sensation and memory in the effects of the vacant sound of a word and the subsequent images that function "visually" as a virtual effect of echoing light correspond to Taine's theory of image resurrection. Mallarmé had been aware of Taine's ideas at least since 1864.

38. The *Oxford English Dictionary* defines "vision" as "the faculty of sight; intellectual perception, conception, or foresight; a mental image produced by the imagination; a mystical experience of seeing as if with the eyes; and, a person or thing of extraordinary beauty, the term vision itself destabilizes its own meanings in the passage cited."

39. In *Stéphane Mallarmé* (1942), Grange Woolley points out that these conjunctions, associations in Igitur's thinking, are "compared by means of the term 'marine complexity' to the sparkling of the moonlit, white capped waves of the ocean. This image forms the background of the poem 'Un coup de dés'" (145).

40. The point is also relevant with regard to Roland Barthes's (questionable) assertions, in *La chambre claire,* of the photographic image as "authentification" (133–39). In *The Burden of Representation* (1988), John Tagg argues against Barthes that photography can aspire to no more and no less than any kind of other representation in its claims to truth and evidentiary qualities. The photographic process, however, can only be considered truthful as the graphic presentation of a distribution of light waves that can be objectified and observed. This view provides a particularly apt metaphor for Igitur's experience with the mirror, how the text "Igitur" seems to envision the workings of the faculty of intelligence, and how it aspires to sketch the process and event of its own production.

41. In *L'univers imaginaire de Mallarmé* (1961), Jean-Pierre Richard notes a similar effect

of crystallization in Mallarmé's work, emphasizing the importance of the diamond in the text (187).

42. Woolley remarks that "the mirror in Igitur's room fills a very important role. It is the pool in which this intellectual Narcissus contemplates the drama of his consciousness. . . . The gradual purification of being which is described in the drama takes place in the mirror. Igitur watches with horror (all is imaginary) the rarifaction of his body in the mirror until it has become a thing of horror" (146).

43. As Block remarks, "Igitur's monologue in justification of his existence is, in fact, a dialogue with his unseen but present ancestors. Overwhelmed by the past of his race, by his acute consciousness of the finite, and by the increasing pressure of emptiness and ennui, Igitur seeks to penetrate the mystery of life" (39).

44. For Mallarmé, fabric provides an archetypal analogy for the writing process. Aside from his elaborate descriptions and obvious fascination with fabrics, lace, and other intricate *tissus,* he often described textual production as the fabrication of delicately and densely woven threads. See Gayle Zachmann, "La Décoration!" (1999).

45. The illusion consists in appropriating a dream of an absolute for the subject in order to survive. This adept observation expressed in Hegelian terms anticipates the logic of what Althusser was later to discuss and reify as the imaginary constructions that enable the subject to exist in society. For as Igitur comes to terms with his self, he also becomes once again aware of his place in context: "Tout ce qu'il en est, c'est que sa race a été pure: qu'elle a enlevé à l'Absolu sa pureté, pour l'être, et n'en laisser qu'une Idée elle-même aboutissant à la Nécessité: et que quant à l'Acte, il est parfaitement absurde sauf que mouvement (personnel) rendu à l'Infini: mais que l'Infini est enfin *fixé*" (*MOC* 1:477, emphasis in original)

46. As Marchal notes: "Il fallait qu'Igitur poussât jusqu'à l'absurde la logique de l'Acte pour guérir de sa maladie d'idéalité, cette névrose de l'absolu. La folie méthodique d'Igitur liquide ainsi l'héritage littéraire du spleen baudelairien et débarrasse Mallarmé de l'hypothèque métaphysique qui le vouait jusque-là au vertige de l'impuissance. Désormais peut commencer le jeu de la Littérature" (*Lecture de Mallarmé,* 267).

47. See Nathaniel Wing, *The Limits of Narrative* (1986) and Ross Chambers, "1851, 2 December, Literature Deterritorialized" (1989).

48. Critics such as Claudel have related Mallarmé's spiritual search, as well as the dilemma of his struggle with chance ("le hasard"), to that of Pascal (114). Bersani and others have related his aesthetic of difficulty to that of "les précieux." Blanchot, explaining certain artistic processes, refers to the classical writing subject in France: "L'écrivain qu'on appelle classique—du moins en France—sacrifie en lui la parole qui lui est propre, mais pour donner voix à l'universel. Le calme d'une forme réglée, la certitude d'une parole libérée du caprice, où parle la généralité impersonnelle, lui assure un rapport avec la vérité. Vérité qui est au-delà de la personne et voudrait être au-delà du temps" (*L'espace littéraire,* 22–23).

CHAPTER 4

Chapter title fragment is from "The Impressionists and Edouard Manet," *MOC* 2:470.

1. The article "The Impressionists and Edouard Manet" (*MOC* 2:444–70), to which I will refer throughout this chapter, was first published in translation in *The Art Monthly Review* (London: September 30, 1876). Although the original has never been found, Mallarmé approved Robinson's English translation in a letter to Arthur O'Shaughnessy (see *Corr* 2:129–30). Although it was recently included in French and in English for the 2003 edition of the *Oeuvres complètes*, for as long as the French manuscript remains lost, the English text remains, as Carl Paul Barbier states: "le seul valable" (*Documents Stéphane Mallarmé* 1:62). An abridged version of the text was retranslated into French by Marilyn Barthelme. See *Nouvelle revue française* (August 1, 1969): 375–85. Philippe Verdier's complete retranslation may be found in the *Gazette des Beaux Arts* (November 1975), 147–56.

2. For studies of Mallarmé and the painters of his generation, see L. J. Austin, "Mallarmé Critique d'Art" (1974), Penny Florence, *Mallarmé, Manet and Redon: Visual and Aural Signs and the Generation of Meaning* (1986), Wallace Fowlie, "Mallarmé and the Painters of his Age" (1966), James Kearns, *Symbolist Landscapes: The Place of Painting in the Poetry and Criticism of Mallarmé and His Circle* (1989), Jacques Lethève, *Impressionists et symbolistes devant la presse* (1959), Rosemary Lloyd, *Mallarmé: The Poet and His Circle* (1999), Jean-Michel Nectoux, *Un clair regard dans les ténèbres, poésie, peinture, musique* (1998), Jane Mayo Roos, ed., *A Painter's Poet: Stéphane Mallarmé and His Impressionist Circle* (1999), Marilyn Stokstad and Bret Waller, eds., *Les Mardis: Stéphane Mallarmé and the Artists of His Circle* (1965).

3. My use of the term "poet-critic" in this chapter refers quite simply to his role as an interartistic aesthetician; my reading does not exclude Albert Sonnenfeld's use of "poète-critique" to describe Mallarmé's process of *translatio,* self-censorship, and secondary and tertiary elaboration, on the contrary. See Sonnenfeld, "Elaboration secondaire du grimoire: Mallarmé et le poète-critique" (1978).

4. See Elwood Hartman, "Mallamé and Whistler: An Aesthetic Alliance" (1975).

5. In *La révolution du langage poétique* (1974), Julia Kristeva notes this reconception and transgression of mimésis as it is articulated in modern poetic language: "Imitant la constitution du symbolique . . . le langage poétique moderne va plus loin que toute *mimésis* classique (théâtrale ou romanesque). . . . La *mimésis* nous paraît se placer en ce lieu de la transgression du thétique, lorsque la vérité n'est plus un renvoi à un objet identifiable en dehors du langage, mais à un objet constructible à travers le réseau sémiotique, posé cependant dans le symbolique et dès lors toujours vraisemblable" (58).

6. See chapter 5. Kristeva theorizes the possibility of such a passage from one system of signs to another as well as its implications for mimesis: "Le terme d'*inter-textualité* désigne cette transposition d'un (ou de plusieurs) système(s) de signes en un autre; mais puisque ce terme a été souvent entendu dans le sens banal de 'critique

des sources' d'un texte, nous lui préférons celui de *transposition,* qui a l'avantage de préciser que le passage d'un système signifiant à un autre exige une nouvelle articulation du thétique" (59–60, emphasis in original).

7. Until recently, criticism relating Mallarmé work to the visual arts remained primarily anecdotal.

8. Although Austin, who discussed the relationship between Mallarmé and the painters of his era, states that the 1876 article remains one of Mallarmé's most important pieces, he devotes only two paragraphs to its summary (153–62). Fowlie delineates the personal associations of Mallarmé and certain artists (542–48), but does not focus on or analyze his critical writing. Kearns provides one of the few detailed studies of the significance of symbolist theories of painting and poetry. His book offers a veritable trove of historical and anecdotal detail. Though his chapter on Mallarmé is a flashback in a book that discusses the painters and poets of Mallarmé's circle rather than Mallarmé, his adept study of the relationship between Manet's art and the later revisions of Mallarmé's *L'après-midi d'un faune,* has the merit of resituating Mallarmé's production within artistic thought of the period. Florence's book, to which I will return, addresses the significance of the 1876 article in relation to "Crise de vers" and *Un coup de dés.* The book examines some of the analogous operations of visual and aural signs and offers an excellent study of intertextuality in painting and poetry. Though both of the latter works demonstrate that the significance of Mallarmé's art theory is beginning to receive critical attention, neither work attempts an overall examination of the impact of critical art and literary discourse on the *development* of Mallarmé's poetic theory, nor do they systematically study how such influences may have affected his own place within the tradition of *ut pictura poesis.* While readings of this piece will no doubt become more common with the addition of the article in French and in English in the 2003 Gallimard/Pléiade edition of the *Oeuvres complètes,* Pascal Durand's insightful analysis of the piece alongside Mallarmé's "Crise de vers" remains, along with the earlier version of this chapter, my article "Developing Movements," one of the most detailed readings of the article's significance for Mallarmé's corpus.

9. "Trois lettres sur l'exposition Internationale de Londres," *MOC* 1945:666. Cited by Kearns, 95. Letters also found in *MOC* 2:365–79.

10. "L'armature intellectuelle . . . se dissimule" (*MOC* 2:659); "L'art suprême, ici, consiste à laisser voir . . . sans avoir montré comment on s'élevait vers ces cimes" (*MOC* 1:657); "Nul vestige d'une philosophie . . . ne transparaîtra" (*MOC* 2:659). Like the absence of attention to Mallarmé's specific writings on art's commercialization in contemporary criticism, the absence of critical consideration of photography's possible impact on the 1876 article is curious. One possible reason is that the traces of photography's influence are purposefully erased, much as was reference to Panama as the inspiration for Mallarmé's well-known text "Or"—a reference that, after all, remained undetected for almost a century, until Barbara Johnson's admirable study of the text. See her "Erasing Panama: Mallarmé and the Text

of History" (1987), 57–67. Though Johnson's article deals specifically with the text, it should be noted that reference to Panama was also made in Jacques Derrida's "La double séance," *La dissémination* (1972) 199–319.

11. Though Barbier's reproduction of the text mentions the full title, it is never addressed and no study has discussed the implications of "the photo" and "the graphic" in light of the pictorial arts' relationship to photography as a possible influence on Mallarmé's poetics.

12. "The Impressionists and Edouard Manet," *MOC* 2:147.

13. Hartman points to this same insistence as one of the key aesthetic alliances between Whistler and Mallarmé. Whistler proposes that the artist is he who chooses from infinite possibilities to create his art: "Nature contains the elements, in colour and form, of all pictures, as the keyboard contains the notes of all music. But the artist is born to pick, and choose, and group with science, these elements, that the result may be beautiful—as the musician gathers his notes, and forms his chords, until he brings forth from chaos glorious harmony. To say to the painter that Nature is to be taken as she is, is to say to the player, that he may sit on the piano" (cited by Hartman, 551).

14. "Mishaps" refers to distortions found in photographs that, though unintentional and most often the result of poor developing processes, revealed new information about reflection and the movement of light and physical matter in nature.

15. Roland Barthes also develops this idea in *La chambre claire* (1980), 16–17.

16. Florence's evocation of the analogy with photography refers specifically to Mallarmé's description of Manet's use of "sources," his "reinvention of painted signs which should be capable of assimilating and transforming their constituents into a point of intersection, a new sign" (39). However, the potential and the depersonalization of the texts to which Florence alludes are not only analogous to photographic texts in the banal sense of creating an "other" art object rather than imitating one's model.

17. Halation, an effect of light most noticeable in photographs after the advent of glass plates (the late 1840s), occurs when light areas encroach on adjacent darker forms, causing a loss of definition due to the erosive power of light. The calotype produced similar effects. See Aaron Scharf, *Art and Photography* (1986), 89.

CHAPTER 5

Chapter title fragment from "Ses purs ongles," *MOC* 1:98.

1. "Le pitre châtié," *MOC* 1:74.

2. Richard Stamelman, *Lost Beyond Telling* (1990).

3. Cf. "Igitur." For a reading of the mirroring function with respect to Mallarmé's "Mimique," see Jacques Derrida's discussion of the text in "La double séance"

(1972) and Mark Franko's "Mimique" (1995), which provides a reading of Mallarmé's mimesis and an insightful critique of "La double séance."

4. See Roland Barthes, "Rhetoric of the Image," 269–86.

5. I am referring here once again to one of the three genres of iconicity (imagistic, metaphoric, and diagrammatic) outlined by Wendy Steiner in her discussion of Charles Sanders Peirce and the contributions of sign theory to the study of the interartistic analogy (*The Colors of Rhetoric,* 19–32).

6. "Sur la philosophie," *MOC* 2:659.

7. "Perhaps, if we imagine the distinctness with which an object is reflected in a positively perfect mirror, we come as near the reality as by any other means. For, in truth, the Daguerreotype plate is *infinitely* (we use the term advisedly) . . . in its representation than any painting by human hands" (Edgar Allen Poe, "The Daguerreotype," 38).

8. See, in particular, Marta Braun, *Picturing Time* (1994) and Jonathan Crary, *Techniques of the Observer* (1995).

9. "Salut," *MOC* 1:4.

10. Derrida's study of Mallarmé's "Mimique" abolishes the temporal sequence of imitated/imitating.

11. In Plato's *Philebus,* the poet and the painter are both equally secondary as regards the temporality of their representations of ideas. Nonetheless, Plato declared the relationship of the painter to the carpenter as one of a copier of copies.

12. The superiority of the visual, which dates back to Plato and stresses seeing as knowing and knowledge as light, is characteristic of theories of perception of the period. The idea of the painting of sensations on the mind's eye was a commonplace.

13. "Igitur," *MOC* 1:498, emphasis in original.

14. For discussions of ekphrasis, see James Heffernan's *Museum of Words* (1993), Murray Kreiger's *Ekphrasis: The Illusion of the Natural Sign* (1992), W. J. T. Mitchell's *Picture Theory* (1994), and Wendy Steiner's *The Colors of Rhetoric* (1982).

15. Again, the term "aspect" here is used in its fullest sense. The French "aspect" is defined by Littré as "L'état d'être sous l'oeil, devant les yeux, vue, orientation // Apparence, dehors, extérieur//faces diverses par lesquelles une chose se présente // Syn. Vue. Aspect est purement objectif, vue est purement subjectif."

16. I am using "graphic" in the fullest sense of the word.

17. "Hérodiade," *MOC* 1:17, 85.

18. See Rae Beth Gordon's analyses of "Ses purs ongles" in "Aboli bibelot?" (1985) and *Ornament, Fantasy, and Desire* (1992). Games with sonority may also have a visual effect in Mallarmé's texts, through his play with word shape and rhyme, for example.

19. "Frisson d'hiver," *MOC* 1:416.

20. Franko defines primary mimesis as "the taking of bodily form by bodies, the material occasion for the representation and transmission of behavior" (209). Relying on Spariosu's distinction between "mimesis-play" and "mimesis-imitation," Franko's study of Mallarmé's "Mimique" (and Derrida's reading of it in "La double séance") critiques the progressive disappearance of primary mimesis and performance in Derrida's analysis. Franko insists that "between self-referential mimicry and trace lies performance as what can materialize, and therefore 'retain' what is not, re-call it. [He] invoke[s] memory not as representation (copy) but as the capacity to perform anew, although always differently, to reproduce by repetitive otherness. In other words, time in performance is not only given as 'spacing out' passing toward itself as nothing, but also as a 'spacing in,' an introjection of uncertainty about something to be readdressed (redressed)" (211).

21. "Autre étude de danse: Les fonds dans le ballet," *MOC* 2:175.

22. André Levinson, in his 1923 essay, "Mallarmé, métaphysicien du ballet," was one of the first to signal the significance of Mallarmé's theory of dance. Following suit, writers and critics such as Suzanne Bernard, Deirdre Priddin, and Paul Valéry, as well as more recent critics such as Dominique Fisher, Mark Franko, Evlyn Gould, Felicia McCarren, Dee Reynolds, and Mary Shaw have highlighted this poet's contributions to the theoretical underpinnings and readings of modern dance and the significance of his writings on dance for his own aesthetic, visions of the female dancer, and discussions of dance and rite.

23. "Ballets," *MOC* 2:173.

24. See "Choreographies" by Jacques Derrida and Christie V. McDonald (1995) and Evlyn Gould's "Penciling and Erasing Mallarmé's Ballets" (1993). Derrida's "incalculable choreographies" and Evlyn Gould's "choreographic syntax" both spring from Mallarmé's own insistence on a "mobilité chorégraphique" and a "synthèse mobile" (*MOC* 2:176, 170). Gould's "choreographic syntax," as it applies to the ever-shifting translation of "Ballets," is also aptly described by calling on Derrida in *The Post Card* where, quoting himself, he writes: "by means of a switch point, I will send them elsewhere" (xi).

25. In his essay "Some Statements and Truisms" (1989) Derrida also addresses the jetty (*jetée*) as a type of *jeté* or jumping off point that calls up how moments of indecision become structures of openness and to send you elsewhere (cf. the parergon).

26. "Sa fusion aux nuances véloces muant leur fantasmagorie oxyhydrique de crépuscule et de grotte, telles rapidités de passions, délice, deuil, colère" ("Les fonds dans le ballet," *MOC* 2:175). Clearly Mallarmé here calls up the play of reflective shadows in the cave ("grotte") of the mind discussed in "Le mystère dans les lettres" and evoked in "Igitur."

27. "Imprinted" is meant to suggest not only an analogical origin in conceptions of visual processing and the visual arts; it is also meant to allude to the disposition of the printed text. "Blueprinted" calls up the diagrammatic iconicity previously discussed.

CHAPTER 6

Chapter title fragment is from "A Henri de Regnier," *Corr* 2:306.

1. Paul Verlaine, "Art poétique," 326.

2. In "Existence du symbolisme," Paul Valéry notes: "Le problème de toute la vie de Mallarmé . . . était . . . de rendre à la Poésie le même empire que la grande musique moderne lui avait enlevé" (700), an obvious reprise of Mallarmé's words in "Crise de vers": "nous en sommes là, précisément, à rechercher . . . un art d'achever la transposition, au Livre, de la symphonie ou . . . *de reprendre notre bien*" (*MOC* 2:212, emphasis added).

3. For studies of Mallarmé and music, see Deborah A. K. Aish, *La métaphore dans l'oeuvre de Stéphane Mallarmé* (1981); L. J. Austin, "Mallarmé on Music and Letters" (1959), 19–39; Suzanne Bernard, *Mallarmé et la musique* (1959); Joshua Landy, "Music, Letters, Truth and Lies" (1994); Aimé Patri, "Mallarmé et la musique du silence" (1952), 101–11; David Powell, "Shadows of Desire: Mallarmé and Debussy Searching for Pleasure" (1994); Richard Seiburth, "1885, Symbolists publish *La Revue Wagnérienne,* the Music of the Future" (1989), among others. Bernard explicitly notes that Mallarmé's interest in music comes later in his career, in the mid-1880s (21).

4. Speaking of English literature, Wendy Steiner states that the romantics' "concern with art's expressiveness rather than mimetic capacity made the painting-literature analogy decidedly marginal in nineteenth century criticism" (*The Colors of Rhetoric,* xii). M. H. Abrams supports the marginality of the painting–literature analogy in nineteenth-century criticism, especially among the romantics: "The use of painting to illuminate the essential character of poetry (*ut pictura poesis*) so widespread in the eighteenth century, almost disappears in the major criticism of the romantic period, the comparisons between poetry and painting that survive are casual, or, as in the instance of the mirror, show the canvas reversed in order to image the inner substance of the poet. In place of painting, music becomes the art frequently pointed to as having a profound affinity with poetry. For if a picture seems the nearest thing to a mirror image of the external world, music, of all the arts is the most remote" (*The Mirror and the Lamp,* 50).

5. "Berthe Morisot," *MOC* 2:151.

6. In "Les fenêtres," where Mallarmé announces: "Que le vitre soit l'art," one finds a dense grouping of such associations (*MOC* 1:9).

7. "A Henri de Regnier," *Corr* 2:306.

CODA

1. For an excellent reading and resource on the rapid development of symbolist journals, "la guerre des petites revues," and symbolism (and Mallarmé's place within this context), see Pamela Genova's *Symbolist Journals* (2002).

2. Damian Catani in *The Poet in Society* (2003) also remarks on the links between these letters, *La dernière mode*, and the discourse of "Etalages." His focus is on how the texts articulate a democratic aesthetic.

3. See Rosalind Williams, *Dream Worlds* (1982) and Patricia Mainardi, *Art and Politics of the Second Empire* (1987), among others.

BIBLIOGRAPHY

Abastado, Claude. "Doctrine symboliste du langage poétique." *Romantisme* 25–26 (1979): 75–106.

Abrams, M. H. *The Mirror and the Lamp.* New York: Oxford University Press, 1953.

Aish, Deborah A. K. *La métaphore dans l'oeuvre de Stéphane Mallarmé.* Geneva: Slatkine Reprints, 1981.

———. "Le rêve de Stéphane Mallarmé." *PMLA* 55 (September 1941): 874–84.

Albert, Pierre, and Fernand Terrou. *Histoire de la presse.* 4th ed. Paris: Presses Universitaires de France, 1970.

Althusser, Louis. "Contradiction et surdétermination." In *Pour Marx,* 85–128. Paris: François Maspero, 1965.

———. "Idéologie et appareils idéologiques d'état." In *Positions: 1964–1975,* 67–125. Paris: Editions Sociales, 1976.

Ambrière, Madeleine, ed. *Précis de la littérature française du XIXe siècle.* Paris: Presses Universitaires de France, 1990.

Anderson, Jill, ed. *Australian Divagations: Mallarmé and the 20th Century.* New York: Peter Lang, 2002.

———. "Mallarmé millénaire: An Exquisite Crisis." In Anderson, *Australian Divagations,* 3–15.

Armstrong, Carol. "Reflections on the Mirror: Painting, Photography, and the Self-Portraits of Edgar Degas." *Representations* 22 (Spring 1988): 108–41.

Audi, Paul. *La tentative de Mallarmé.* Paris: Presses Universitaires de France, 1997.

Audin, Marius. *Histoire de l'imprimerie par l'image.* Vol. 4. Paris: H. Jonquières, 1929.

Auerbach, Erich. *Mimesis: The Representation of Reality in Western Literature.* Translated by Willard R. Trask. Princeton: Princeton University Press, 1991.

Austin, L. J. "Mallarmé Critique d'Art." In *The Artist and the Writer in France,* 153–62. Oxford: Clarendon Press, 1974.

———. "Mallarmé on Music and Letters." *Bulletin of The John Rylands Library* 42, no. 1 (September 1959): 19–39.

———. *Poetic Principles and Practice.* Cambridge: Cambridge University Press, 1987.

Barko, Carol. "The Dancer and the Becoming of Language." *Yale French Studies* 54 (1977): 173–87.

Barthes, Roland. *La chambre claire: Note sur la photographie.* Paris: Gallimard/Le Seuil, 1980.

———. *Image, Music, Text.* Translated by Stephen Heath. London: Fontana, 1977.

———. "Rhetoric of the Image." In Trachtenberg, *Classic Essays on Photography,* 269–86.

Baudelaire, Charles. *Oeuvres complètes.* Edited by Claude Pichois. 2 vols. Paris: Gallimard, 1975 (Vol. 1), 1976 (Vol. 2).

Beausire, Pierre. *Mallarmé: Poésie et poétique.* Paris: Honoré Champion, 1974.

Bellanger, Claude, Jacques Godechot, Pierre Guiral, and Fernand Terrou, eds. *Histoire générale de la presse française.* Vol. 2 (1815–1871). Paris: Presses Universitaires de France, 1972.

Bellet, Roger. *Presse et journalisme sous le Second Empire.* Paris: Armand Colin, 1967.

Bénichou, Paul. *Selon Mallarmé.* Paris: Gallimard, 1995.

Benjamin, Walter. *Charles Baudelaire: A Lyric Poet in the Era of High Capitalism.* Translated by Harry Zohn. London: New Left Books, 1973.

———. "On Some Motifs in Baudelaire." In *Illuminations,* edited by Hannah Arendt, translated by Harry Zohn, 155–200. New York: Schocken Books, 1969.

———. "Paris, Capital of the Nineteenth Century." In *Reflections,* edited by Peter Demetz, translated by Edmund Jephcott, 146–62. New York: Schocken, 1986.

———. "The Work of Art in the Age of Mechanical Reproduction." In *Illuminations,* 217–52.

Benoît, Eric. *Mallarmé et le mystère du livre.* Paris: Champion, 1998.

Bernard, Suzanne. *Mallarmé et la musique.* Paris: Nizet, 1959.

Berretti, Jany. "La prose réconciliée: Mallarmé architecte et musicien." In Scepi, *Mallarmé et la prose,* 21–35.

Bersani, Leo. *The Death of Stéphane Mallarmé.* Cambridge: Cambridge University Press, 1982.

Birkett, Mary Ellen. "Pictura, Poesis and Landscape." *Stanford French Review* 2, no. 2 (Fall 1978): 235–46.

Blanchot, Maurice. *L'espace littéraire.* Paris: Gallimard, 1955.

———. *Le livre à venir.* Paris: Gallimard, 1959.

———. "Mallarmé et le langage." *Arche* 14 (April 1946): 134–46.

Block, Haskell M. *Mallarmé and the Symbolist Drama.* Detroit: Wayne University Press, 1963.

Bloom, Harold. *The Anxiety of Influence.* London: Oxford University Press, 1973.

Bonnefoy, Yves. "Igitur and the Photographer." *PMLA* 114 (May 1999): 329–46.

———. "The Poetics of Mallarmé." Translated by Elaine Ancekewicz. *Yale French Studies* 54 (1977): 9–21.

———. "La poétique de Mallarmé." *Critique* 31 (1975): 1053–74.

Bourdieu, Pierre. *The Field of Cultural Production: Essays on Art and Literature.* Edited by Randal Johnson. New York: Columbia University Press, 1993.

Bourgain-Wittiau, Anne. *Mallarmé ou la création au bord du gouffre: Entre litterature et psychanalyse.* Paris: L'Harmattan, 1996.

Bowie, Malcolm. *Mallarmé and the Art of Being Difficult.* Cambridge: Cambridge University Press, 1978.

———. "Towards a Poetics of Mallarmé's Late Prose." *Yearbook of Comparative and General Literature* 42 (1994): 29–37.

Braun, Marta. *Picturing Time: The Work of Etienne-Jules Marey (1830–1904).* Chicago and London: University of Chicago Press, 1992.

Brown, Peter. "*La Dernière Mode* ou le premier mode de Mallarmé." In Anderson, *Australian Divagations,* 182–205.

———. *Mallarmé et l'écriture en mode mineur.* Paris and Caen: Lettres Modernes Minard, 1998.

Brunel, Pierre. *Les poésies de Stéphane Mallarmé ou échec au néant.* Paris: Editions du Temps, 1998.

Burt, Ellen. "Mallarmé's 'Sonnet en yx': The Ambiguities of Speculation." *Yale French Studies* 54 (1977): 55–81.

Catani, Damian. *The Poet in Society: Art, Consumerism, and Politics in Mallarmé.* New York: Peter Lang, 2003.

Caws, Mary Ann. "Dancing with Mallarmé and Seurat (and Loïe Fuller, *Hérodiade* and La Goulue)." In *Artistic Relations: Literature and the Visual Arts in Nineteenth-Century France,* edited by Peter Collier and Robert Lethbridge, 291–302. New Haven: Yale University Press, 1994.

———. *The Eye in the Text: Essays on Perception, Mannerist to Modern.* Princeton: Princeton University Press, 1981.

———. "Mallarmé Here and Now." *L'Esprit Créateur* 40, no. 3 (Fall 2000): 6–13.

———. "Translation and the Art of Friendship, Signed Mallarmé and Whistler." *Yearbook of Comparative and General Literature* 42 (1994): 109–26.

Chambers, Ross. "An Address in the Country: Mallarmé and the Kinds of Literary Context." *French Forum* 2 (1986): 199–25.

———. "1851, 2 December, Literature Deterritorialized." In Hollier, *A New History of French Literature,* 710–16.

Charle, Christophe. "L'expansion et la crise de la production littéraire (2e moitié du 19è siècle)." *Actes de la recherche en sciences sociales,* no. 4 (1975): 44–65.

Chautard, Emile. *Glossaire typographique.* Paris: Denoël, 1936.

Chiari, Joseph. *Symbolism from Poe to Mallarmé: The Growth of a Myth.* 2d ed. New York: Gordian Press, 1970.

Chrisholm, A. R. "Substance and Symbol in Mallarmé." *French Studies* 5, no. 1 (January 1951): 36–48.

Cim, Albert. *Le livre.* Paris: Ernest Flammarion, 1906.

Clark, T. J. *The Absolute Bourgeois: Artists and Politics in France 1848–1851.* Princeton: Princeton University Press, 1982.

———. *The Painting of Modern Life: Paris in the Art of Manet and His Followers.* New York: Alfred A. Knopf, 1985.

Claudel, Paul. "La catastrophe d'Igitur." In *Oeuvres complètes,* Vol. 5, 111–17. Paris: Gallimard, 1959.

Cohn, Robert Greer. "The Mallarmé Century." *Stanford French Review* 3, no. 2 (Winter 1978): 431–49.

———. *Mallarmé's "Divagations": A Guide and Commentary.* New York: Peter Lang, 1990.

———. *Mallarmé's "Igitur."* Berkeley, Los Angeles, and London: University of California Press, 1981.

———. "Mallarmé's Windows." *Yale French Studies* 54 (1977): 23–31.

———. *Toward the Poems of Stéphane Mallarmé.* Berkeley and Los Angeles: University of California Press, 1965.

Copeland, Roger, and Marshall Cohen, eds. *What Is Dance? Readings in Theory and Criticism.* New York: Oxford University Press, 1983.

Cornell, Kenneth. *The Symbolist Movement.* New Haven: Yale University Press, 1951.

Crary, Jonathan. *Techniques of the Observer: On Vision and Modernity in the Nineteenth Century.* Cambridge and London: MIT Press, 1990.

Crowley, Roseline. "Toward the Poetics of Juxtaposition: *L'Après-midi d'un faune.*" *Yale French Studies* 54 (1977): 33–44.

Daulte, Olivier, and Manuel Dupertuis. *Correspondance de Stéphane Mallarmé et Berthe Morisot 1876–1895.* Lausanne: Bibliothèque des Arts, 1995.

Davies, Gardner. *Mallarmé et le drame solaire.* Paris: José Corti, 1959.

———. *Mallarmé et le rêve d'Hérodiade.* Paris: José Corti, 1978.

———. "Note on Mallarmé et Banville." *Australian Modern Languages Association* 19 (1963): 107–11.

———. *"Les Tombeaux" de Mallarmé.* Paris: José Corti, 1950.

Dayan, Peter. *Mallarmé's Divine Transposition: Real and Apparent Sources of Literary Value.* Oxford: Clarendon Press, 1986.

Deguy, Michel. "Mallarmé: Prose, phrase et périphrase." In Scepi, *Mallarmé et la prose,* 9–19.

Delèque, Yves. *Mallarmé: Le suspens.* Strasbourg, France: Presses Universitaires de Strasbourg, 1997.

Delfel, Guy. *L'esthétique de Stéphane Mallarmé.* Paris: Flammarion, 1951.

Derrida, Jacques. "La double séance." In *La dissémination,* 198–319. Paris: Le Seuil, 1972.

———. *The Post Card: From Socrates to Freud and Beyond.* Translated by Alan Bass. Chicago and London: University of Chicago Press, 1987.

———. "Some Statements and Truisms About Neo-Logisms, Newisms, Postisms, Parasitisms, and Other Small Seisisms." In *The States of 'Theory' and the Future of History and Art,* edited by David Carroll, translated by Anne Tomiche, 63–94. New York: Columbia University Press, 1989.

Derrida, Jacques, and Christie V. McDonald. "Choreographies." In Goellner and Murphy, *Bodies of the Text,* 141–56.

Dragonnetti, Roger. *Un fantôme dans le kiosque.* Paris: Le Seuil, 1992.

Ducros, Franc. *Pour Mallarmé. Trois études: Toast funèbre / Le Tombeau de Charles Baudelaire / Un Coup de Dés.* Saint-Maximin: Théétète, 1998.

Dujardin, Edouard. *Mallarmé, par un des siens.* New York: AMS, 1980 (c. 1936).

Durand, Pascal. *Crises: Mallarmé via Manet.* Leuven: Peeters Vrin, 1998.

———. "De 'l'universel reportage' au poème univers: L'hybridation." In Théranty and Vaillant, *Presse et plumes,* 339–50.

———. *Poésies de Stéphane Mallarmé.* Paris: Gallimard, 1998.

Duranty, Louis Edmond. *La nouvelle peinture: A propos du groupe d'artistes qui expose dans les galeries Durand-Ruel (1876).* Caen: L'Echoppe, 1988.

Edelstein, Dan. "Moving through the Looking-Glass: Deleuzian Reflections on the Series in Mallarmé." *L'Esprit Créateur* 40, no. 3 (Fall 2000): 50–60.

Ellison, David. "A Reading of Mallarmé's 'Hommage' (à Richard Wagner)." *Yearbook of Comparative and General Literature* 42 (1994): 46–56.

Ellmann, Maud. "Spacing Out: A Double Entendre on Mallarmé." *Oxford Literary Review* (1978): 22–31.

Elson, Christopher. "A Poetics of Summing-up and Making-away-with: Michel Deguy and Stéphane Mallarmé." *L'Esprit Créateur* 40, no. 3 (Fall 2000): 86–96.

Finke, Ulrich, ed. *French Nineteenth Century Painting and Literature.* Manchester, UK: Manchester University Press, 1972.

Fisher, Dominique D. *Staging of Language and Language(s) of the Stage: Mallarmé's Poëme Critique and Artaud's Poetry-Minus-Text.* New York: Peter Lang, 1994.

Florence, Penny. *Mallarmé, Manet and Redon: Visual and Aural Signs and the Generation of Meaning.* Cambridge: Cambridge University Press, 1986.

Fowlie, Wallace. *Mallarmé.* Chicago: University of Chicago Press, 1970.

———. "Mallarmé and the Painters of his Age" *The Southern Review* (Summer 1966): 542–48.

Franklin, Ursula. *An Anatomy of Poesis: The Prose Poems of Stéphane Mallarmé.* Chapel Hill: University of North Carolina Press, 1976.

Franko, Mark. "Mimique." In Goellner and Murphy, *Bodies of the Text,* 205–16.

Frappier-Mazur, Lucienne. "1843, 9 June, Publishing Novels." In Hollier, *A New History of French Literature,* 693–98.

———. "Narcisse travesti: Poétique et idéologie dans *La Dernière Mode* de Mallarmé." *French Forum* 11 (1986): 41–57.

Gallardo, Jean-Luc. *Mallarmé et le jeu suprême.* Orléans: Paradigme, 1998.

Garelick, Rhonda K. "Electric Salome: Loïe Fuller at the Exposition Universelle of 1900." In *Imperialism and Theatre: Essays on World Theatre, Drama and Performance,* edited by J. Ellen Gainor, 85–103. London and New York: Routledge: 1995.

Gauthier, Michel. *Mallarmé en clair.* Saint-Genouph: Nizet, 1998.

Gavronsky, Serge. "Borrowing Mallarmé." *L'Esprit Créateur* 40, no. 3 (Fall 2000): 72–85.

Gebauer, Gunter, and Christoph Wulf. *Mimesis: Culture—Art—Society.* Translated by Don Reneau. Berkeley and Los Angeles: University of California Press, 1992.

Genette, Gérard. "Bonheur de Mallarmé?" In *Figures* 1, 91–100. Paris: Le Seuil, 1966.

Genova, Pamela. *Symbolist Journals: A Culture of Correspondence.* Burlington, VT: Ashgate, 2002.

———. "Word, Image, Chord: Stéphane Mallarmé and the Interrelationships of the Arts in Late Nineteenth-Century French Symbolist Reviews." *Dalhousie French Studies* 36 (Fall 1996): 79–102.

Godefrey, Sima. "1874, Haute Couture and Haute Culture." In Hollier, *A New History of French Literature,* 761–68.

Goebel, Gerhard. "'Poésie et littérature' chez Baudelaire et Mallarmé, analyse du changement d'un concept." *Romantisme: Revue du dix-neuvième siècle* 39, no. 12 (1983): 73–83.

Goellner, Ellen W., and Jacqueline Shea Murphy, eds. *Bodies of the Text: Dance as Theory, Literature as Dance.* New Brunswick, NJ: Rutgers University Press, 1995.

Goodkin, Richard E. *The Symbolist Home and the Tragic Home: Mallarmé and Oedipus.* Amsterdam and Philadelphia: John Benjamins, 1984.

Gordon, Rae Beth. "Aboli Bibelot? The Influence of the Decorative Arts on Stéphane Mallarmé et Gustave Moreau." *Art Journal* 45 (Summer 1985): 105–12.

———. "'Le Faune.' Illusion, and Unconscious Perception." *Yearbook of Comparative and General Literature* 42 (1994): 100–8.

———. *Ornament, Fantasy, and Desire in Nineteenth-Century French Literature.* Princeton: Princeton University Press, 1992.

Gould, Evlyn. "Penciling and Erasing Mallarme's Ballets." *Performing Arts Journal* 15.1 (January 1993): 97–105.

———. *Virtual Theater from Diderot to Mallarmé.* Baltimore: Johns Hopkins University Press, 1989.

Guyaux, André. *Mallarmé*. Paris: Presses de l'Université de Paris-Sorbonne, 1998.

Hagstrum, Jean. *The Sister Arts: The Tradition of Literary Pictorialism and English Poetry from Dryden to Gray*. Chicago: University of Chicago Press, 1958.

Hameury, Jean-Paul. *L'échec de Mallarmé*. Bédée, France: Folle Avoine, 1998.

Harris, Margaret Haile. *Loïe Fuller: Magician of Light*. Richmond: Virginia Museum, 1979.

Hartman, Elwood. "Mallarmé and Whistler: An Aesthetic Alliance." *Kentucky Romance Quarterly* 22, no. 4 (1975): 543–60.

Heffernan, James A. W. *Museum of Words: The Poetic of Ekphrasis from Homer to Ashbery*. Chicago and London: University of Chicago Press, 1993.

Hollier, Denis, ed. *A New History of French Literature*. Cambridge: Harvard University Press, 1989.

Imbs, Paul, ed. *Trésor de la langue française: Dictionnaire de la langue du XIXe et du XXe siècle (1789–1960)*. Vol. 4. Paris: Centre national de la recherche scientifique, 1975.

Jean-Aubry, G. *Une amitié exemplaire*. Paris: Mercure de France, 1942.

Johnson, Barbara. *Défigurations du language poétique*. Paris: Flammarion, 1979.

———. "1885, June, The Liberation of Verse." In Hollier, *A New History of French Literature*, 798–800.

———. "1866, The Dream of Stone." In Hollier, *A New History of French Literature*, 743–47.

———. "Erasing Panama: Mallarmé and the Text of History." In *A World of Difference*, 57–67. Baltimore: Johns Hopkins University Press, 1987.

———. "Les Fleurs du mal armé: Some Reflections on Intertextuality." In *Lyric Poetry: Beyond New Criticism*. Ithaca: Cornell University Press, 1985.

Jouve, Séverine. *Obsessions et perversions dans la littérature et les demeures à la fin du dix-neuvième siècle*. Paris: Hermann, 1996.

Kafalenos, Emma. "Purification of Language in Mallarmé, Dada, and Visual Poetry." In *Visual Literature Criticism: A New Collection*, edited by Richard Kostelanetz, 51–60. Carbondale: Southern Illinois University Press, 1979.

Kaiser, John. "Baudelaire, Manet, Rossetti et Mallarmé." *Bulletin Baudelairien* 14, no. 2 (Winter 1979): 14–16.

Kaufmann, Vincent. *Le Livre et ses adresses*. Paris: Méridiens-Klincksieck, 1986.

Kearns, James. *Symbolist Landscapes: The Place of Painting in the Poetry and Criticism of Mallarmé and his Circle*. London: Modern Humanities Research Association, 1989.

Kelly, David. "'Modernité' in Baudelaire's Art Criticism." In *The Artist and the Writer in France: Essays in Honor of Jean Seznec*, edited by Francis Haskel, Anthony Levi, and Robert Shackleton, 138–52. Oxford: Clarendon Press, 1974.

Kermode, Frank. "Poet and the Dancer Before Diaghilev." In *Puzzles and Epiphanies*, 1–28. London: Literistic, 1962.

Klein, Richard. "Straight Lines and Arabesques: Metaphors of Metaphor." *Yale French Studies* 45 (1970): 64–86.

Kravis, Judy. *The Prose of Mallarmé.* New York: Columbia University Press, 1976.

Krieger, Murray. *Ekphrasis: The Illusion of the Natural Sign.* Baltimore and London: Johns Hopkins University Press, 1992.

Kristeva, Julia. *La révolution du langage poétique: L'avant-garde à la fin du XIXe siècle: Lautréamont et Mallarmé.* Paris: Le Seuil, 1974.

Lacan, Jacques. "Le stade du miroir comme formateur du Je." In *Ecrits,* 93–100. Paris: Le Seuil, 1966.

La Charité, Virginia. *The Dynamics of Space: Mallarmé's "Un Coup de dés jamais n'abolira le hasard."* Lexington, KY: French Forum, 1987.

Lamartine, Alphonse de. "De la politique rationnelle." *La revue européenne* (1831) 2:125–43.

Landy, Joshua. "Music, Letters, Truth and Lies: 'L'Après-Midi d'un Faune' as an *ars poetica.*" *Yearbook of Comparative and General Literature* 42 (1994): 57–69.

Leaky, F. W. *Baudelaire and Nature.* Manchester, UK: Manchester University Press, 1969.

Lee, Rensselaer W. Ut Pictura Poesis: *The Humanistic Theory of Painting.* New York: Norton, 1976.

Lethève, Jacques. *Impressionists et symbolistes devant la presse.* Paris: Armand Colin, 1959.

Levinson, André. "Mallarmé, métaphysicien du ballet." *La revue musicale* 5 (1923): 21–33.

Littré, Emile, ed. *Dictionnaire de la langue française.* Paris: Gallimard-Hachette, 1965.

Lloyd, Rosemary. *Baudelaire's Literary Criticism.* Cambridge: Cambridge University Press, 1980.

———. "La Divine Transposition: Mallarmé and Banville." *French Studies Bulletin* 9 (Winter 1983–84): 3–6.

———. *Mallarmé: The Poet and His Circle.* Ithaca: Cornell University Press, 1999.

———. "Notes in View of a Book on Mallarmé." In Anderson, *Australian Divagations,* 1–2.

Lyu, Claire. "Stéphane Mallarmé as Miss Satin: The Texture of Fashion and Poetry." *L'Esprit Créateur* 40, no. 3 (Fall 2000): 61–71.

Macé, Gérard. "Mallarmé (1)." *La nouvelle revue française* 321 (October 1979): 88–102.

———. "Mallarmé, mort en miroir (2)." *La nouvelle revue française* 322 (November 1979): 75–86.

Mainardi, Patricia. *Art and Politics of the Second Empire: The Universal Expositions of 1885 and 1867.* New Haven, CT, and London: Yale University Press, 1987.

Mallarmé, Stéphane. *Correspondance.* Vol. 1 (1862–1871). Edited by H. Mondor. Paris: Gallimard, 1959.

———. *Correspondance.* Vol. 2 (1871–1885). Edited by Henri Mondor and Lloyd James Austin. Paris: Gallimard, 1965.

————. *Correspondance.* Vol. 3 (1886–1889). Edited by Henri Mondor and Lloyd James Austin. Paris: Gallimard, 1969.

————. *Correspondance complète (1862–1871), suivi[e] de lettres sur la poésie (1872–1898), avec des lettres inédites.* Edited by Bertrand Marchal. Paris: Gallimard, 1995.

————. *Les gossips de Mallarmé.* Edited by Henri Mondor and Lloyd James Austin. Paris: Gallimard, 1962.

————. "The Impressionists and Edouard Manet, 1876." In *Documents Stéphane Mallarmé,* Vol. 1, edited by Carl Paul Barbier, 69–86. Paris: Nizet, 1968. (Retranslated into French by Philippe Verdier, *Gazette des Beaux Arts,* November 1975: 147–56.)

————. *Lettres à Méry Laurent.* Edited by Bertrand Marchal. Paris: Gallimard, 1996.

————. *Mallarmé: Selected Prose, Poems, Essays, and Letters.* Translated by Bradford Cook. Baltimore: Johns Hopkins Press, 1956.

————. *Oeuvres complètes.* Edited by H. Mondor and G. Jean-Aubry. Paris: Gallimard, 1945.

————. *Oeuvres complètes.* Edited by Bertrand Marchal. 2 vols. Paris: Gallimard, 1998 (Vol. 1), 2003 (Vol. 2).

————. *Propos sur la poésie.* Edited by Henri Mondor. Monaco, France: Editions du Rocher, 1945.

Marchal, Bertrand. *Lecture de Mallarmé: Poésies, "Igitur," "Le Coup de dés."* Paris: Corti, 1985.

————. "Mallarmé and 'Le Signe par Excellence.'" *Yearbook of Comparative and General Literature* 42 (1994): 38–45.

————. *Mallarmé: Mémoire de la critique.* Paris: Presses de l'Université de Paris-Sorbonne, 1998.

————. *La religion de Mallarmé.* Paris: Corti, 1988.

Marcussen, Marianne, and Hilde Olrik. "Le réel chez Zola et les Impressionnistes: Perception et représentation," *Revue d'histoire littéraire de la France* 6 (1980): 965–77.

Martino, Pierre. *Parnasse et symbolisme.* 2d ed. Paris: Armand Colin, 1970.

Mattiussi, Laurent. "Hors-lieu et hors-temps de la fiction chez Mallarmé et Villiers de l'Isle-Adam: Décentrements et irradiations." *Nineteenth-Century French Studies* 27 (Spring/Summer 1999): 346–55.

Mauron, Charles. *Introduction to the Psychoanalysis of Mallarmé.* Translated by Archibald Henderson Jr. and Will L. McLendon. Berkeley and Los Angeles: University of California Press, 1963.

————. *Mallarmé par lui-même.* Paris: Le Seuil, 1966.

McCarren, Felicia. "Mallarmé at the Movies." *L'Esprit Créateur* 40, no. 3 (Fall 2000): 25–38.

————. "Stéphane Mallarmé, Loïe Fuller, and the Theater of Femininity." In Goellner and Murphy, *Bodies of the Text,* 217–30.

McCauley, Elizabeth Anne. *Industrial Madness: Commercial Photography in Paris, 1848–1871*. New Haven and London: Yale University Press, 1994.

McLuhan, Marshall. "Joyce, Mallarmé, and the Press." *The Sewanee Review* 62 (1954): 38.

Meitinger, Serge. "Baudelaire et Mallarmé devant Richard Wagner." *Romantisme* 33, no. 2 (1981): 75–90.

———. *Stéphane Mallarmé*. Paris: Hachette, 1995.

Meltzer, Françoise. "Color as Cognition in Symbolist Verse." *Critical Inquiry* 5, no. 2 (1979): 253–73.

———. "1892, Writing and Dance." In Hollier, *A New History of French Literature*, 813–19.

———. *Salome and the Dance of Writing: Portraits of Mimesis in Literature*. Chicago: University of Chicago Press, 1987.

Michaud, Guy. *Mallarmé*. Paris: Hatier, 1971.

———. *Mallarmé: L'homme et l'oeuvre*. Paris: Hatier-Bovin, 1953.

Millan, Gordon, ed. *Documents Stéphane Mallarmé*. N.s. Vol. 1. Saint-Genouph, France: Nizet, 1998.

Milner, Jean-Claude. *Mallarmé au tombeau*. Lagrasse, France: Verdier, 1999.

Miner, Margaret. *Resonant Gaps: Between Baudelaire and Wagner*. Athens: University of Georgia Press, 1995.

Mitchell, W. J. T. *Picture Theory: Essays on Verbal and Visual Representation*. Chicago and London: University of Chicago Press, 1994.

Mondor, Henri. *Mallarmé lycéen*. Paris: Gallimard, 1954.

———. *Mallarmé plus intime*. Paris: Gallimard, 1944.

———. *Vie de Mallarmé*. Vol. 1. Paris: Gallimard, 1941.

Nectoux, Jean-Michel. *Mallarmé: "Un clair regard dans les ténèbres," poésie, peinture, musique*. Paris: Adam Biro, 1998.

Nelson, Robert J. "Mallarmé's Mirror of Art: An Explication of 'Ses purs ongles.'" *Modern Language Quarterly* 20, no. 1 (1959): 49–56.

Nochlin, Linda. *Realism*. Middlesex, UK: Penguin, 1990.

Olds, Marshall C. *Desire Seeking Expression: Mallarmé's "Prose pour des Esseintes."* Lexington, KY: French Forum, 1983.

Ortel, Philippe. *La littérature à l'ère de la photographie: Enquête sur une révolution invisible*. Nîmes: Jacqueline Chambon, 2002.

Oster, Daniel. *La gloire*. Paris: P.O.L., 1997.

———. "Quelques réflexions sur le proaïsme de Stéphane Mallarmé." In Scepi, *Mallarmé et la prose*, 103–17.

Patri, Aimé. "Mallarmé et la musique du silence." *La revue musicale* 210 (January 1952): 101–11.

Pearson, Roger. *Mallarmé and Circumstance: The Translation of Silence.* Oxford: Oxford University Press, 2004.

———. *Unfolding Mallarmé: The Development of a Poetic Art.* New York: Oxford University Press, 1996.

Pierssens, Michel. *Savoirs à l'œuvre: Essais d'épistémocritique.* Lille: Presses Universitaires de Lille, 1990.

———. *The Power of Babel: A Study of Logophilia.* London and New York: Routledge & Kegan Paul, 1980.

———. "Le signe et sa folie: Le dispositif Mallarmé/Saussure." *Romantisme: Revue de la société des études romantiques* 25–26 (1979): 49–55.

———. *La Tour de Babil: La Fiction du signe.* Paris: Minuit, 1976.

Poe, Edgar Allen. "The Daguerreotype." In Trachtenberg, *Classic Essays on Photography,* 38.

Powell, David A. "Shadows of Desire: Mallarmé and Debussy Searching for Pleasure." *Yearbook of Comparative and General Literature* 42 (1994): 83–91.

Prendergast, Christopher. *The Order of Mimesis: Balzac, Stendhal, Nerval, Flaubert.* Cambridge: Cambridge University Press, 1986.

Pridden, Deirdre. *The Art of Dancing in French Literature from Théophile Gautier to Paul Valéry.* London: Adam and Black, 1952.

Ramsey, Warren. "A View of Mallarmé's Poetics." *The Romanic Review* 46, no. 3 (October 1955): 178–91.

Rancière, Jacques. *Mallarmé: La politique de la sirène.* Evreux, France: Hachette, 1996.

Randall, John Herman Jr. *The Making of the Modern Mind: A Survey of the Intellectual Background of the Present Age.* 5th ed. New York: Columbia University Press, 1976.

Regnier, Henri de. *Nos rencontres.* Paris: Mercure de France, 1931.

Renéville, Roland de. *L'expérience poétique.* Paris: Gallimard, 1938.

Reynolds, Dee. "The Dancer as Woman: Loïe Fuller and Stéphane Mallarmé." In *Impressions of French Modernity: Art and Literature in France 1850–1900,* edited by Richard Hobbs, 155–72. Manchester, UK, and New York: Manchester University Press, 1998.

Richard, Jean-Pierre. *L'univers imaginaire de Mallarmé.* Paris: Le Seuil, 1961.

Riffaterre, Michael. *Semiotics of Poetry.* Bloomington: Indiana University Press, 1978.

Robb, Graham. *Unlocking Mallarmé.* New Haven: Yale University Press, 1996.

Rogers, Nathalie Buchet. "L'or du poète et l'or du financier: Une lecture de *Chatterton,* de Vigny, avec Mallarmé." *Nineteenth-Century French Studies* 31 (Fall/Winter 2002–2003): 84–103.

Roos, Jane Mayo, ed. *A Painter's Poet: Stéphane Mallarmé and the Impressionist Circle.* New York: Hunter College Art Gallery, 1999.

Roubaud, Jacques. *La vieillesse d'Alexandre: Essai sur quelques états récents du vers français.* Paris: Ramsay, 1988.

Roujoun, Jacques. "Whistler et Mallarmé 1888–1898." *Mercure de France* 1, no. 12 (1955): 631–60.

Saint-Gérand, Jacques-Philippe. "'Comme une araignée sacrée . . .' : Note sur Stéphane Mallarmé et les sciences du langage contemporaines (1842–1898)." In Scepi, *Mallarmé et la prose,* 51–82.

Saisselin, Rémy G. *The Bourgeois and the Bibelot.* New Brunswick, NJ: Rutgers University Press, 1984.

Sartre, Jean-Paul. Preface to *Poésies: Poésies, choix de vers de circonstance, poèmes d'enfance et de jeunesse* by Stéphane Mallarmé. Paris: Gallimard, 1945.

Scepi, Henri, ed. *Mallarmé et la prose.* Licorne, no. 45. Poitiers, France: Université de Poitiers, UFR de Langues et Littérature, 1998.

Scharf, Aaron. *Art and Photography.* New York: Viking Penguin, 1974.

Scherer, Jacques. *Grammaire de Mallarmé.* Paris: Nizet, 1977.

Scott, David. *Pictorialist Poetics: Poetry and the Visual Arts in Nineteenth-Century France.* Cambridge: Cambridge University Press, 1988.

Sieburth, Richard. "1885, February, The Music of the Future." In Hollier, *A New History of French Literature,* 789–97.

———. "Ms Fr 270: Prelude to a Translation." *L'Esprit Créateur* 40, no. 3 (Fall 2000): 97–107.

Shaw, Mary Lewis. *Performance in the Texts of Mallarmé: The Passage from Art to Ritual.* University Park: Pennsylvania State University Press, 1993.

Snyder, Joel, and Neil Walsh Allen. "Photography, Vision and Representation." In *Reading into Photography,* edited by Thomas F. Barrow, Shelley Armitage, and William E. Tydeman, 61–91. Albuquerque: University of New Mexico Press, 1982.

Sollers, Philippe. *Logiques.* Paris: Le Seuil, 1968.

———. *L'écriture et l'expérience des limites.* Paris: Le Seuil, 1971.

Sonnenfeld, Albert. "Elaboration secondaire du grimoire: Mallarmé et le poète-critique." *Romanic Review* (January-March 1978): 72–89.

Sontag, Susan. *On Photography.* New York: Picador USA; Farrar, Strauss and Giroux, 2001, c. 1977.

Spariosu, Mihai. *Dionysus Reborn: Play and the Aesthetic Dimension in Modern Philosophical and Scientific Discourse.* Ithaca: Cornell University Press, 1989.

———. Introduction and "Mimesis and Contemporary French Theory." In *Mimesis in Contemporary Theory: An Interdisciplinary Approach.* Vol. 1, *The Philosophical and Literary Debate,* edited by Spariosu, i–xxix, 65–108. Philadelphia: John Benjamins, 1984.

Stafford, Hélène. *Mallarmé and the Poetics of Everyday Life: A Study of the Concept of the Ordinary in his Verse and Prose.* Amsterdam and Atlanta: Rodopi, 2000.

Stamelman, Richard. *Lost Beyond Telling: Representations of Death and Absence in Modern French Poetry.* Ithaca and London: Cornell University Press, 1990.

Steiner, Wendy. *The Colors of Rhetoric: Problems in the Relation between Modern Literature and Painting.* Chicago: University of Chicago Press, 1982.

Steinmetz, Jean-Luc. "Hommages: Mallarmé et la *Nouvelle Revue Française.*" In Anderson, *Australian Divagations,* 103–14.

———. *Stéphane Mallarmé: L'absolu au jour le jour.* Paris: Arthème Fayard, 1998.

Stétié, Salah. *Mallarmé sauf azur.* Cognac, France: Fata Morgana, 1999.

Stokstad, Marilyn, and Burt Waller, eds. *Les Mardis: Stéphane Mallarmé and the Artists of His Circle.* Lawrence: Kansas University Museum of Art, 1965.

Sugano, Marian Zwerling. *The Poetics of the Occasion: Mallarmé and the Poetry of Circumstance.* Stanford: Stanford University Press, 1992.

Suter, Patrick. "Presse et invention littéraire. Mallarmé et ses 'héritiers' futurists, Dada et surréalists." In Thérenty and Vaillant, *Presse et plumes,* 351–64.

Symington, Micéala. "Poétique de la critique picturale symboliste." *MLN* 114 (December 1999): 1110–18.

Tagg, John. *The Burden of Representation: Essays on Photographics and Histories.* London: Macmillan, 1988.

Taine, Hippolyte. *De l'intelligence.* 18th ed. Paris: Librairie Hachette, n.d.

———. *Philosophie de l'art.* Tours: Arthème Fayard, 1985.

Temple, Michael. *Meeting with Mallarmé in Contemporary Culture.* Exeter, UK: University of Exeter Press, 1998.

Terdiman, Richard. *Discourse/Counter- Discourse: The Theory and Practice of Symbolic Resistance in Nineteenth-Century France.* Ithaca and London: Cornell University Press, 1985.

———. "1848, Class Struggles in France." In Hollier, *A New History of French Literature,* 705–10.

———. "1852, 2 December, Bonapartism." In Hollier, *A New History of French Literature,* 717–22.

Thélot, Jérôme. *Les inventions littéraires de la photographie.* Paris: Presses Universitaires de France, 2003.

Thérenty, Marie-Eve. "L'invention de la fiction d'actualité." In Thérenty and Vaillant, *Presse et plumes,* 414–27.

Thérenty, Marie-Eve, and Alain Vaillant, eds. *Presse et plumes: Journalisme et littérature au XIXè siècle.* Paris: Nouveau Monde, 2004.

Trachtenberg, Alan, ed. *Classic Essays on Photography.* New Haven, CT: Leete's Island Books, 1980.

Vaillant, Alain. "Le journal, creuset de l'invention poétique." In Thérenty and Vaillant, *Presse et plumes,* 317–28.

Valéry, Paul. *Ecrits divers sur Stéphane Mallarmé.* Paris: NRF, 1950.

———. "L'âme et la danse." In *Oeuvres,* edited by Jean Hytier, Vol. 2, 148–76. Paris: Gallimard, 1957.

———. "Existence du symbolisme." In *Oeuvres,* edited by Jean Hytier, Vol. 1, 686–706. Paris: Gallimard, 1957.

Verlaine, Paul. "Art poétique." In *Oeuvres poétiques complètes,* edited by Y.-G. le Dantec, revised and augmented by Jacques Borel, 326–27. Paris: Gallimard, 1965.

Villiers de l'Isle-Adam, Auguste, comte de. *Oeuvres complètes.* Edited by Alan Raitt and Pierre Georges Castex. 2 vols. Paris: Gallimard, 1986.

Wall-Romana, Chistophe. "Mallarmé's Cinepoetics: The Poem Uncoiled by the Ciné-matographe, 1893–98." *PMLA* 120 (January 2005): 128–47.

Wayland-Smith, Ellen. "Passing Fashion: Mallarmé and the Future of Poetry in the Age of Mechanical Reproduction." *MLN* 117 (September 2002): 887–907.

Welch, Liliane. "Mallarmé and the Experience of Art." *The Journal of Aesthetics and Art Criticism.* 3, no. 33 (Spring 1972): 369–76.

Williams, Rosalind H. *Dream Worlds: Mass Consumption in Late-Nineteenth-Century France.* Berkeley: University of California Press, 1982.

Wing, Nathaniel. "1859, 7 December, Exile from Within, Exile from Without." In Hollier, *A New History of French Literature,* 737–43.

———. *The Limits of Narrative: Essays on Baudelaire, Flaubert, Rimbaud and Mallarmé.* Cambridge: Cambridge University Press, 1986.

Wittgenstein, Ludwig. *Remarks on Frazer's Golden Bough.* Edited by Rush Rhees. Translated by A. C. Miles. Atlantic Highlands, NJ: Humanities Press, 1970.

Woolley, Grange. *Stéphane Mallarmé 1842–1898.* New York: AMS, 1981 (c. 1942).

Zachmann, Gayle. "La Décoration! Figuring the Feminine and the Writing of Mallarmé." In *Corps/Décors: Femmes, Orgie, Parodie: Hommage à Lucienne Frappier-Mazur,* edited by Catherine Nesci, Gerald Prince, and Gretchen Van Slyke, 285–301. Amsterdam and Atlanta: Rodopi, 1999.

———. "Developing Movements: Mallarmé, Manet, the 'Photo' and the 'Graphic.'" *French Forum* 22, no. 2 (1997): 181–202.

———. "Frameworks for Mallarmé's Photo-Graphics." *L'Esprit Créateur* 40, no. 3 (Fall 2000): 39–49.

———. "Offensive Moves in Mallarmé: Dancing with *des astres.*" In *Confrontations: Politics and Aesthetics in Nineteenth-Century France,* edited by Kathryn M. Grossman, Michael E. Lane, Bénédicte Mouret, and Willa Z. Silverman, 187–200. Amsterdam and Atlanta: Rodopi, 2001.

INDEX

Page numbers in italics refer to illustrations.

Abrams, M. H., 187n4

afterimage, 12, 41, 45, 56, 66, 76, 88, 93, 137, 140, 152, 177n11. *See also* Mallarmé: "Igitur"; optical perception; psychic process; Taine; visual: models of psychic, perception

Aish, Deborah A. K., 4, 187n3

Allen, Neil Walsh, 179n32

Althusser, Louis, 173n15, 181n45

Ambrière, Madeleine, 173n7

Armstrong, Carol, 152

Arago, François, 129

Aristotle, 29, 174n22

art criticism, 3, 10, 22, 27, 39, 45, 52, 59, 91–121, 123, 127–133, 135, 150, 160, 161, 173n11. *See also* Mallarmé: "Impressionists and Edouard Manet"

"art for art's sake," 24, 33–34. *See also* Parnasse; *Parnasse contemporain, Le*

art market, 2, 3, 6, 10, 94, 110. *See also* commercialization; consumer culture; literary market

Art Monthly Review, The, 95, 182n1

Artiste, L', 36

Athenaeum, 174n5

Aubanel, Théodore, 124, 175n15

Auerbach, Erich, 173n18

Austin, Lloyd James, 155, 156, 158, 159, 160, 182n2, 183n8, 187n3

Balzac, Honore de, 50, 52, 176n4

Banville, Théodore de, 24, 33, 35, 173n13

Barbier, Carl Paul, 182n1, 184n11

Barthelme, Marilyn, 182n1

Barthes, Roland, 4, 80, 106, 107, 108, 125, 180n40, 184n15, 185n4

Baudelaire, Charles, 12, 25, 26, 27–32, 34–35, 37–38, 48, 52, 95, 99, 100, 111, 128, 129, 150, 151, 161, 173n13, 173n19, 173n21, 174n2; "Le confiteor de l'artiste," 52; "*Madame Bovary* by Gustave Flaubert, " 12, 28; Nadar image of, *31;* Puisque réalisme il y a," 28; "Théophile Gautier" 32–33, 174n2; *Salon de 1846,* 27; *Salon de 1859,* 27–32

Bellanger, Claude, 172n5

Benichou, Paul, 7

Benjamin, Walter, 17–18, 45, 173n21

Benoit, Eric, 171–172n4

Bernard, Suzanne, 186n22, 187n3

Bersani, Leo, 11, 87, 179n33, 181n48

Blanc, Charles, 152, 175n12

Block, Haskell, 85, 178n25, 181n43